D0926983

VINE'S

EXPOSITORY COMMENTARY ON
GALATIANS

W.E. VINE
with C. F. Hogg

VINE'S

EXPOSITORY COMMENTARY ON
GALATIANS

W.E. VINE
WITH C. F. HOGG

THOMAS NELSON PUBLISHERS
Nashville ▪ Atlanta ▪ London ▪ Vancouver

All rights reserved. No part of this book may be used or reproduced in any manner whatsoever without written permission of the publisher, except for brief quotations in critical reviews or articles.

Published in Nashville, Tennessee, by Thomas Nelson, Inc. and distributed in Canada by Nelson/Word, Inc.

Copyright © 1997. W. E. Vine Copyright Ltd. of Bath, England.

Library of Congress Cataloging-in-Publication Data

Vine, W. E. (William Edwy), 1873–1949.
   [Expository commentary on Galatians]
   Vine's expository commentary on Galatians / W. E. Vine
with C. F. Hogg.
     p.   cm.
   ISBN 0-7852-1172-1
   1. Bible. N.T. Galatians—Commentaries. I. Hogg, C. F.
II. Title.
BS2685.3.V56 1997
227'.407—dc20   96–36201
                                               CIP

Printed in the United States of America.
1 2 3 4 5 — 00 99 98 97 96

Galatians

with

C. F. Hogg

CONTENTS

■ LIST OF ABBREVIATIONS ■

The undernoted abbreviations are used in the Notes.

A.V.	Authorized Version
chh.	chapters
ca., circa	about the year
cp.	compare
ct.	contrast
e.g.	for example
Eng.	English
et al.	and other passages
Gk.	Greek
Heb.	Hebrew
i.e.	that is
in orig.	in the original
lit.	literally
LXX.	the Septuagint, a translation of the Old Testament from Hebrew into Greek, made between 250 and 150 B.C.
marg.	margin
MS., MSS.	manuscript(s)
N.T.	New Testament
O.T.	Old Testament
R.V.	Revised Version
vv.	Verses
viz.	namely

|| at the end of a paragraph or note indicates that all the New Testament occurrences of the Greek word under consideration are mentioned in it.

"Qualified in Many Fields, Narrow in None"

Undoubtedly William Edwy Vine was qualified in many fields. As well as being a theologian and a man of outstanding academic intellect, he had a heart for all humanity that made him a master of communication.

Born in 1873, at the time when C. H. Spurgeon, D. L. Moody and F. B. Meyer were enjoying popularity on both sides of the Atlantic, Vine was brought up in a boarding school owned by and governed by his father as its headmaster. This factor was a major contribution to his interest in teaching. At the age of 17 he was a teacher at his father's school while attending the University College of Wales in preparation for his eventual London University degree, an M.A. in classics.

At the age of twenty-six he spent an Easter vacation at the home of a godly couple, Mr. and Mrs. Baxendale, where he met their daughter Phoebe; a few years later, they married. It was a marriage made in Heaven. They had five children: Helen, Christine, Edward (O.B.E.), Winifred, and Jeanette. During the time of their engagement, Vine's reputation as a clear Bible expositor was growing. It was not long before he accepted the joint headmastership of the school with his father. In 1904, after his father died, his brother Theodore then became joint headmaster with him.

It was during this time, in conjunction with Mr. C. F. Hogg, that he produced three classic works which are contained in this collection: Commentaries on 1 and 2 Thessalonians, followed by Galatians. These master works display the full scope of Vine's scholarship.

While Vine was teaching in the school, preparing for his M.A. and writing in-depth commentaries, he also developed a lifetime habit of teaching classes in New Testament Greek grammar. This laid the foundation for his all-time classic work, *An Expository Dictionary of New Testament Words,* and later, *An Expository Dictionary of Old Testament Words.* His Dictionaries are classics—copies are in excess of three million worldwide. They are available today in the best-selling *Vine's Complete Expository Dictionary of Old and New Testament Words* (published in a separate volume by Thomas Nelson Publishers)—proof that his scholarship and clarity of expression is as relevant as when first published.

"One who, in his less humble moments fancies himself to be something of a specialist in this field, must bear witness that the reading of the greater part of the *Expository Dictionary* in typescript and in proof before publication was for him a real education in New Testament usage."   Professor F. F. Bruce

A Bridge Builder between this Century and the Next Millennium

To own this extensive library is to have tools that can only bring practical and spiritual insight both for new and mature Christians.

Expository Commentaries

Vine applies a "microscopic" approach to expository teaching—a word approach that takes into consideration every reference to that word in the Bible as well as its use in contemporary and classic Greek.

The value of these books alone make this collection a must. They stand up with other great commentaries, such as J. Armitage Robinson on Ephesians, Lightfoot on Colossians, and Westcott on John's Gospel and Hebrews, to name but a few.

"For the student of the English New Testament these commentaries will long remain standard works."   Professor F. F. Bruce

Vine's verse-by-verse exposition reveals a depth of understanding that commentaries many times their size fail to give. He explains the meaning of the key words in each verse and links them with the complete passage.

"Here we have some of the most distinctive features of Mr. Vine's exegesis, which stamp him as a truly biblical theologian."   Professor F. F. Bruce

A Bridge Builder between Mind and Heart

Concerning the man himself, I have come to know more of him through two of his daughters as well as from the local Christian church that he and his wife attended for so many years. Many of the members still remember the Vines, known for their hospitality, humor, hard work, and commitment to the Word of God and missionary enterprise. The writings of W. E. Vine come from the finest intellect in combination with a devoted missionary heart, truly a rare combination.

"The Scriptures' chief function is to bear witness of Christ, and the chief end of their study and exegesis is to increase our inward knowledge of Him, under the illumination of the Spirit of God. Nor would Mr. Vine, in all his study and writing, be content with any lower aim than this, for himself and his readers alike."   Professor F. F. Bruce

Robert Hicks   Bath, England
                                                                                        1996

The reception given to the volume of "Notes on the Epistles to the Thessalonians" encourages us to offer a companion exposition of the epistle to the Galatians to fellow students of the great documents which contain the earliest, and, as we are constrained to believe, the final and authoritative interpretation of "The Gospel of God concerning His Son."

The Galatian epistle differs from those to the Thessalonians, not at all in its presentation of the substance of the gospel, but very markedly in its treatment thereof. There Paul is concerned mainly for the spiritual well-being of those to whom he writes; here for the integrity of the gospel he preached. There he aims at the confirmation of the gospel in the hearts of the believers; here he is set for its defense against an attack which he was persuaded, and rightly as we can perceive, would have made Christianity a mere sect of the Jews.

The interest of the apostle in the persons to whom he writes is the same. They all belonged to Christ. Their churches were of his own founding. But if writing to the Thessalonians he is affectionate, and concerned for their well-being, writing to the Galatians he is indignant and reproachful, and concerned lest they should prove disloyal to Christ.

At the outset the gospel was everywhere proclaimed under the protection of the Roman authorities, as the narrative in Acts witnesses. The interest of these authorities, however, was not at all in the gospel, but in the preservation of the peace within the territories for which they were responsible. The religion of the Jews was recognized by the State, but the officers of the State were careless of the finer distinctions the Jews might make among themselves. The Gallios cared for none of these things (Acts 18:12–17). Hence Christianity, as a Jewish sect, as the Pharisees and the Sadducees were sects (Acts 5:17; 15:5; 24:5), was entitled to such official protection as was accorded to the Jews generally in the practice of their religion.

One of the immediate effects of the apostle's strenuous battle with the Judaizers was to make it clear that Christianity claimed to be something very different from a sect of the Jews, while the Jews themselves were emphatic in their repudiation of it. "The Way which they call a sect" (Acts 24:14), Paul asserted, while it preserved the essentials of Judaism, superseded it. So far from being merely Judaism seen from a new angle, a new interpretation of the ancient faith, Christianity antiquated it and replaced it, leaving no excuse for the continued existence of what, in the new light, was seen to be a "beggarly element," and which could only hinder, instead of serving, the double end of glorifying God and saving men. Indeed, the essentials of the conflict may be summed up in the question: Was salvation for a nation or for the nations? was redemption accomplished by a Jew for Jews, or by a Man for men?

If, however, Christianity was not a sect of the Jews it followed that it must be an unauthorized religion, and, if so, then it fell under the ban of the State, for the practice of a religion not recognized by the State was a criminal offense in Roman law. As soon as this was realized it became evident that if the gospel was still to be preached it must be preached in despite of Roman authority. Henceforth the Christian might at any moment be faced with the alternatives, apostasy or death. This development took place, apparently, toward the end of Nero's reign and of Paul's ministry. It is reflected in Peter's Epistles, particularly the first, and in the Letters to Seven Churches of Asia.

The battle for the faith of the gospel is perennial, in one form or another it must be fought out in each generation, for the antagonism of the human mind to the Cross and its implications is inveterate. The gospel as Paul preached it, and in this epistle he insists that there is no other carrying the Divine approval, or in itself worthy of the name, lays the axe to the root of human merit, and demands that men acknowledge their share in the sinfulness that brought the Son of God to the Cross. On the other hand, such is the desperate case of the human race, the consequence of the intrusion of sin, that only through the death of the Son of God on the Cross can any man, in any age, be saved, whatever his race, his history, or his condition.

Attacks on the gospel from the beginning have run along two lines. There were, as there are, those who would remove some vital element from it, as, e.g., the doctrine of the Deity, or of the humanity, of the Lord, or of the Cross as the instrument of redemption. But these are the elements that inspire devotion in the hearts of men; when they are omitted the Gospel becomes dull, lifeless, unattractive.

The other line of attack is by the addition of something extraneous to the gospel. Circumcision, and the lawkeeping of which it is the symbol, is the typical case with which this Epistle is primarily concerned. All such accretions obscure the characteristic of the gospel and rob it of its power, so "making void the grace of God."

Pursuing the natural trend of the mind, men seek some refuge from the implication of guilt involved in accepting a salvation provided in grace, and available to faith alone. Hence they are forever adding something thereto in which a merit of their own, however attenuated, is implied. In Paul's day it was circumcision of Gentile believers, indeed, but there are those who preach salvation through sacraments, baptism and the holy eucharist, through membership in some religious community, through keeping the law, generally, or the fourth commandment, specifically, or through following an inner light, which may or may not coincide with the light of the Holy Scriptures. But in no case is faith in Christ, as essential to salvation, repudiated. There must be faith in Christ indeed, but there must be something besides. And that something invariably implies merit on the part of him who has it, or who does it. This, affirms the apostle, is to make the Cross of Christ of none effect.

The apostle thoroughly understood the Jews' repugnance to the Cross. He had felt it himself to the bottom of his soul. It became a passion with him, stirring to its depths a nature capable of unqualified surrender to any cause that might lay a spell upon his mind, of unlimited response to whatever demands his ideals might make upon him. But, in the height of his recoil from the Cross, he had had an experience which not only served to evoke even more strongly the devotion of his whole being to an end that seemed to him supremely worthy, it gave to that devotion a direction the opposite of that along which it had been finding its expression. Compromise was to him impossible, inconceivable even. The surrender of the Judaizers must be as complete as his own or it would avail them nothing. Christ, whether as Savior or as Lord, must be all or He could be nothing. The emphasis with which he declared that along this path alone they must find their way to salvation was the index to the certainty to which he had himself attained that in all the world there is no other.

Men had crucified Christ; God had raised Him from the dead. Their ignorance and wickedness (Acts 3:17; 4:16, 17) accounted for what men had done, Jews and Gentiles, malicious and callous, in a common mind for once at the Cross. That by men in their wicked folly He should be "numbered with the transgressors," or that by God He should be "separated from sinners, and made higher than the Heavens," is readily understood. The Cross is the mystery. Why did God forsake Him? Why did God spare Israel and Rome and allow His Son to be murdered? The question was, in its essence, the problem that had distressed the saints through the ages. It is the unresolved problem of Job, and of Asaph (Ps. 73), and of Jeremiah (ch. 12), and of many others. But never before had it pressed for a solution with such a poignant appeal as now, when the Holy Son of God is put to open shame and a violent death by malignant men. In the light of the Resurrection the problem so far as it concerned Him had been solved. The Lord Jesus Christ had given "Himself for our sins, that He might deliver us out of this present evil age," or, as in his later and personal declaration of his own interest in the matter, Paul declares, "the Son of God, Who loved me, and gave Himself up for me." The Cross is thus God's answer to man's sin; the Death of Christ is at once the irrefragable proof of God's love to men, and the adequate ground of reconciliation between God and men. Plainly, then, the Cross stands in solitary isolation from aught that men can do. The sufficiency of the Cross is its glory. To add anything to it, however innocent or however laudable in itself, is to rob the Cross of that glory, and to do despite to the grace of God revealed in it.

To establish his contention Paul does not appeal, either in the argument of the epistle, or in his contention with Peter at Antioch recorded therein, to the Encyclical Letter of the Jerusalem Council (Acts 15:23–29). This may have been partly because he felt the inconsistency of appealing to an authority which he had already repudiated with much particularity; partly because he perceived that authority of any kind could not give a final decision in a matter of such vital moment as he knew this to be; partly because he perceived how inadequate that decision was which said no more than that Gentiles need not keep the law, whereas he insisted that they must not undertake any obligation in relation to it whatever.

Neither in the epistle to the Galatians, nor in that to the Romans, in which the same "Gospel of God concerning His Son" is expounded at greater length, and with more expository calm, if with less controversial warmth, does the apostle provide his readers with a treatise on theology. Theology systematized is theology crystalized, moribund. Here, rather, is the truth of God working itself out through love. Truth that saves is truth warm from the heart of God, glowing with the love that proved itself at the Cross, the love of God in Christ Jesus our Lord.

It is not necessary to repeat here what was said in the foreword to our previous volume of the principles that underlie this study, or of the methods by which it has been brought to its present form. This volume also is the product of our separate studies and experiences, compared, corrected, and combined. In order to avoid increasing the dimensions of the book we have not repeated the matter already printed in the *Notes on the Thessalonians,* but have instead made frequent reference to it. It remains only to acknowledge gratefully the valued help of several friends. Among these we may mention Mrs. Herbert Jenkyn, B.A., who read a considerable portion of the manuscript; to Mr. J. C. M. Dawson, B.A., and to Mr. W. R. Lewis, who read the whole of it, we are indebted for valuable criticisms and suggestions. Mr. Harold St. John verified the references in proof and supplied the Indexes. To each of these our fellow workers we tender our thanks. The shortcomings of the volume, and we are painfully conscious that they must be many, are entirely our own.

Such as it is we lay it at the feet of the Lord, knowing that there could be no richer reward for our labors than that what we have done should prove, in His grace, to be "useful to the Master."

May, 1922.*

---

*The text of the epistle is printed from the Revised Version of 1881, with the kind permission of the Syndics of the University Press.

The Writer

Paul, a Roman name = "little," always used by the apostle himself, cp. 2 Peter 3:15, was also called Saul, a Hebrew name = "asked for." It is possible he bore both from childhood; at any rate it was not unusual for one man to bear a Jewish and a Gentile name, cp. Simon Peter, Matthew 10:2; Jesus Justus, Colossians 4:11. In this case, however, the two are never so joined. The Hebrew name appears for the last, the Gentile for the first time in Acts 13:9.

It is not possible to fix with certainty the dates of Paul's birth, conversion, and death, but 1 B.C., A.D. 32 and 67, respectively, may be taken as approximating closely to them. He would thus be slightly younger than the Lord Jesus, Who was born from four to eight years before the account called Anno Domini. Paul was born at Tarsus in Cilicia, Acts 21:39, and was probably executed at Rome. If these dates are even approximately correct he must have been a little over fifty years old, and must have had about twenty years' experience in missionary work, when he wrote his Epistle to the Galatians. See also comment on *1 Thessalonians*.

Galatia and Galatians

These terms were used in two senses, one official, one popular. The Galatians proper originally belonged to migratory Celtic tribes which, early in the third century B.C., invaded Greece from the north. A considerable host of these separated from the main body and, about 280 B.C., crossed over into what is now known as Asia Minor, in the center of which they established themselves. In the apostolic age "Galatians" and "Galatia" were still popularly used for this people (with the substratum of native Phrygians whom they had subdued), and for that part of the country in which they had settled.

A hundred years after their settlement in Asia Minor the Galatians themselves were conquered by the Romans, 189 B.C., Galatia ultimately becoming a Roman province. Its boundaries were defined in 25 B.C., but were again and again enlarged, and in A.D. 41 were extended southward to include Derbe and the adjacent territory. Thus the terms were used officially to designate far more than the original Galatian country and people, for the population of Derbe, Lystra, and Iconium were Lycaonians, those of Pisidian Antioch were Phrygians.

The southern part of the Roman province was the more populous, it had long had colonies of Greeks and Jews; commerce and emigration were encouraged by the safety of the great Roman road which ran through the cities just named.

The Destination of the Epistle

The ambiguity of the words "Galatia" and "Galatians" makes it difficult to determine the destination of the epistle and the time of its writing. The matter is surprisingly complicated. An attempt may, however, be made here to give the more important of the reasons usually adduced for and against two conflicting theories. If the apostle used the term "Galatia" in its more popular sense he must have intended the epistle for churches in some unnamed cities, perhaps Ancyra, Pessinus, and Tavium; this is the "North Galatian" theory. If, however, he used it in the official sense (i.e., as the designation of the Roman province), he addressed the churches in Antioch, Iconium, Lystra, and Derbe; this is the "South Galatian" theory.

In favor of the former it is urged that all the Fathers refer it to the northern cities; but, even so, the existence of churches in them is merely conjectural. Lightfoot, who supports this theory, writes: "It is strange [that] . . . not a single name of a person or place, scarcely a single incident of any kind connected with the apostle's preaching in Galatia should be preserved in either the history, i.e., Acts, or the Epistle." And yet the work there must have been of a strikingly successful character. Those who advocate this theory find room for a visit to these cities in Acts 16:6 (where Asia is not the continent now so-called, but Proconsular Asia, a Roman Province west of Galatia), and for a second visit, implied in 4:13, Acts 18:23. But the way from Syrian Antioch through Galatia and Phrygia to Ephesus does not seem to lie through North Galatia, even though the apostle reached his destination, not by Colossae and Laodicea, but by "the upper country," 19:1.

The other theory is also beset with difficulties. It is stated in support of it that Paul, being a Roman citizen, would use the official designation of the countries to which he makes reference. He does not always do so, however, Pisidia, Phrygia, and Mysia, 14:24; 16:6–8, e.g., are geographical rather than official names for these countries. Moreover, Lystra and Derbe are styled by Luke "cities of Lycaonia," 14:6, and Antioch is described as "of Pisidia," 13:14, but they are not called Galatian.

It may be gathered from the epistle itself that the churches addressed were in the main Gentile, though there was a Jewish element among them. According to Acts the churches at Derbe and the neighboring towns were also mixed— Jew and Gentile. Antioch, 13:14, and Iconium, 14:1, had synagogues, and there is other and non-Biblical testimony to the presence of Jews in South Galatia. On the other hand, there is no trace of any considerable settlement of Jews in North Galatia.

Again, the mention of Barnabas, 2:13, suggests that he was known to the readers of the Epistles; but Barnabas was not with Paul when he is supposed to have visited the northern cities, Acts 16:6; whereas they were fellowtravelers when the churches in the southern cities were formed, chapters thirteen and fourteen. Against this, of course, it may be urged that Barnabas is mentioned in much the same way in 1 Corinthians 9:6, though he was not with Paul when the church was founded there.

Other arguments there are, on either side, of greater weight or less, but perhaps what has been written is sufficient for the present purpose. The conclusion cannot be said to be emphatic either way, but the balance on the whole is favorable to the view that the epistle was addressed to the churches of South Galatia, i.e., those of Antioch, Iconium, Lystra, and Derbe.

Authenticity of the Epistle

The genuineness of this epistle has seldom been called in question. The elements of personal character reflected in it are in accord with what we know of the apostle from other sources. Here are the same cogent reasoning, the same warmth of feeling, the same capacity for indignation, and for tenderness, that characterize his other writings, but all heightened and emphasized by the circumstances that called forth the epistle. Here, too, is Paul's theology, his characteristic insistence on the doctrines of grace, of salvation by faith apart from works; while at the same time his exhortations to good works are as marked as in all his other writings.

Ancient testimony, direct and indirect, is as complete as could be expected, considering how few writings of the subapostolic age remain. Among direct testimonies may be mentioned the list of books accepted by Marcion, the heretic, circa A.D. 140; the epistle was also accepted by his orthodox opponents. It is included in the "Muratorian Fragment" about the end of the second century A.D. The Syrian and Old Latin Versions contain it; these were made probably before the second century closed.

Date of the Epistle

The subject matter of the epistle, the battle between those who contended that the Gentiles must become Jews in order to become Christians, and those who claimed that the Gentiles could become Christians directly, itself fixes the period to which the epistle must belong. It could not have been written after A.D. 70, when Jerusalem fell and the Jewish religion lost its national status, nor could it have been written before the preaching of the gospel to the Gentiles had become fairly general, say about A.D. 48–49, cp. Acts 13:46. These obvious considerations bring the epistle well within the period of the apostle's active labors (see the section on "Authenticity" above) but the difficulties that beset the attempt to fix a date for it during that period are very perplexing. For instance, if he wrote after the Council at Jerusalem, Acts 15, why does he not refer to its decrees, which indeed he himself delivered to the churches over an area including the Galatian cities, Acts 16:1-6, whether the "Northern" or "Southern" theory is accepted? This consideration points to a date preceding the Council, and would make the epistle the earliest of all Paul's writings.

On the other hand, if Paul had already written the epistle, which contains such words as these, "I Paul say unto you, that, if ye receive circumcision, Christ will profit you nothing," 5:2, how could he himself thereafter have circumcised Timothy, as it is recorded, Acts 16:3, that he did? But this consideration would make the epistle later than the Second Missionary Journey, and seems quite inconsistent with the former.

Again, the epistle could hardly have been written later than Paul's imprisonment at Caesarea, A.D. 57-59, see Acts 23:33, for internal evidence suggests that it belongs not to the period of Ephesians, Philippians, and Colossians, but to that of Corinthians and Romans.

The words "the first time" (marg., "the former time"), 4:13, seem to indicate that the apostle had visited the Galatian churches at least once since he planted them. He did not, however, visit the northern cities at all until after the Council, Acts 16:6, and not again till his Third Missionary Journey, 18:23, in which case the epistle must have been written later in that journey. But it will be remembered that whether the northern cities are intended in these two passages is merely conjecture, see the section on "Destination."

The first visit to the southern cities belongs to the First Missionary Journey, see Acts 13:13; 14:7, the second was made on the way back to Syrian Antioch, 14:21. In that case the epistle may have been written from that city, and so even earlier than the Council of Acts 15. If, however, the second visit is that mentioned in 16:6, the epistle may belong to the Second Missionary Journey, and may have been written at Corinth, before or after the epistles to the Thessalonians, 18:11, or at Ephesus, 19:10. The subscription to the epistle in A.V., found in a few MSS. and versions, stating that it was written at Rome, is of no authority.

Of all Paul's epistles the Galatians most resembles 2 Corinthians and Romans. It is like the former in its defense of the writer's apostleship, and like the latter in its doctrinal statements. In Romans, however, the argument of Galatians is developed and elaborated, and is stated in a more dispassionate way. This resemblance would point to the apostle's three months' stay in Corinth, Acts 20:3, during which Romans was written, as the date of Galatians also. Arguments based on internal considerations, however, are precarious; on the whole it may be assumed that the epistle was written from Corinth, Acts 18:11, or Ephesus, 19:10, as mentioned above.

Occasion and Purpose of the Epistle

The beginning of the gospel in Galatia had not been without opposition from the Jews, 3:4, cp. Acts 13:50; like the "Hebrews" the Galatians had suffered for the faith, and now, like them, they were tempted "to cast away their boldness" and so to lose their reward, Hebrews 10:34, 35. The truth of the message had at first been denied, Acts 13:45, and those favorably disposed to it either threatened or actually injured; now it was perverted and adherence to the spurious substitute encouraged and applauded. Where the blustering storm of opposition failed the subtle influences of persuasion had met with more success. Violence and guile are the chief resources of the adversary in his opposition to the gospel, and in this order. Where the endurance of affliction makes evident that the progress of the gospel cannot be prevented, an attempt is made to alter its character by plausible argument.

There is indeed a third and even more effective way whereby the gospel is hindered; a spirit of indifference is induced, first among those who profess it and then among those who hear it. This comes later, however, cp. 2 Peter 3:1-7; apparently the apostle Paul did not encounter it at any period of his career, unless indeed it has left traces in such a passage as 2 Timothy 4:10.

At the outset the relation of the apostle with the Galatian churches was of a peculiarly tender character. Overtaken by some physical infirmity his course had been deflected into their midst when it had not been his purpose to visit them at all.* But God overruled his movements for their salvation, and this they had acknowledged with many spontaneous tokens of affection for the apostle, 4:12-15. But in a short time a great change had come over them. He was their enemy, 4:16; he was a dissimulator, pretending to oppose circumcision whereas he himself preached it where it suited him to do so, 5:11, cp. 1:10; he was merely a subordinate of the twelve, 1:17; 2:1, 2, 9, 11; perhaps not really an apostle at all, 1:1, cp. 6:17. Such were their new thoughts about the man of whose apostleship they were themselves the seal, cp. 1 Corinthians 9:2, inasmuch as they, like the Corinthians, were his own children in the faith, cp. 4:19 with 1 Corinthians 4:15 and Philemon 10.

The trouble was not primarily personal. Paul had been discredited only that his doctrines might be discredited. He had taught that the death of Christ answers every claim of the Divine Justice upon men; that Christ Himself is the sole and sufficient Savior. The Judaizers did not deny Christ, they taught that Christ plus the law was the complete gospel; the death of Christ plus the circumcision of the believer, the ground of salvation. In such an association, the apostle asserts, Christ profits nothing, 5:2, it is as though He were not; "if righteousness is through the law, then Christ died for naught," 2:21.

This was the condition that called forth the Epistle, which deals first with the

---

*Prof. Ramsay, "St. Paul the Traveller and Roman Citizen," p. 94, suggests that this "infirmity" was an attack of malarial fever, contracted during his stay in the low-lying and notoriously unhealthy district of Pamphylia on the south coast; see Acts 13:13. Such an illness would certainly incapacitate him from work, and it would be natural enough for him to go as far north as to Antioch to escape the miasma and to recuperate. Then with returning strength he would find opportunity to preach the gospel to the Galatians; see Acts 13:14. The narrative is of course very much condensed, and all attempts to fix the nature of this illness, and of Paul's "thorn in the flesh," whether or no they were one and the same thing, are purely speculative.

apostleship, chapters 1 and 2, then with the ground of justification, chapters 3—5:12. As is customary with the apostle, he announces informally in the opening verses the subjects with which he intends to deal, but in no other of his Epistles does he hold so closely to his theme right to the end.

Writing to the Thessalonians Paul does not designate himself an apostle, as he does in all his later Epistles, save those to the Philippians and to Philemon. Writing to the Galatians he claims the dignity in his opening words, and at once digressed into an emphatic assertion of the divine origin and the divine mediation of His call. He had never seen the Lord, so, it was reported to him, his detractors said, how then could he be an apostle, seeing that the Lord had appointed His apostles in His lifetime? "Had the death of the Lord Jesus put a period to His authority? Had they forgotten His Resurrection?" he replies. His appointment was directly from God through the Risen Lord, Who still rules in the churches.

In this emphatic statement of his independence of men the apostle does not intend to ignore or deny the claims of fellowship. His was a unique case; he was independent of men solely because of his direct dependence upon Christ. Even so, he shows, later in the letter, how careful he had been to maintain fellowship with those who were apostles before him, 2:2, 9. Indeed, under circumstances somewhat similar to the present, he had gone up to Jerusalem and obtained a considered judgment from the apostles, and had himself delivered their decrees to the churches, Acts 15—16:4. The true servant of Christ does not set his claim to be directly responsible to his Lord in antagonism with the claim of his brethren on his fellowship. On his willingness and power to show himself responsive to both, the efficiency of his service must largely depend.

Paul's ordinary salutation, "grace," again affords him the opportunity of saying in a few words what, if they had rightly apprehended it, would have shown the Galatians the radical impossibility of any combination of law and gospel, verse 4. The Lord Jesus Christ, the Son of God, gave Himself, in the will of God, to accomplish the salvation of men. Is it conceivable that anything, old or new, must be added thereto in order to effect that purpose? Never! To God alone is the eternal glory of the deliverance of all such as trust in the Lord Jesus Christ.

Analyses of the Epistle

Summary

    Chapters 1 and 2—Christian Experience.
    Chapters 3 and 4—Christian Doctrine.
    Chapters 5 and 6—Christian Character

Outline

Ch. 1:1–5. Salutation.
    6–10. Occasion of the Epistle.
    11–

Ch. 2:10 The writer's apostolic credentials.

    1-15. The dispute with Peter.

    16-21. The general principle of the gospel discussed and applied.

Ch. 3:1-5. Appeal to the experiences of the Galatians at their conversion.

    6-29. An illustration—Abraham.

Ch. 4:1-7 Contrast between servanthood under the law, and sonship under the gospel.

    8-11. The Galatians, being Gentiles, in submitting to the law, were merely exchanging one form of bondage for another.

    12-20. Appeal to the experiences of the Galatians at their conversion.

    21-31. An illustration—Sarah and Hagar.

Ch. 5:1. Exhortation to maintain freedom.

    2-6. Warning lest liberty be surrendered.

    7-12. Expostulation.

    13-15. Warning lest liberty degenerate into license.

    16-24. Walking by the Spirit—individual.

    25.

Ch 6:5- Walking by the Spirit—collective.

    6-10. Counsel and encouragement.

    11-16 Final warning.

    17-18. Conclusion.

Detailed Analyses of 1:11—2:21

1. 11, 12 The Proposition.

13-2:14 Historical.

 15-16 Doctrinal.

The Proof

17-20 Experimental.

21 Conclusion.

1:11, 12. The Proposition: the gospel of grace is of divine, not of human, origin.

13, 14. The Proof: Historical; Paul's history; his religious prepossessions antagonistic to the gospel.

15. The unsuspected purpose of God.

16a. Paul's experience on the Damascus road.

16b, 17. His subsequent course; any contact with The Twelve impossible for three years thereafter.

18-21. His first contact with The Twelve was limited to Peter; and in time to fifteen days.

22-24. Thus for many years he was unknown, save by repute, to Christians in the land in which the gospel originated and which The Twelve, up to that time, had not left.

Clearly then he owed neither his gospel nor his authority to The Twelve. It remains to declare what his relations with them actually were.

2:1–21. Paul's relations with The Twelve.

1. His first official visit to Jerusalem.

2. Its purpose, not to learn, but to negotiate concerning a practical difficulty.

3, 4. Even at Jerusalem he refused consent to the circumcision of a Gentile convert,

5. lest the gospel should be compromised.

6. He learned nothing, and received no authority, from the recognized leaders there.

7–10. On the contrary, they fully and publicly recognized the divine origin and authority of Paul's gospel and of his mission.

11–14. Far from deriving authority from The Twelve, he contended with their leader, Peter, and rebuked him publicly for disloyalty to the gospel of grace.

15, 16. Doctrinal: summary of his argument with Peter,

17, 18. which passes, imperceptibly, into an address to the Galatians.

19, 20. Experimental: personal testimony to the purpose and effect of the gospel.

21. Conclusion: either the gospel of grace is the sole gospel, or the death of Christ was superfluous.

The Marginal Notes

Readings and Renderings. No autograph MS. of any part of the New Testament is known to exist. The MSS. that have been preserved are all copied from copies of those actually written by the men whose names they bear, or by others at their dictation, Romans 16:22. Experience teaches us that it is hardly possible to copy a lengthy document without making what are called "clerical," i.e., clerks', errors. These are of different kinds, repetitions, omissions, misspellings, confusion of words and of phrases, and so forth. In these and in other ways mistakes have so multiplied that no two manuscripts of the New Testament agree in every particular.

In the providence of God, however, so many ancient copies of the whole, or of parts, of the New Testament have been preserved, that careful comparison of their contents, by persons qualified for the work by knowledge and training, has resulted in the elimination of the great majority of these errors, so that but few passages remain really doubtful, and on none of these does any vital matter of fact or teaching depend. In the appendix to their small edition of the Greek Text, Drs. Westcott and Hort write, "the words in our opinion still subject to doubt can hardly amount to more than a thousandth part of the whole New Testament."

Ancient MSS. containing the whole, or any part, of the New Testament in the original, i.e., the Greek, language, early translations into other languages, such as Syriac, Egyptian, and Latin, and quotations from any of these in the writings of early Christians ("the Fathers"), are called the "authorities" for the text. The differences found in these in any particular passage are called "readings." It is, however, misleading to quote a long list of "authorities" for or against a "reading," inasmuch as the subject is one of great complexity, and the ability to discriminate among "readings" is acquired only by long practice; "authorities" have to be weighed rather than counted.

The margin of the R.V. contains "notes specifying such differences of reading as were judged by the Revisers to be of sufficient importance to require particular notice"; see Preface to R.V., which, like that to A.V. (now seldom printed), is an interesting and informing document, and should be read throughout. Wherever, then, "many authorities," or a like phrase, occurs in the margin, what follows is called a "various reading" (often written "var. lect.," or "v.l.," a contraction of the equivalent Latin words *varia lectio*), and all these are of sufficient likelihood and importance to have commanded the votes of at least the majority of the Revisers.

Other marginal notes are introduced by "or," these are called "alternative renderings," and indicate that there is some uncertainty about either the meaning of a word or the grammar of a sentence.

Thus the presence of a "various reading" shows that there is some uncertainty as to what the writer said, an "alternative rendering" that there is some uncertainty as to what he meant.

A third class of marginal notes is introduced by "Gr.," a contraction of the word "Greek"; this indicates that the translation adopted is more or less idiomatic, and therefore, as a guide to the reader, the literal translation is also supplied.

GALATIANS

CHAPTER ONE

Verses 1–24

1:1 Paul,—see Introductory Note, and comment on *1 Thessalonians* 2:4.

an apostle—see comment on *1 Thessalonians* 2:6.

(not from—*apo,* pointing to the source of authority.

men,—i.e., any body of men who might be assumed to have authority to appoint apostles, such as the Twelve, Acts 6:3-6; 8:14; 11:22, or the Council at Jerusalem, 15:6, or the prophets and teachers at Antioch, 13:1-3.

neither through—*dia,* with genitive case, pointing to the medium by which authority is ordinarily conveyed.

man,—i.e., any person who might act on behalf of such a body, as Ananias, through whom his commission from the Lord was confirmed at the first, cp. Acts 22:12:15 with 26:15-18, or as Barnabas, who sought him out at Tarsus and brought him to the work among Gentiles at Antioch, 11:25. The phrase, "through man," stands in contrast with "through Jesus Christ," thus suggesting that He is not to be classed with merely human agents, and preparing the way for the implication of His Deity in the succeeding words.

but through—*dia,* as above.

Jesus Christ,—see comment on *1 Thessalonians* 1:1.

and God the Father,—i.e., of the Lord Jesus Christ, cp. 1 Corinthians 8:6 with Ephesians 1:3, where this title is given in full, and see further *1 Thessalonians* 1:1. Here the repetition of "from," *apo,* might have been expected to complete the chiasm* thus:

a, not from men,
b, neither through man,
b, but through Jesus Christ,
a, and (from) God the Father.

Its absence, however, hardly impairs the symmetry of the sentence, while the effect of uniting both names under the government of one preposition is to suggest the unity of authority and of action of the Father and the Son, corre-

---

*Chiasm, from a Greek word = "crosswise," like the letter X, in Greek pronounced *chi,* is a figure of speech of frequent occurrence in Scripture, cp., e.g., Is. 55:8, 9; Matt. 12:22; John 10:14, 15; Rom. 10:9, 10; 3 John 11. Sometimes the chiasm extends to more than two or three double statements, as in Rom. 2:6-11, a section in which seven pairs of corresponding lines are found, cp. also Num. 15:35, 36.

sponding with their unity of Being in the Godhead. The repetition of "from" would have dissociated the name of the Son from that of the Father in a way quite unusual with Paul. See verse 3, where the two are again united under "from," *apo*. See also comment on *1 Thessalonians,* 1:1; 3:11. The apostle does not always draw a strict line as between source and mediation when speaking of God, cp., e.g., Romans 11:36 with 1 Corinthians 8:6.

who—whereas in the preceding phrase the Father and the Son are most intimately associated, here they are as sharply distinguished. It was the Son Who died, it was the Father Who raised Him from among the dead. The same distinction is made in verse 4, cp. also John 1:1, "the Word was with God, and the Word was God."

raised him—this is the sole direct reference in the Epistle to the resurrection of the Lord.

from the dead),—*ek nekrōn,* lit., "from among dead ones," this is the apostle's usual expression; once he adds the article *ek tōn nekrōn,* Colossians 1:18. See comment on *1 Thessalonians.*

1:2 and all the brethren—see comment on *1 Thessalonians* 1:4.

which are with me,—in Philippians 4:21, 22 the apostle distinguishes between his colleagues in labor and the church in Rome, the city from which he wrote; he does not associate a church with himself in any other of his Epistles. In view of these facts, these words are best understood as referring to his fellow workers. Apparently the apostle was usually accompanied on his journeys by a little band of helpers, cp. Acts 20:4, e.g., where seven are named, besides Luke who was also with him, verse 5. This was a special occasion, however, for some of these had been delegated by certain churches to carry their offerings to Jerusalem, cp. 1 Corinthians 16:3; ordinarily, the number may not have been as large. Here he mentions that his companions, without exception, are with him in what he is about to say; but he leaves them unnamed because the responsibility, and the arguments, are his own. Moreover, it was his apostleship that had been called in question; hence his use of the singular pronoun throughout the Epistle.

unto the churches—see comment on *1 Thessalonians* 1:1; 2:14.

of Galatia:—cp. 1 Corinthians 16:1, and see Intro. Note. This is the only letter of the apostle Paul addressed to a group of churches, though the Corinthian Epistles contemplate a wider circle than the church at Corinth, see the opening verses. This is, moreover, the only Epistle in which he does not add any qualifying epithet, cp. "of God," 1 Corinthians 1:1, "in God the Father and the Lord Jesus Christ," 1 Thessalonians 1:1. It is usual for him to incorporate in the address some recognition of the Christian calling of those to whom he writes, cp. 1 Corinthians 1:2, e.g., and v. 22, or some commendation of their Christian graces, see Romans 1:8, *e.g.* The omission of such expressions here is to be accounted for by the circumstances that called for the Epistle and that caused the apostle to be "perplexed," 4:20, about the standing and the state of those to whom he wrote.

1:3 Grace to you and peace from God the Father, and our Lord Jesus Christ, 1:4, who—here the Father and the Son are first intimately associated as the source of grace, and then sharply distinguished by an historical statement true only of the latter.

gave—*didōmi,* used again in this connection by the apostle Paul in 1 Timothy 2:6, with the words "a ransom," and in Titus 2:14, where, as here, there is no defining clause.

himself—cp. 2:20, Hebrews 9:14. Here the apostle seems to have in mind the Lord's own words, "The Son of Man came—to give His live (*psuche* = soul, cp. John 12:27) a ransom for many," Matthew 20:28; "I will give . . . My Flesh for the life of the world," John 6:51; "My Body which is given for you," Luke 22:19, cp. Heb. 10:10.
    These three words of the Lord are instances of a figure of speech called synecdoche, in which a part is put for the whole, or the whole for a part; thus by the "Soul," the "Flesh," the "Body" of the Lord Jesus, He Himself is meant.

for—the ancient authorities are about evenly divided here between *peri* and *huper,* which are frequently interchanged in the New Testament, see comment on *1 Thessalonians* 5:10, where the different prepositions used in the New Testament to describe the purpose of the death of Christ are defined.

our sins,—*hamartia,* cp. 1 Corinthians 15:3, "Christ died for our sins," the closest parallel in Paul's Epistles. See also Hebrews 5:1, 3; 7:27, from which the ellipsis may be supplied, "as a sacrifice for our sins." *Hamartia, is* lit. "a missing of the mark," but this etymological meaning is for the most part quite lost sight of in the New Testament where it is the most comprehensive of the many words used for general moral obliquity.

that—pointing to the purpose of the sacrifice.

he might deliver us out of—*exaireō,* here only in Paul's Epistles; it signifies to pluck out of, Matthew 5:29; 18:9, and hence to rescue, as from danger, Acts 12:11; 23:27, and to deliver, as from bondage, 7:10, 34; 26:17, and here. See comment on *1 Thessalonians,* v. 10.‖ The verb is in the middle voice, suggesting that He who thus delivers us has an interest in the result of His own act. Thus in Ephesians 1:4 there is the thought that God "chose us for Himself" in Christ, i.e., that we might be His sons, verse 5. So here. The words may be paraphrased, "Who gave Himself for our sins, in order that He might deliver us out of this present evil age that so we might belong to Him."

this present—*enistēmi* = "to set in," is used of the present in contrast with the past, Hebrews 9:9, and with the future, Romans 8:38, 1 Corinthians 3:22, 2 Thessalonians 2:2, and here, or with both, 1 Corinthians 7:26. In 2 Timothy 3:1, lit., "shall be present," a period future when the words were written is in view.‖ *Nun.* = *"now,"* a synonym of *enistemi*, appears in 1 Timothy 6:17, 2 Timothy 4:10, Titus 2:12; in Romans 12:2 the phrase is simply "this age." In all these places a contrast is suggested with another period called "that age," Luke 20:35, et al., "the age to come," Mark 10:30, et al., "the age [which is about] to come," Matthew 12:32, Hebrews 6:5, *et al.;* the difference being that this present age is under the control of its "god," 2 Corinthians 4:4, whereas the coming age will be under the control of the Lord Jesus Christ.

evil—*poneros*, see comment on *1 Thessalonians* 5:22.

world,—*aiōn* (as an Eng. word, written "aeon"), an age, a period of time, past, Ephesians 3:9, present, 1:21, or future, 2:7; not the duration of the period but its spiritual and moral characteristics are in view where the word appears. See comment on *1 Thessalonians* 1:9. The number and length of the aeons, or ages, to which reference is made in the New Testament, e.g., Jude 25, have not been revealed, but their succession has been fixed by God, Hebrews 1:2, Whose purpose runs throughout them, Ephesians 3:11, and Who is called "King of the Ages," 1 Timothy 1:17, Revelation 15:3, cp. Psalm 10:16. Apparently the ultimate ages, in which the purposes of God will be fully developed, Ephesians 2:7, are now drawing on, since Paul speaks of himself as among those on whom "the ends of the ages are come," 1 Corinthians 10:11.

The "consummation of the ages" was marked by the Cross of the Son of God, Hebrews 9:26; to that former ages led up, and to it subsequent ages will look back as the pivotal point on which all God's dealings with His creatures turn. This phrase is not found elsewhere in the New Testament

The present age began with the creation of man, Luke 1:70, John 9:32, and will end with the harvest from the seed sown in the hearts of men during its course, Matthew 13:39. Since the Fall it is an age of spiritual darkness, Ephesians 6:12, and is subject to the "authority of darkness," Colossians 1:13; its "sons," i.e., those who embody its spirit and express its characteristics (see comment on *1 Thessalonians* 5:4), are guided only by a wisdom drawn from experience, Luke 16:8, cp. 1 Corinthians 3:18, the while they are blinded to the light of the gospel of the glory of Christ by its "god," 2 Corinthians 4:4, and hence escape neither its cares, Mark 4:19, nor its doom.

A synonym of *aiōn, kosmos,* occurs 4:3; 6:14. Sometimes the words seem to express the same idea, as in 1 Corinthians 3:18, *aiōn,* and 19, *kosmos,* but not always, for while God seeks to reconcile the world, *kosmos,* to Himself, 2 Corinthians 5:19 (see comment on *1 Thessalonians* 2:4), He is never said to reconcile the *aiōn* to Himself. The words are found together in Ephesians 2:2, lit., "the age, *aiōn,* of this world, *kosmos.*"

The only other word translated "world" in the New Testament is *oikoumenē,* = "the inhabited earth." In many of its occurrences it is used of the Roman Empire, the world as the men who spoke knew it, see Luke 2:1, Acts 11:28, e.g., while in others the world as God sees it is intended, see Matthew 24:14, Acts 17:31, e.g. Paul uses *oikoumenē* once only, in a quotation from Psalm 19:4, LXX.

This deliverance may be understood in two ways: *a,* that it refers to present salvation from the evil tendencies and influences which characterize the world, *kosmos,* in this age or period of its history; *b,* that it refers to deliverance out of it when the saints are caught away at the coming of the Lord Jesus, 1 Thessalonians 4:17.

Of these alternative interpretations, *a* seems preferable since it is in harmony with 2:20, and with the prayer of the Lord in John 17, and with such passages as Romans 12:1, 2. In Colossians 1:13 this deliverance is looked upon as actually accomplished, but the law of the kingdom is that what is true of the believer in the grace and purpose of God must be made true in his experience by faith and obedience, cp. the call to separation in 2 Corinthians 6:17, 18, addressed to a "church of God," ch. 1:1.

according to the will—*thelēma,* see comment on *1 Thessalonians* 5:18. This refers alike to the end, the deliverance of men, and the means of its accomplishment, the sacrifice of Christ, Hebrews 10:5–10.

Of our God—who is the God of all men, Numbers 16:22, Acts 17:22–31, Romans 3:29, inasmuch as He is their Creator, Genesis 1:27, Revelation 4:11, and Sustainer, Psalm 145:15, 16, Acts 14:15–17.

and Father:—the Fatherhood of God is asserted only in relation to those who have been born anew, 3:26, John 1:12, 13, 1 John 3:1; 5:1. See comment on *1 Thessalonians* 1:1.

The will of God is moved by His love, Ephesians 2:4, guided by His wisdom, and accomplished by His power, 1 Corinthians 1:24, and administered under His authority, John 17:2. The gospel has its origin in the love of God the Father, cp. John 3:17 with 1 John 4:14, "Who reconciled us to Himself through Christ," 2 Corinthians 5:18. Hence it is plain that Christ did not die in order that God might love men, or that it might become His will to save them. Christ died because God loved men and because it is His will to save them, 1 Timothy 2:3, 4.

1:5 to whom—i.e., to God the Father.

be—the verb is wanting in orig.; it is noteworthy that in 1 Peter 4:11, the writer himself supplies "is."

the glory—*doxa,* see comment on *1 Thessalonians* 2:14. Similar doxologies (so-called from this Greek word) occur in Paul's Epistles, Romans 11:36; 16:27, Ephesians 3:20, 21, Philippians 4:20, 2 Timothy 4:18, but here only in the opening verses, taking the place of the usual thanksgiving.

There is an omission here of some such word as "ascribed." The creature does not give glory to the Creator in the sense of adding anything to Him, but only by acknowledging what He is and what He has done.

forever and ever.—lit., "unto the ages of the ages," a phrase used by Paul only in his doxologies, of God, Philippians 4:20, 1 Timothy 1:17, and of Christ, 2 Timothy 4:18. It occurs in the same connection, of God, Hebrews 13:21, 1 Peter 4:11; 5:11, Revelation 4:9, 10; 7, 12; 10:6, 15, 7; and of the Lord Jesus, 1:6; and of both, 5:13. It is used of the duration of the resurrection life of Christ, 1:18 (which is said to be "endless," or "indissoluble," Heb. 7:16, marg.), and of His reign, 11:15, and of that of the redeemed with Him, 22:5. Finally, the same phrase is used to describe the duration of the punishment of the Great Harlot, 19:3, and of the Devil, the Beast, and the False Prophet, 20:10. The articles are dropped in 14:11, which describes the punishment of the worshipers of the Beast, but this apparently does not alter the meaning. The same words, but both in the singular number, "unto the age of the age," appear in Hebrews 1:8, quoted from Psalm 45:6, LXX, with apparently the same meaning, cp. Luke 1:33, Revelation 11:15. Paul's most comprehensive form of this description of eternal duration occurs in Ephesians 3:21, "unto all the generations of the age of the ages."||

"Unto the ages" occurs in Luke 1:33, quoted from Isaiah 9:7, LXX, and is explained immediately by the words "there is no end." It occurs elsewhere of God, Romans 1:25; 11:36, 2 Corinthians 11:31, and of Christ, Hebrews 13:8, "who is over all, God blessed forever," Romans 9:5. Plainly this shorter form carries just the same weight of meaning as the longer.||

"Unto the age" is found in Matthew 21:19, Mark 3:29, John 4:14; 12:34, 2 Corinthians 9:9, Hebrews 5:6, 1 Peter 1:25, 1 John 2:17, etc., where the same idea, that of permanence and finality, is also evident. Here again the singular form is no less forceful than the plural, cp. Luke 1:33 with John 12:34.

"Unto [an] age" occurs in Jude 13; "unto all the ages" in Jude 25; "unto [the] day of an age" in 2 Peter 3:18; the only occurrences of these forms.

These phrases are idiomatic, and hence literal translations are likely to prove misleading, and are often quite impossible, see John 13:8, 2 Peter 3:18, e.g.* One and all connote the idea of infinity, eternity, unendingness, as their use with infinite, unending, persons and things shows.

Amen.—A Hebrew word, the meaning of which may be seen in such passages as Deuteronomy 7:9, "the faithful God," Isaiah 49:7, "Jehovah that is faithful," and 65:16, "the God of truth," marg., "the God of Amen." And if God is faithful His testimonies and precepts are "sure," Psalm 19:7; 111:7, as are also His

---

*An idiom is a form of expression in one language which cannot be rendered literally to convey the same sense in another. Literal translations are frequently either misleading or meaningless, e.g., in John 1:15, 30, "before me" is, literally and word for word, "first of me," a combination which in English does not convey any sense.

warnings, Hosea 5:9, and promises, Isaiah 33:16; 55:3. "Amen" is used of men also, Proverbs 25:13, e.g.

Very frequently the word is transliterated, not translated, both into Greek and into English. These are cases where the people used it to express their assent to a law and their willingness to submit to the penalty attached to the breach of it, Deuteronomy 27:15, cp. Nehemiah 5:13. It is also used to express acquiescence in another's prayer, 1 Kings 1:36, where it is defined as = "[let] God say so too," or in another's thanksgiving, 1 Chronicles 16:36, whether by an individual, Jeremiah 11:5, or by the congregation, Psalm 106:48.

Thus "Amen" said by God = "it is and shall be so," and by men, "so let it be."

Once in New Testament "Amen" is a title of Christ, Revelation 3:14, because through Him the purposes of God are established, 2 Corinthians 1:20.

The early Christian churches followed the example of Israel in associating themselves audibly with the prayers and thanksgivings offered on their behalf, 1 Corinthians 14:16, where the article "the" points to a common practice. Moreover this custom conforms to the pattern of things in the Heavens, see Revelation 5:14, etc.

The individual also said "Amen" to express his "let it be so" in response to the divine "thus it shall be," Revelation 22:20. Frequently the speaker adds "Amen" to his own prayers and doxologies, as is the case here and at Ephesians 3:21, e.g.

The Lord Jesus often used "Amen," translated "verily," to introduce new revelations of the mind of God. In John's Gospel it is always repeated, "Amen, Amen," but not elsewhere. Luke does not use it at all, but where Matthew, 16:28, and Mark, 9:1, have "Amen," he has "of a truth"; thus by varying the translation of what the Lord said (if, as seems probable, He spoke in Aramaic) Luke throws light on His meaning.

1:6 I marvel—*thaumazō* = surprise at the unexpected, whether regretful, as here, or pleasurable, as at 2 Thessalonians 1:10, the only occurrences in Paul's epistles; but see also Acts 13:41.

that ye are . . . removing—metatithēmi = to remove a person or thing from one place to another, Acts 7:16, Hebrews 11:5, to change the character of anything, Hebrews 7:12, Jude 4, to desert, here, cp. 1 Kings 21:25, LXX, to the effect of Jezebel's influence over Ahab, "as his wife Jezebel changed him."||

The present tense of the verb suggests that the defection of the Galatians from the truth was not yet complete, and that it would continue, unless of course they were brought to a better mind by this letter. Whether or not this was the case is not known. The form of the verb (middle voice = "removing yourselves"), suggests that not those who had influenced them but the Galatians themselves were responsible for their own declension from the faith. Adam sought in vain to lay the blame for his fall on Eve, as Eve pleaded in vain the wiles of Satan.

so quickly—*tacheōs,* as at 2 Thessalonians 2:2. This may mean either, *a,* that their action had been hasty, taken without due consideration, cp. Exodus 32:8; 1 Timothy 5:22, or, *b,* that but little time had elapsed between their acceptance of the gospel and their desertion of it, cp. Philippians 2:19. On the whole, *a* seems more probable. If, on the other hand, the reference should be to the time rather than to the manner of their defection, then "so soon after the arrival of the false teachers" is more likely than "so soon after your conversion." The apostle may have intended a hint that he had not found them so ready to accept the true gospel as the false teachers had found them ready to accept a perversion of it.

from him that called you—i.e., God, to Whom Paul attributes the call of believers to salvation, cp. v. 15, and see comment on *1 Thessalonians* 2:12; 5:24. Romans 1:6; Ephesians 4:4 are best understood in harmony with these more definite statements.

These words reveal in a flash the gravity of the situation. The Galatians were not merely exchanging one set of opinions for another, they were not merely preferring an alternative way of access to Him. If they left the grace of God they left God Himself.

in the grace of Christ—the means whereby the call of God is mediated, cp. Romans 1:5; 5:15, "the grace of God, and the gift by [lit., "in," as here] the grace of the one Man Christ Jesus." The grace of Christ is defined in 2 Corinthians 8:9. Hence the gospel is not only "of the grace of God," Acts 20:24, it is also "the word of His grace," i.e., of the grace of the Lord Jesus, 14:3, cp. 15:11. See further comment on *1 Thessalonians* 5:28.

unto a different [*heteros*] gospel; 1:7, which is not another [*allos*] gospel:—the words *heteros* and *allos* are synonyms = "other," "another."

Synonyms are words with similar, but not necessarily the same, meaning. Hence synonymous words are sometimes interchangeable, sometimes not.

Heteros and *allos* are interchanged in 1 Corinthians 1:16 and 6:1; 12:8–10; 14:17 and 19, e.g., where both are used of believers, members of the same church. But they are not interchangeable in 1 Corinthians 15:39–41, where *heteros* is used to distinguish the heavenly glory from the earthly, for these differ in genus, and *allos* to distinguish the flesh of men, birds, and fishes, which, however, is in each case flesh, differing not in genus but in species. *Allos* is used again to distinguish between the glories of the heavenly bodies, for these also differ not in kind but in degree only.

Guided by Paul's usage elsewhere the words may be paraphrased, "Unto a gospel which differs so radically from that which I preached to you that it is not another gospel, for it is not a gospel at all." This was the explanation of the Judaizers, theirs was a gospel with a difference; and this the reply of the apostle, so great is the difference that what they preach is not a gospel at all. He cannot allow them even the name. He preached salvation by grace through faith, they preached salvation by law through works; the two, he asserts, are incompatible, and must be antagonistic to the end, cp. Romans 11:6. Thus at the outset he closes the door against compromise, and throughout the epistle this severity of tone is maintained. This new teaching is "bondage," 2:4, and "entanglement," 5:1, and could not result in "justification," 2:16, or "freedom," 5:1; it made Christ to be of no profit, 5:2, and the death of Christ, which is of the essence of the Gospel, a mere embellishment, a superfluous thing of no account, 2:21; so far from bringing blessing to men it put them "under a curse," 3:10, and all who accepted it fell away instantly from grace, 5:4.

only there are some—here the apostle is admittedly difficult to follow: ordinarily his style is both parenthetical and elliptical, much more is it likely to be so where his feelings are strongly moved. The sense may be completed by supplying such words as "you would never have heard of this other gospel if it were not that there are some," etc.

Paul's style is said to be parenthetical because he frequently embellishes and extends his thought by adding words which do not form part of his main argument, see Ephesians 1:21–23; 3:2–21; Philippians 3:18–19, e.g. It is said to be elliptical because he frequently omits words necessary to the continuity of his argument, see Romans 5:18; 9:32, Ephesians 2:1, e.g. See further comment on *2 Thessalonians* 1:11.

that trouble you,—*tarassō,* the word used in the letter from the Jerusalem Council, Acts 15:24, where the meaning is defined by the addition of "subverting your souls."

and would—*thelō* = to desire or design to do anything.

pervert—*metastrephō,* to transform into something of an opposite character, as the sun into darkness, Acts 2:20, laughter and joy into mourning and heaviness, James 4:9.||

These Judaizers, then, were not merely perplexing the minds of the converts, they were seeking to remove the foundation on which alone men may rest for salvation.

the gospel of Christ.—i.e., the gospel concerning Christ, which, under their treatment of it, becomes no gospel at all.

The rendering suggested by the American Revisers, and strongly supported by many European scholars, is, "unto a different gospel, which is nothing else save that there are some that trouble you and would pervert the gospel of Christ." As thus translated the meaning of the apostle seems to be that this professed gospel was simply an attempt on the part of some to make mischief by perverting the true gospel of Christ.

1:8 But though—"but even if," suggesting that the contingency was very remote.

we,—i.e., "Paul and his company," which included Barnabas, on their first visit, Acts 13:13, and, on a later occasion, Silas and Timothy, 15:40; 16:3-6.

or an angel from heaven,—a contingency even more remote. There may be here an allusion to the incident recorded in Acts 14:11-13, when on their first visit to Lystra, a Galatian city, the people supposed them to be gods. Apart from this, however, the words suggest the highest conceivable authority.

should preach unto you any gospel other than that which we preached unto you,—*para,* rendered "other than" may be rendered "beside," "contrary to." Paul's claim was that the gospel as he and his colleagues had preached it was complete, absolute, final.

Here, and in vv. 9, 16, 23; 4:13, "preached the gospel" represents one word, *euangelizō,* i.e., "to gospel"; see at v. 11 and cp. 2:2, below.

let him be anathema.—this word, which is translated from the Greek, occurs frequently in LXX, where it is used to translate the Hebrew *cherem,* a thing devoted to God, whether, *a,* for His service, as the sacrifices, Leviticus 27:28, or, *b,* for destruction, as an idol, Deuteronomy 7:26, or Jericho, Joshua 6:17. Then later, *cherem* took on a wider, more general meaning, the disfavor of Jehovah, see Isaiah 34:5; Zechariah 14:11; Malachi 4:6. This latter is the New Testament sense of anathema.

In Luke 21:5, "offerings," the good sense, *a,* above, appears, but there the spelling is *anathēma.*

Apart from the present context "anathema" occurs in Paul's writings only in Romans 9:3; 1 Corinthians 12:3; 16:22; elsewhere only in Acts 23:14, where it is joined with the verb "anathematize."||

To say "Anathema Jesus" was to make a solemn declaration that Jesus of Nazareth had died for His own sins, and so under a curse deserved and abiding; to say "Lord Jesus" was to acknowledge that He died for the sins of others, 1 Corinthians 12:3. And if any man fail to be attracted by the character, the "glory and virtue," 2 Peter 1:3, of Christ, surely such a man, inasmuch as he refuses the blessing, is preparing himself for the curse, the doom of the lost at the coming of the Lord Jesus in glory, 1 Corinthians 16:22.

The words of the apostle in Romans 9:3 are reminiscent of those of Moses, Exodus 32:32. Perhaps the love of Paul for his fellow countrymen can be fully comprehended only by those with love as great as his, but whatever he might find in his heart to wish in order that they might be saved, two things are plain— first, that the wish was impossible of accomplishment, and second, that had it been possible it could not have availed to secure the end he desired.

Here the meaning is that any who thus pervert the gospel of Christ shall for so doing incur the disfavor of God.

1:9 As we have said before,—*prolegō,* used in 2 Corinthians 13:2, as here, of a former occasion; in 1 Thessalonians 3:4, it = "plainly," as margin.||

so say I now again,—"now," *arti,* implies a lapse of time and a contrast between the present and the past. Its use here makes quite clear that Paul refers not to what he had just written, v. 8, but to earlier warnings given by himself and his colleagues on former visits.

If any man—lit., "if anyone."

preacheth unto you—whereas in the previous verse the verb is in the subjunctive mood, here it is in the indicative; the former is purely hypothetical, = "if by any chance anyone should preach," whereas the latter is more direct and concrete, = "if, as a matter of fact, anyone is preaching."

any gospel other than that which ye received,—in v. 8 the standpoint is that of the missionaries, "we preached," here it is that of the converts, "ye received." The gospel for which he was so jealous was not merely that which he had proclaimed at the outset, it was that which they had accepted, which had lightened their darkness, and freed them from their sins, cp. 1 Corinthians 15:1 and 1 Thessalonians 2:13.

let him be anathema.—the repetition of the curse shows he had pronounced it not passionately but deliberately, as a matter not of feeling but of judgment.

1:10 For—the strength of his language requires justification, this he proceeds to supply.

am I . . . persuading—*peithō,* = to bring about a change of mind by the influence of reason, or of moral considerations, as at 2 Corinthians 5:11, cp. also Acts 13:43, "urge." It also = "to conciliate," "to make a friend of," as in Acts 12:20, and should probably so be understood here.

now—*arti,* as in v. 9; the contrast is not with his life before his conversion, when, indeed, he showed no conciliatory spirit, but rather with the general course of his ministry. His traducers suggested that he was a trimmer who sought to ingratiate himself by "becoming all things to all men," 1 Corinthians 9:22; in support of this contention they could point to the circumcision of Timothy as a bid for Jewish favor, and to his repudiation of law as an attempt to conciliate the Gentiles. So the emphasis is thrown on "now," as though he would say, "never mind the past, at least in this repeated statement my meaning is not to be mistaken or misrepresented."

men, or God?—the answer intended is, of course, "not men, but God!" Certainly, there is some incongruity in the thought of conciliating God, but this boldness is accounted for by the circumstances under which he wrote, and by the fact that he is not making a statement, nor even asking a question to elicit information. The passage is not logical but rhetorical, and may be paraphrased, "in thus saying do I seek to conciliate men at the expense of my veracity, as some have suggested? Have I not, on the contrary, regard solely to God?"

or am I seeking to please men?—the answer expected is in the negative; in full it would run, "No, not to please men, but to please God."

if I were still pleasing men,—in his pre-Christian days he had shared the common motives of men, see Acts 22:5; Philippians 3:4-6 for hints of this; now he no longer courted popularity, 1 Thessalonians 2:4; he shared with all Christians the new motive made possible by the gift of the Spirit, Romans 8:8, 9, cp. 1 Thessalonians 4:1.

In these passages the contrast is between pleasing God and pleasing men. Elsewhere a contrast is made between pleasing, or gratifying, oneself, and gratifying others, 1 Corinthians 10:33. In such cases the Christian is to "please his neighbor, for that which is good, unto edifying," in which Christ Himself is our Example, for He "pleased not Himself," Romans 15:1-3. If indeed Christ had pleased Himself, that being the motive of One Himself intrinsically holy, could only have been a holy motive. But since, notwithstanding the purity and perfection of His character, "He pleased not Himself," much more should Christians, conscious of the deceitfulness of their own hearts, beware of pleasing themselves.

I should not be a servant—*doulos* = bondservant, i.e., a servant viewed in his relationship to his master. For New Testament synonyms of *doulos* see comment on *1 Thessalonians* 3:10.

of Christ.—that popularity and the service of Christ are incompatible Paul knew from experience, for immediately he entered the service of Christ his former friends took counsel to kill him, and even yet persecution had not ceased, cp. 5:11, Acts 9:23.

In Titus 1:1, Paul calls himself "a servant of God and an apostle of Jesus Christ," and since no man can serve, *douleuō,* two masters, there is in this description of himself incidental evidence that the Lord Jesus occupied in the apostle's thoughts a place indistinguishable from that of God.

1:11 For—the writer now begins to deal with the first of his main themes, his credentials as an apostle.

I make known unto you, brethren,—*gnōrizō,* a word which Paul sometimes used for the communication of things before unknown, 2 Corinthians 8:1, sometimes for the recapitulation of things already well-known, here and 1 Corinthians 15:1, cp. 1 Corinthians 12:3, and its use of prayer to God in Philippians 4:6. Plainly it is not intended to suggest that the Galatians had not before known the ground of Paul's claim to apostleship, but to remind them of the facts.

as touching—these words are not in the original; Paul's elliptical style makes it necessary to supply them in order to complete the sense, for he is not about to restate the gospel but to describe his own relation to it.

the gospel [*euangelion*] which was preached [*euangelizō*] by me—Paul uses the word "gospel" of two closely allied but quite distinct things, *a,* of the facts of the death, burial, and resurrection of the Lord Jesus, as in 1 Corinthians 15:1-3; *b,* of the interpretation of these facts, as in v. 8; 2:2, and here, cp. "my gospel" in Romans 2:16, *et al.* In *a* the gospel is viewed historically, in *b* doctrinally. Not the facts but the interpretation of them was in dispute among the Galatians. Hence *b* is the meaning here.

that it is not—the change from the past to the present tense is a reminder that the gospel had not changed its character in the meantime.

after man.—*kata,* "according to," i.e., not of man's device, not even in harmony with man's ideas. The interpretation put upon the facts of the gospel by the Judaizers was "after man," human alike in its origin and its object.

1:12 For neither did I receive it—the pronoun is emphatic, suggesting a contrast with the Judaizers, who probably professed to come from James, as they did who taught the same things at Antioch, see 2:12, and denying any inferiority in this respect to those apostles who had companied with the Lord and had been directly commissioned by Him before His ascension. But while Paul thus "glorifies his ministry," Romans 11:13, when speaking of himself personally he uses very different language, "I am the least of the apostles, that am not meet to be called an apostle," 1 Corinthians 15:9, cp. 2 Corinthians 12:11.

from man,—suggesting again the contrast noticed at v. 1 between the Lord Jesus and "man"; a contrast even more marked if the margin, "a man" is adopted.

nor was I taught it,—the apostle continues to clear the ground of all possible alternatives before declaring the means whereby he learned the meaning of the facts of the gospel.

but *it came to me*—another instance of Paul's elliptical style. As the italics indicate, the words are not found in the original but are added to complete the sense. "It came to me" = "I received and was taught it."

through revelation—*apokalupsis,* i.e., a direct communication of the mind of God, cp. the words of the Lord to Peter, Matthew 16:17. See further at v. 16.

of Jesus Christ.—the words, taken apart from their context, may mean either, *a,* the making visible of the Lord Himself in glory, as at 1 Corinthians 1:7; 2 Thessalonians 1:7; 1 Peter 1:7, 13, or, *b,* a communication from Him, as in 2 Corinthians 12:1; Revelation 1:1, cp. Ephesians 3:3. The context makes plain that the latter is intended here. Both are illustrated at the conversion of the writer who saw the Lord and heard His voice, Acts 22:14. There is no indication, here or elsewhere, of the time at which this revelation of the meaning of the facts of the gospel was given, or whether it was given at once or on several occasions.

Since the revelation was from the Lord risen and ascended, the order of the name and title is in harmony with the context.

1:13 For ye have heard—or, as the point tense indicates, "ye heard," i.e., from the writer when he first preached the gospel to them. The proof of his statement that his gospel was not from a human but from a divine source is involved in his history, of which he proceeds to give a very condensed account.

of my manner of life—*anastrophē* = the general ordering of one's conduct in relation to others. The word occurs elsewhere in Paul's epistles only in Ephesians 4:22; 1 Timothy 4:12, the corresponding verb only in 2 Corinthians 1:12; 1 Timothy 3:15, "behave," Ephesians 2:3, "live."

Paul uses a synonym, *biōsis,* in Acts 26:4, which refers to one's course of life viewed in itself, not in relation to others.||

in time past—i.e., prior to his conversion.

in the Jews' religion,—*Ioudaismos* = Judaism, and in v. 14; it occurs frequently in the Apocrypha, where it = "the government, laws, institutions, and religion of the Jews." Thus it refers not to religious beliefs but to religious practices, and to these not as they were instituted by God, but as the Pharisees and their scribes had developed and enlarged them by their traditions. See Matthew 23.||

The Apocrypha is a collection of the noncanonical books of the Jews, historical, political, moral, and predictive. They are known to exist only in the Greek language, and in this and other respects are separated by a wide gulf from the canonical Hebrew Scriptures. The Apocrypha is of great literary and historical value, but its religious authority is nil.

how that—or simply "that," as the word is most frequently rendered, see 2 Corinthians 13:5, e.g. Here again there is an ellipsis, which may be supplied by "and ye heard," repeated from the beginning of the sentence, or, but less simply, by such words as "and what that manner of life was may be judged from the fact that."

beyond measure—*kata huperbolē,* a phrase Paul uses in 2 Corinthians 1:8 of the afflictions which he suffered at the hands of others, illustrating the principle that "whatsoever a man soweth, that shall he also reap," 6:7, below. He uses it also of the glory that awaits those who suffer for the Lord's sake, 2 Corinthians 4:17, and of the sinfulness of sin, Romans 7:13, and of the superiority of love to all "gifts" or forms of service, however desirable, 1 Corinthians 12:31.

The word *huperbolē* occurs also in 2 Corinthians 4:7 of the power of God, and in 12:7 of the revelations given to Paul.||

I persecuted—*diōkō* = to pursue earnestly, whether with a good purpose, as 1 Thessalonians 5:15; Philippians 3:12, 14, "press on," or an evil, as Philippians 3:6, and here. He refers to the incidents recorded in Acts 8:1–3; 9:1, 2.

the church of God,—i.e., at Jerusalem. See Acts 9:13; 26:10, 11; see 1 Thess. 2:14.

and made havock of it,—*portheo,* to lay waste, to ruin, as in v. 23, Acts 9:21. "To the death" is his own statement of the only limit he had set for himself in his self-appointed task, Acts 22:4.||

1:14 and I advanced in the Jews' religion—*porkoptō,* lit., "to strike forward," i.e., to make progress, whether in a good sense, as of the Lord Jesus, Luke 2:52, or in an evil sense, 2 Timothy 2:16; 3:9, 13, or in a sense quite neutral, as here and Romans 13:12.||

The corresponding noun, *prokopē,* "progress," is used only in a good sense; of the gospel in the world, Philippians 1:12; of believers in the faith, 1:25; and of the servant of Christ in his qualification for service, 1 Timothy 4:15.||

The tense of the three words Paul uses is "continuous," lit., "was persecuting," "was making havock," "was advancing," indicating that each was being actively pursued, but that none were brought to completion.

beyond many of mine own age among my countrymen,—he had attained to a good standing among his fellow-students in the rabbinical schools, alike on account of his mental abilities and of his zeal, though, naturally, he mentions only the latter, cp. Acts 22:3.

being—*huparchō,* lit., "to be from the beginning," i.e., naturally, and hence "confessedly"; the fact was acknowledged by all who knew him.

more exceedingly—i.e., in comparison with the others of his own age.

zealous—*zēlōtēs,* lit., "zealot" = an uncompromising partisan. By this name an extreme section of the Pharisees, characterized by bitter antagonism to the Romans, came to be known; "Cananaean" was the equivalent Hebrew term, Matthew 10:4. To this section one of the apostles, Simon, had belonged, Luke 6:15; Acts 1:13. Here and in all other New Testament occurrences *zēlōtēs* is an adjective; Paul does not mean that he belonged to "the Zealots," any more than he meant that the Jews to whom he spoke at Jerusalem belonged to them, Acts 22:3, cp. 21:20. He is reminding his readers of his unquestioned loyalty to Judaism in the days before he became a Christian. *Zēlōtēs* is also capable of a good sense; Christians are to be "zealous of good works," Titus 2:14, and of "spiritual gifts," 1 Corinthians 14:12, though this latter passage is probably slightly ironical.||

for the traditions—i.e., interpretations of the law of Moses to which the Lord Jesus said the virtual abrogation of that law among the Jews was due, Mark 7:3–13.

of my fathers.—*patrikos,* "paternal." Paul was by descent a Pharisee, one of "the straitest sect of our [the Jews'] religion," Acts 26:5. But in addressing the Jewish mob he declared that he had been instructed in "the strict manner of the law of our fathers," *patrōos,* i.e., the law of Moses which was acknowledged by all alike.||

1:15 But when—up to this point in Paul's life all had been of man and by man; now God intervened, and everything was changed. The reference to his conversion, however, is quite incidental here; his purpose is to describe the course he pursued thereafter. Hence the connection is "when . . . immediately."

it was the good pleasure of God,—*eudokeō,* see comment on *1 Thessalonians* 2:6. These words are to be connected directly with "to reveal His Son in me." The intervention of God in the life of Paul was neither sought nor deserved by him; his salvation, alike in its purpose and in its accomplishment, was of God.

who separated me, *even* **from my mother's womb,**—*aphorizō* = to mark off from; see at 2:12, below. The purpose of God is thus shown to be independent alike of Paul's character and of his actions, cp. Romans 9:11. For a parallel case, see Jeremiah 1:5, and for similar language concerning the Messiah, Isaiah 49:1. Inasmuch as the word Pharisee = "a separated person," it is at least possible that the apostle here suggests a contrast with his former associations. But whereas formerly he was "a separated one" by his birth and by his own convictions, now he knew that he had been separated to a different object before he was born at all.

and called me—"point" tense, referring to what occurred on the Damascus road, Acts 9:1–9.

through his grace,—cp. v. 6; this sums up in one comprehensive word, *a,* the motive of God in His own good pleasure, *b,* the purposive act of God in setting Paul apart before his birth, and, *c,* his actual call of God in time. And as in his case so also in that of every one partaking of the salvation provided in the gospel, "grace reigns."

1:16 to reveal his Son—*apokaluptō,* "to uncover," "to unveil"; from *kaluptō,* "to cover"; both words are used in Matthew 10:26, "there is nothing covered *(kaluptō),* that shall not be revealed *(apokaluptō)*"; see also Luke 12:2. New Testament occurrences of this word fall under two heads, subjective and objective. The subjective use is that in which something is presented to the mind directly, as:
  a, the meaning of the acts of God, Matthew 11:25, Luke 10:21;
  b, the secret of the Person of the Lord Jesus, Matthew 16:17, John 12:38;
  c, the character of God as Father, Matthew 11:27; Luke 10:22;
  d, the will of God for the conduct of His children, Philippians 3:15;
  e, the mind of God to the prophets, of Israel, 1 Peter 1:12, and of the Church, 1 Corinthians 14:30; Ephesians 3:5.

The objective use is that in which something is presented to the senses, sight or hearing, as: referring to the past,

f, the truth declared to men in the gospel, Romans 1:17; 1 Corinthians 2:10; Galatians 3:23;

g, thoughts before hidden in the heart, Luke 2:35; referring to the future,

h, the coming in glory of the Lord Jesus, Luke 17:30;

i, the salvation and glory that await the believer, Romans 8:18; 1 Peter 1:5; 5:1;

j, the true value of service, 1 Corinthians 3:13;

k, the wrath of God (at the Cross, against sin, and, at the revelation of the Lord Jesus, against the sinner), Romans 1:18;

l, the Lawless One, 2 Thessalonians 2:3, 6, 8.

"Reveal" here is "point" tense, referring to a definite occurrence, viz., Paul's experience on the way to Damascus. For an analysis of the New Testament occurrences of the corresponding noun, *apokalupsis,* see comment on *2 Thessalonians* 1:7.‖

in me,—*en emoi,* these words have been understood in three ways:

a. Instrumentally, = "by" or "through me," as, apparently the same words are to be understood in 2 Corinthians 13:3.

There is, however, no other passage in the New Testament that bears this meaning. The gospel of God concerning Christ was revealed to the apostle, see at v. 12, but in no place is it suggested that the Son of God Himself was revealed to others through any man. God did, indeed, reveal Himself to men in and through Christ, but no man could conceivably be to Christ what Christ was to God.

b. Subjectively, = "within me," i.e., in his heart or soul, to his inner consciousness.

But it is plain that Paul here refers to what occurred on the way to Damascus, and it is equally plain that on that occasion he saw the Lord outwardly, in actual presence. Had his intention been to give the ground of his claim to be a Christian, he might perhaps have appealed to an inward experience, as he does at 2:20, but an inward experience would be valueless in support of a claim to apostolic authority.

c. Objectively, = "in my case," as the same words are sometimes translated; in such places, as here, a contrast is suggested. Thus in 1 Corinthians 9:15, the meaning is that while the apostle did not wish the Corinthian church to undertake responsibility in temporal things in his case, they should be prepared to do so in the case of other laborers in the gospel. In v. 24 of this chapter, obviously the meaning is "they glorified God in my case," i.e., in contrast with that of the other persecutors who remained unconverted. Cp. 1 Corinthians 14:11, marg., 1 Timothy 1:16; 1 John 2:8; 4:9, 16, marg.

So here; whereas in the case of all other Christians salvation is through the word preached and heard, Romans 10:14, 15, in Paul's case it pleased God to reveal His Son to him. If then, to have seen the Lord was a necessary qualification for apostolic authority, in this also Paul was not inferior to the Twelve. But whereas in their case the Lord Jesus had been seen in the days of His flesh, in Paul's case He was revealed in glory.

Neither in Luke's narrative, Acts 9:1-9, nor in Paul's own accounts of the occurrence, chapters twenty-two and twenty-six, is it stated that Paul actually saw the Lord Jesus; but Ananias, who had been made acquainted with the facts by direct communication from the Lord in a vision, spoke to him of "the Lord, even Jesus, Who appeared unto thee," 9:17, and Paul himself recounted the words of Ananias thus: "The God of our fathers hath appointed thee . . . to see the Righteous One," 22:14. And writing to the Corinthians, he exclaims, "have I not seen Jesus our Lord?" and later states categorically that last of all, as unto one born out of due time, "He appeared to me also," 1 Corinthians 9:1; 15:8. In these passages, the word translated "appear," "see," is that used lower down, v. 19, of "seeing" the apostles.

Moreover in the only other New Testament passage in which the verb "reveal" is used of the Lord Jesus, an objective, i.e., a real external appearance in person is certainly intended, Luke 17:30.

The language of Paul in 1 Corinthians 15:8, where he refers to the experience of which he speaks here, suggests that there is a relationship between the revelation of the Lord Jesus to Paul, and that yet future consummation when He will be revealed to the nation of the Jews. "One born out of due time," or prematurely, is not one born after, but before, the full or due time. The apostle then does not intend in these words to describe himself in relation to the Twelve, whose calling preceded his, neither does he wish to suggest that as compared with them he was either weak, sickly, or deformed in a spiritual sense. Rather he seems to have in mind such passages as Zechariah 12:10, and the salvation of Israel when the Lord Jesus is revealed from heaven, 2 Thessalonians 1:7. As he was saved so shall they be saved; his experience anticipated theirs.

that—"in order that."

I might preach—*euangelizo,* as at vv. 8, 9, 11, = "to proclaim good news"; see comment on *1 Thessalonians* 3:6.

Paul was called in order that he might become a Christian; God revealed His Son to him in order that he might have apostolic authority to preach the gospel. The tense is "continuous," for though the revelation was a definite and completed act, the commission to preach was for his lifetime.

him—as to its source and authority the gospel is "the gospel of God," as to its substance it is "concerning His Son . . . Jesus Christ our Lord," Romans 1:1, 3. Here, however, in view of the fact that his detractors also claimed to preach the gospel, the apostle adds an unambiguous reference to Christ Himself, the center, substance, and circumference of the good news he carried.

among the Gentiles;—*ethnos,* see comment on *1 Thessalonians* 2:16.

immediately—i.e., after his experience on the way to Damascus, and its sequel in Damascus; the word is to be read with "I went away," v. 17. "Immediately" is an elastic term, and must be understood here in the light of the facts related in Acts 9:19-25, and of the purpose of this section of the Epistle to demonstrate Paul's independence of men in the matter of his apostolic authority. "Immediately" admits of "certain days" having been spent by him in Damascus, and probably includes the "many days" of v. 23 which were devoted to testimony among the Jews. The word is used merely to show that he had not had any opportunity of learning either the facts of the gospel or their meaning from the recognized, accredited apostles.

I conferred not—*prosanatithēmi*, lit., "to put before," i.e., to lay any matter before others with a view to obtaining advice or instruction. Cp. 2:6, "they who were of repute laid nothing before me," i.e., imparted nothing to me.||

In 2:2 a shorter form, *anatithēmi*, is used; the writer may have selected the less intensive word for use there in order to suggest that he described the character of his teaching to the apostles, not in order to obtain their approval of it or any advice as to modifying it, but simply that they might be made conversant with the facts of the case on which they were shortly to adjudicate. See Acts 25:14.||

with flesh and blood:—by synecdoche (a figure of speech in which a part is put for the whole, or the whole for a part), = man, human beings; the phrase ordinarily emphasizes the inevitable limitations of humanity. It occurs again with the same meaning in Matthew 16:17. In 1 Corinthians 15:50 the language is not figurative, the reference is to the physical part of man, his body, which in its corruptible and mortal state is unfit for the spiritual realm, the kingdom of God in its future manifestation. In Hebrews 2:14, Ephesians 6:12, the order in orig. is "blood and flesh."||

1:17 neither went I up to Jerusalem to them which were apostles before me:—Paul gave full recognition to the apostolic authority of the Twelve, and to the precedence of their apostleship in time, while he so strenuously insists on his independence of them. So far negatively, what he did not do; now he proceeds to declare the course that he actually did pursue.

but—*alla;* the conjunction is strongly adversative, and indeed may be intended not only to introduce the contrast between the objective of the journey which he did not take, Jerusalem, and that of the journey which he did take, Arabia, but also to suggest a contrast between the object that might have taken him to Jerusalem, viz., conference with men, and the object that may have taken him into Arabia, viz., solitary meditation and communion with God.

I went away—there is no other reference to this journey in the New Testament It may have been made immediately after his baptism and before the "certain days" of Acts 9:19. Or the narrative of Acts may be continuous, Paul may have remained in the city until after the "many days" of v. 23, which were brought to a close by an attempt to arrest him, v. 25, cp. 2 Corinthians 11:32, 33. The "immediately" of v. 16 is not really inconsistent with either hypothesis, though it seems to favor the former, as the narrative in Acts seems to favor the latter.

As to the duration of the apostle's stay in Arabia there is no information. The language used may suggest that it was brief; on the other hand it may have occupied the larger part of the three years of the following verse.

into Arabia;—in the first century the northern confines of the district so named were quite near to the city of Damascus.

and again I returned unto Damascus.—implying that it was from Damascus he set out, though he does not mention the fact; it was not necessary to do so, for he was writing to those already acquainted with the story. His purpose in referring to the city at all is to account for his movements at the time, and to show that even then he had not put himself in the way of the Twelve.

This quite incidental reference to Damascus is what is termed an "undesigned coincidence" with Acts 9:3, "undesigned" because, of course, "Acts" was not written until long after this Epistle.

Damascus, the capital of Syria, is situated on the banks of the river Abana, see 2 Kings 5:12. It was a place of note in the time of Abraham, Genesis 14:15; 15:2. The inhabitants were subdued by David, 2 Samuel 8:5, 6, but revolted under Solomon, 1 Kings 11:24. It passed under the rule of the Hadads, the foes of Israel, 1 Kings 15:18, and was afterwards taken by Tiglath Pileser, King of Assyria, 2 Kings 16:9; Isaiah 17:1-3. Its importance at the time of the captivity is noted in Ezekiel 27:18. It was conquered by the Greeks under Alexander the Great in 333 B.C., and by the Romans under Pompey in 64 B.C., and remained in their hands till A.D. 37, when the Emperor Caligula seems to have restored it to Aretas IV, King of Arabia, to whose father it had previously belonged. Damascus was in the possession of Aretas in the time of Paul's stay there, 2 Corinthians 11:32, 33.

1:18 Then after three years I went up to Jerusalem—i.e., three years elapsed after his conversion before he saw any of the apostles at all.

to visit—*historeō,* = to visit with a view to becoming acquainted with, see marg.||

Cephas,—the Aramaic equivalent of the Greek name "Peter," = "a stone." His original name was Simon, or Symeon, Acts 15:14, but he was renamed Cephas, or Peter, by the Lord Jesus, first, apparently, prophetically, "Thou shalt be called," John 1:42, then actually, "thou art," Matthew 16:18. Paul is the only other writer who uses the Aramaic name, but he does not use it exclusively, see 2:7. Peter was the leader and chief spokesman of the twelve apostles.

and tarried with him fifteen days.—this was, apparently, the visit of Acts 9:26-30; 22:17-21; his zeal in the preaching of the gospel provoked opposition, before which God, in a vision given him while in a trance, called him to retire that he might engage in a wider sphere of service. Here, however, the apostle refers to the visit merely lest he should lay himself open to the charge of suppression of a salient fact that might be used against him.

For "with," *pros,* see comment on *1 Thessalonians* 3:4.

1:19 But other—*heteros,* as at v. 6; here plainly = "other of the same order."

of the apostles saw I none,—if, as is highly probable, this visit is to be identified with that of Acts 9:26–30, it may seem strange that Luke should say that Barnabas brought Paul to "the apostles," whereas Paul himself declares that he saw only Peter and James. It is quite possible, however, that Peter, who himself went shortly after on an extended preaching tour, v. 32, may have been the only one of the Twelve in Jerusalem at the time, and in that case Barnabas would introduce Paul to him as their representative. And if James is to be reckoned an apostle, Luke's words are quite consistent, for though he says "the apostles," he does not add "all." For the purpose of the historian it was not necessary to amplify the narrative, but for Paul, whose aim is to show that he could not have been a disciple of the Twelve, detail is essential.

save James—lit., "if not," = except; this may be taken as implying that James was an apostle whether, *a,* in the more restricted sense, making him one of the Twelve, and in that case presumably the son of Alphaeus, Matthew 10:3, or *b,* in the wider sense in which the word is sometimes used, see note on v. 1. Or the words may be translated as margin, "but only," (cp. 2:9) when the meaning will be, *c,* "I saw no other apostle unless indeed it be James, who, though not an apostle, is reputed to be a pillar in the church," cp. 2:9.

Of these *a* is to be rejected, see below; *b* and c, which cover the same ground, seem to express the writer's meaning.

the Lord's brother.—this relationship has been understood in three ways:

a. That "brother" is a general term, = kinsman, cousin, cp. Genesis 13:8; 29:15, and that the James intended is the son of Alphaeus, whose wife was Mary, this Mary being a sister of Mary the mother of the Lord. This is known as the "Hieronymian" theory, since Jerome, or Hieronymus, was its author, *circa* A.D. 383.

While it is true that kinsmen, and even those who were merely fellow country-men, sometimes addressed each other as "brother," there is no other place in Scripture (though 1 Chr. 23:22 may be noted) where such are categorically stated to be brothers, as Paul here states that James was the Lord's brother. Moreover, it is improbable that two sisters would be called Mary, and highly probable that four women, not three, are intended in John 19:25, thus, 1, "His mother," 2, "and His mother's sister," 3, "Mary the wife of Clopas," 4, "and Mary Magdalene." The theory that James and his brothers were really cousins of the Lord, and in only this sense His brothers, is without adequate support in Scripture.

b. That James and his brothers, Matthew 13:55, were sons of Joseph by a former marriage, and so half-brothers of the Lord. This is known as the "Epiphanian" theory, and dates from a very early age. Like the Hieronymian it preserved the doctrine of the "perpetual virginity" of Mary in an age when asceticism was highly esteemed, and it may have been invented with this in view. Thus Origen, *circa* A.D. 253, who himself accepts it, says, "Those who hold this view wish to preserve the honor of Mary in virginity throughout . . . And I think it reasonable . . ."

According to prophecy the Messiah was to be the King of the Jews, see Psalm 2:6-9; Jeremiah 23:5; Zechariah 9:9; Micah 5:2, et al., reigning in virtue of His descent from David, Psalm 132:11. The angel Gabriel identified the promised Son with these prophecies, Luke 1:32; as King of Israel He was acclaimed, John 12:12-15, and as King of the Jews He was crucified, John 19:19. The Lord Jesus was thus indeed "of the seed of David," 2 Timothy 2:8, in virtue of the Davidic descent of His mother, but, of course, could not inherit the throne on this account; for the claim to kingship was based on primogeniture in the male line, save in those specified cases in which it was set aside. Since Joseph was in the direct line, Matthew 1:16, he, and after him his eldest son, were David's heirs. If, however, Joseph had sons by a marriage previous to that with Mary, then the eldest of these would be his heir. Certainly the Lord Jesus was not the son of Joseph, but having been born after Joseph had taken Mary as his wife, vv. 20-24, He was reputed to be his son, and would inherit accordingly, but only as the eldest of his sons, cp. 2 Chronicles 21:3. This theory would, apparently, invalidate the claim of the Lord Jesus to David's throne by descent.

c. That the words are to be taken in their natural sense, i.e., that the brethren and sisters of the Lord were the offspring of the marriage of Joseph and Mary. This is known as the "Helvidian" theory. According to it the Lord was the eldest in the family of Joseph, and hence rightful heir to the throne of David. It may not be without significance that the word "brethren" is defined as the equivalent of "my mother's children" in a Psalm, many parts of which are Messianic, 69, and some parts of which had a detailed fulfillment in the experience of the Lord Jesus, cp. v. 21 with Matthew 27:34, e.g.

This designation is added by Paul to distinguish this James, *a,* from James the son of Alphaeus, one of the Twelve, Mark 3:18, and, *b,* from James the son of Zebedee, another of the Twelve, who was alive at the time of this visit and was subsequently slain by Herod, Acts 12:2. Mention of him in this way implies that he occupied a prominent position in the church at Jerusalem, and this is consistent with Luke's narrative, Acts 12:17; 15:13; 21:18. This James is probably to be identified with the writer of the Epistle.

1:20 Now touching the things which I write unto you, behold, before God, I lie not.—lit., "before God, that I lie not," i.e., *"before* God I declare that," etc.

This solemn protestation witnesses to his apprehension lest the Galatian believers, under the influence of those who were impugning his apostleship, might still be incredulous despite all he had related.

He uses this particular form of asseveration, lit., "in the presence of God," in 1 Timothy 5:21; 6:13; 2 Timothy 4:1. See further comment on *1 Thessalonians* 5:27.

1:21 Then—at the end of the fifteen days, i.e., immediately upon the discovery of the plot against his life, see Acts 9:30.

I came into the regions—*klima*, lit., "slope," in general use = "district," as in Romans 15:23; 2 Corinthians 11:10.

of Syria and Cilicia.—two adjacent provinces, the former situated immediately north of Palestine, with Damascus in the south, and Antioch, the capital, in the north; the latter, the chief town of which was Tarsus, lay northwest again. The order of the names is probably the order of the importance of the provinces, not the order in which the apostle visited them. In Acts 9:30 Luke records that he went from Caesarea to Tarsus, apparently by sea, since both these places are ports. In these provinces he seems to have continued for about ten years, apparently making Tarsus his headquarters, 11:25, and laboring in the gospel in the northern parts of Syria, those adjacent to Cilicia, and in Cilicia itself, and founding churches, 15:41. The apostle's purpose, however, is not to define the sphere of his labors during these ten years, but to show that it lay far from Jerusalem and from the possibility of contact with the Twelve.

1:22 And I was still unknown—continuous tense, "I remained unknown."

by face—*prosōpon*, as in 1 Thessalonians 2:17, i.e., in person.

unto the churches of Judaea—i.e., as distinguished from that in Jerusalem, where, of course, he was known, or at least had been seen, v. 18. These churches appear to have been formed subsequent to his persecution of the church there, v. 13. The statement in Acts 26:20 does not contradict that in the text, for there he is narrating the scope of his missionary labors up to his appearance before Agrippa; hence the ministry "throughout all the country of Judaea" belongs to a time later than that to which he here refers.

which were—the verb is not in orig.; it seems more natural to supply the present tense, "are," since, presumably, these churches were still existent when the words were written.

in Christ:—see note at *1 Thessalonians* 1:1. The addition of these words is a suggestive reminder to the Galatians and their Judaizing teachers that even the churches under the immediate influence of the Twelve were not merely companies of Jews professing a modified form of Judaism; they were "in Christ," i.e., even at the date of which he writes they were already cut off from Judaism altogether. What happened at Ephesus happened in Jerusalem; sooner or later the disciples of Christ were everywhere separated from the Jews, see Acts 19:9. How unreasonable, then, was this attempt, made in the name of the gospel, to lead Gentiles into a bondage from which the gospel had set Jews free!

1:23 but they only heard say,—continuous tense, "they were hearing."

He that once persecuted us—the tense is again continuous, and the form of the verb is the participle, = "the persecutor"; such was the fear in which he had been held by the saints that this had become his distinctive appellation among them.

now preacheth—as at v. 16.

the faith—*hē pistis;* see comment on *1 Thessalonians* 3:3.

of which he once made havock;—verb and tense as in v. *13.* The figure here is metonymy, in which one thing is put for another with which it is closely associated, i.e., *"the* faith" is put for those who hold it. There is no exaggeration in the figure, however, for at that early date when the number of believers was small, and when the faith was still enshrined only in the hearts of men, it may well have seemed practicable to its opponents to stamp it out by energetic attacks upon those who held it.

1:24 and they glorified God—*doxazō,* continuous tense, lit., "were glorifying"; i.e., they ascribed the credit for the transformation of an erstwhile persecutor into a zealous advocate, not to the man in whom the change had been wrought, but to the One Who had accomplished it, God, to Whose Name the emphasis is given by its position at the end of the sentence.

in me.—see at v. 16, under c, and cp. Isaiah 49:3. These words mark a climax in the apostle's argument; the Christians in Judaea had praised God for the preaching of the very same gospel with which those who professed to come from Judaea found fault as inadequate.

GALATIANS

CHAPTER TWO

Verses 1–21

2:1 Then—as in vv. 18, 21, marking another stage in his history.

after the space of—*dia,* a different word from that of 1:18, *meta,* and used to emphasize the length of time that elapsed before it was again possible for him to come into contact with the Twelve.

fourteen years—not necessarily fourteen full years, but any part of one year, however short, then twelve full years, and then any part of another year, however short. These fourteen years may be regarded, *a,* as dating from his conversion, or, *b,* from his visit to Cephas, to which he had just before referred, 1:18. On the whole the latter, though it is not free from difficulty, seems the more natural sense; see further below.

I went up again to Jerusalem—this visit may be that of Acts 11:30—12:25, or that of Acts 15. In favor of the former it is urged that, as Paul is arguing that he never had an opportunity of learning from, or receiving authority from, the Twelve, he could not, in fairness, have omitted a reference to this visit. It is to be noted, however, that Luke does not mention a meeting between Paul and the Twelve, or any one of them on that occasion. He may, indeed, have been in Jerusalem during Peter's imprisonment, 12:4, 5, or during his subsequent absence, vv. 17:19, when the other apostles may also have been absent or greatly preoccupied by the persecution of Herod. In such circumstances it is conceivable that Paul, writing to people acquainted with the facts, may for brevity have omitted any reference to a visit, undertaken for a specific purpose, and evidently of no great duration.

Against it, moreover, are some considerations of weight. King Herod Agrippa I died in A.D. 44, presumably the year of the visit of Acts 11:30—12:25. Fourteen years earlier would be A.D. 31 or 30, a date too early for Paul's conversion, and much too early for Paul's first visit to Jerusalem, that of 1:18. According to the narrative in Acts, Paul's apostolic labors among Gentiles did not begin until after the visit of 11:30, see 13:1., ff., whereas in the epistle it is implied that these labors had continued for some time before the visit to which he refers took place, an argument in favor of its identification with that of Acts 15.

Against the latter, i.e., the visit of Acts 15, it is urged that where Luke speaks of the "appointment" of the brethren, the apostle speaks of "revelation," Acts 15:2 with Galatians 2:2. But these are not mutually exclusive; the revelation may have been given, not directly to Paul, but to one of the brethren, thus securing the fellowship and cooperation of the whole church, and making the way clear to a final settlement of this vexed question. This, moreover, is not an isolated instance of the same event being viewed from different aspects. Thus in Acts 9:29, 30, Luke relates that when the brethren heard of the Jews' plot to kill Paul "they brought him down, . . . and sent him forth," while Paul himself, referring to the same incident, says that he was sent away from Jerusalem by a direct revelation from God, 22:17–21. Cp. 15:28.

Again, Paul says that he took Titus with him to the Jerusalem Council, whereas Luke mentions only Barnabas by name; but Luke does speak of "certain other" who accompanied Paul, and Titus may well have been included in this general description. Paul, moreover, has a purpose in particularizing Titus, see vv. 3–5, who, as the word "take" shows, was rather a subordinate than a colleague. The fact that Luke speaks first of a general gathering of the church, v. 4, and then of the elders, v. 6, whereas Paul mentions only a private interview with the leaders, is readily explicable, if, as would be natural, this consultation preceded the more public discussion.

A more serious objection is that as Paul and Barnabas separated finally very shortly after the Council at Jerusalem, the contention with Peter, at which Barnabas was present, must have taken place immediately thereafter; and that it is inconceivable that Peter would have changed so completely within such a short space of time. To this may be replied either, *a,* that it is not inconceivable, and indeed that Paul's charge is that Peter was glaringly inconsistent, or *b,* that the section beginning at v. 11 does not follow upon 1–10 in chronological order. In favor of the identification of this visit with that of Acts 15 is that the circumstances are similar, the subject of the discussion is similar, the chief persons concerned are the same, and the general agreement finally arrived at between them is the same.

with—*meta,* i.e., as colleague and fellow worker, being an equal in age and experience.

Barnabas,—a Heb. name, *bar* = son, *nabas* = prophecy; Luke gives as the Gk. equivalent "son of exhortation" or "of comfort," Acts 4:36 (*paraklēsis,* see note on the corresponding verb, *parakaleō, 1 Thessalonians* 2:11); the two translations are reconciled by Paul's words, "he that prophesieth speaketh unto men . . . comfort," 1 Corinthians 14:3. This name was given him by the apostles, apparently to describe the prominent characteristic of his ministry. His own name was Joseph; his ancestors, of the tribe of Levi, had settled in Cyprus, where he was born. In the Bible laudatory words are used of few men, and of these Barnabas is one, "he was a good man, full of the Holy Ghost and of faith," Acts 11:24.

It was Barnabas who introduced Paul to the apostles when he returned to Jerusalem after his conversion, vouching for the good faith of the onetime persecutor to those naturally suspicious of him. Barnabas stood high in the confidence of the apostles, and became their delegate when the Greeks began to turn to God at Antioch. Arrived at that city the sight of the grace of God gladdened him; he strengthened the hands of the believers, and many people were "added to the Lord." Feeling the need of a colleague, and, it may be, remembering the word of the Lord concerning Saul at his conversion, that his life work was to lie among the Gentiles, Barnabas sought him out and from henceforth for some years the two were closely associated in the work of the gospel. Later, however, they separated in consequence of a disagreement over a younger fellow worker, John Mark. Thereafter the writer of the Acts is silent about Barnabas, though a brief and friendly reference to him by the apostle Paul at a later date shows him still actively engaged in the work of the Lord, 1 Corinthians 9:6.

taking . . . with me.—one word in orig., *sumparalambanō*, used elsewhere only of John Mark, Acts 12:25; 15:37, 38. Paul makes a difference thus between Barnabas who went with him, and Titus whom he took with him. The younger man was subordinate to the older men, an assistant and attendant, 13:5, rather than a colleague.||

Titus also—a Gentile Christian, a younger fellow worker with the apostle, mentioned only in the Epistles of the latter, viz., in 2 Corinthians nine times, in Galatians twice, and in 2 Timothy 4:10; one of the "Pastoral" Epistles was addressed to him.

2:2 And I went up by revelation; and I laid before—see on "conferred not," 1:16, above.

them—i.e., the church at Jerusalem, see Acts 15:6, 12:22.

the gospel which I preach—*kērussō*, to herald, to proclaim as a herald does, see on 1:11, above.

among the Gentiles,—see on 1:16, above.

but privately—*kat'idian,* as in Matthew 17:19; 20:17, e.g., where the words are rendered "apart." Presumably this interview preceded the gathering of the whole church mentioned in Acts 15:6-29; cp. "before them all," 2:14.

before them who were of repute,—or, simply, "to them of repute," i.e., persons held in consideration. The participle of *dokeō,* "to think," is used, and is, lit. = "persons [well] thought of by others"; it occurs again in v. 6, "those who were reputed to be somewhat," and in v. 9, "James and Cephas and John, they who were reputed to be pillars"; plainly these are the persons intended here also.

The description is not ironical; in Mark 10:42 "they which are accounted to rule over the Gentiles" are not nominal rulers. So here; the apostle recognizes, alike by his actions and in his words, that James, Cephas, and John were what they were reputed in the church at Jerusalem to be, its responsible rulers and guides.

In each case the margin "are" is to be preferred, for though the apostle is describing how the church at Jerusalem at the time of his visit esteemed these men, the thought of how those to whom he was writing esteemed them was uppermost in his mind.

lest by any means—introducing the reason why he had sought an interview with the leaders before laying the matter before the whole church.

I should be running,—continuous present tense, referring to the particular service in which he was then engaged, viz., the mission to Jerusalem.

or had run,—continuous past tense, referring to the attitude he had taken up toward the Judaizing teachers at Antioch, and to his consent to submit the matters in dispute to the judgment of the church in Jerusalem.

The metaphor is drawn from the Greek Stadium in which races were run; see 1 Corinthians 9:26; Philippians 2:16; 3:14; 2 Timothy 4:7.

in vain.—See comment on *1 Thessalonians* 2:1.

These words are not to be understood as indicating any misgiving in the apostle's mind concerning the gospel he preached. They refer to his apprehension of the possibility of nonsuccess in his mission. When "dissension and questioning" arose at Antioch, he had consented to take the judgment of the church at Jerusalem. If then, through any lack of diligence or forethought on his part, a decision adverse to the broader, more liberal gospel were to be given, the work of God among the Gentiles would be set back indefinitely. Hence his precaution that the leaders should be put in possession of all the facts and arguments, so that, if possible, their weighty influence in favor of freedom might be secured before the points in dispute were debated in public. Paul had not come to Jerusalem to obtain sanction for the continuance of his ministry among the Gentiles, indeed, but in view of the efforts that had been made to nullify his labors, to convince the elders and the church there of the validity of the gospel he preached, and to counteract the misrepresentations that had been made. In this aim he seems to have been successful, as subsequent events showed, cp. especially Acts 15:25. Paul and Barnabas seem to have commended themselves as well as their doctrine.

2:3 But—the apostle adduces another proof that he was not an opportunist, preaching or denying the law as suited his circumstances, and that he had never from the first yielded to the claims of the Judaizers; see on 1:17, and Introductory Note.

not even Titus who was with me,—the form of the sentence as well as its wording throws the emphasis on the fact that Titus was actually present at the time of which the apostle is writing. On the one hand, living among Jews whose prejudices, albeit they were Christians, were such as to prevent their eating with an uncircumcised person, to have induced Titus to submit to the rite would have relieved the apostle from some embarrassment. On the other, to have yielded to pressure in the matter might have conciliated the Judaizers somewhat, and so have contributed to the success of his mission.

being a Greek,—and so uncircumcised. The term *Hellēn,* here and at 3:28, was applied only to such Gentiles as spoke the Greek language. Since, however, that tongue was the common medium of intercourse in the Roman Empire, "Greek" and "Gentile" had become more or less interchangeable terms. The nationality of Titus is not stated in the New Testament.

It is possible that the apostle had in mind the use the Judaizers had made of his circumcision of Timothy, Acts 16:3, and that these words are added to differentiate the two cases, for Timothy's mother was a Jewess, though his father was a Greek.

was compelled to be circumcised:—i.e., pressure was brought to bear upon them to this end; by whom is not stated, perhaps by certain believers of the sect of the Pharisees, Acts 15:5, to whose natural prejudices in favor of the law of Moses the "false brethren" may have appealed. If these men claimed that all Gentile converts must be circumcised, the apostle's own companion, Titus, would become a test case. Did Paul yield the point and was Titus actually circumcised? The question has been answered:

a. Affirmatively, that Titus was circumcised, but by a gracious concession on the part of the apostle, not by the compulsion of the Judaizers.

b. Negatively, that the apostle maintained his ground, and that Titus remained uncircumcised.

In support of *a* it is urged that the emphasis falls on the words "compelled" and "by way of subjection," v. 5, and that the apostle's intention is to show that he gave way only as a concession and in order to conciliate the narrower party, not because he recognized the propriety of imposing a purely Jewish ordinance on Gentile converts. Against this, however, it seems conclusive that neither of these words is emphatic by position, as should have been the case on this hypothesis.

Moreover, the apostle can hardly have intended to assert that Titus was circumcised as evidence that he had not yielded on this very point. Surrender is not a proof of victory. Such an admission would weaken his argument just where it ought to gather force.

Paul had shown his desire to promote harmony in consenting to take the judgment of the church at Jerusalem at all; he showed his firmness where essential things are concerned in refusing to have Titus circumcised.

Thus v. 3 stands in contrast with v. 2; the former shows how far the apostle was prepared to go in order to allay any legitimate fear as to his course and to promote a good understanding; the latter shows that his willingness to conciliate did not extend to surrender in any really vital matter.

2:4 and that—there is no word in orig. corresponding to "that."

because of—if "that" be omitted the sentence introduced by "and because of" connects itself naturally with the close of v. 2 as a second reason why the apostle should have sought a private interview with the leaders. Verse 3 would, in that case, form a parenthesis (see note at 1:7).

If, however, "that" be retained, v. 4 is to be read with v. 3, and is to be understood as supplying the reason why the efforts of some at Jerusalem to have Titus circumcised were unsuccessful. In that case the ellipsis may be supplied and the words paraphrased thus: "and that pressure was brought to bear upon us by the Twelve, or others, because of (i.e., in order to conciliate, or to avoid conflict with) the false brethren."

Of these interpretations perhaps the first is to be preferred.

the false brethren—occurs again only at 2 Corinthians 11:26, "in perils among false brethren," with apparent reference to the "false apostles, deceitful workers" of v. 13. Thus "false brethren" = pretended brethren, not Christians at all, but Jews with a subtle design on the integrity and simplicity of the gospel.

privily brought in,—*pareisaktos*, from *para* = "by the side," i.e., not straightforwardly, *eis* = "into," and *ago* = "to bring." The word is used by Strabo, a Greek historian contemporary with Paul, of enemies introduced secretly into a city by traitors within.||

The corresponding verb, *pareisago*, occurs, in 2 Peter 2:1, of false teachers "who privily bring in destructive heresies."||

Presumably these false brethren had been introduced into the church by "them that were of the circumcision," 2:12, mentioned in Acts 15:5. Party zeal often leads to unholy alliances.

who came in privily—*pareiserchomai;* brought in to accomplish the ends of the circumcision party, the establishment of the ceremonial law, or some part of it, in the church, they came in to accomplish their own end, the complete destruction of the faith.

In Romans 5:20, where this word occurs again, it has its literal meaning.||

A similar compound, *pareisduo*, is used in a similar connection in Jude 4, of some who had "crept in privily—ungodly men."||

Cp. John 10:1, where the Lord Jesus describes such men as "thieves and robbers."

to spy out—*kataskopeo*, as in 2 Samuel 10:3, LXX, e.g., to search out with a view to overthrowing.||

our liberty—*eleutheria*, a word here used to describe the unfettered condition of the Christian soul in contrast with the Jewish condition of bondage to law, and so in 5:1. This liberty is said to be "in Christ Jesus," and is secured by the presence and ministry of the Holy Spirit, Who frees the mind from mistaken notions about God and Christ, 2 Corinthians 3:17. It secures to the individual freedom of choice and of action, 1 Corinthians 10:29, but always within the limits imposed by consideration for the welfare of others, Galatians 5:13, and this because Christ's freeman is the bondservant of God, 1 Peter 2:16. Hence

Christian liberty is far removed from the carnal license which false teachers promise their dupes, 2 Peter 2:19. James, speaking of the restraints of the gospel on those who profess it, finely describes Christianity as "the perfect law, the law of liberty," 1:25, and reminds his readers that by this law the Christian is about to be judged for the use of his liberty in his words and deeds, 2:12.

From "the bondage of corruption" the Christian looks for deliverance at the coming of the Lord, Romans 8:21.||

which we have in Christ Jesus, that they might bring us into bondage:—*katadouloō*, = to reduce to slavery, as in 2 Corinthians 11:20. The tense of the verb implies that had it not been for the circumstances he is about to relate the success of the false brethren would have been assured.||

2:5 to whom we—i.e., Paul, Barnabas, and the others, who were sent from Antioch, Acts 15:2.

gave place—*eikō*, to yield, to give way.||

in the way of subjection,—*hupotagē*, used again in 2 Corinthians 9:13 of the submission of Christians to Christ; in 1 Timothy 2:11 of the position of women in the church; and in 1 Timothy 3:4 of the relationship between children and their parents. "Submission" is to be preferred to "subjection" here, inasmuch as to submit is to yield oneself, whereas to subject is to cause another person to yield.||

no, not for an hour;—this emphatic expression implies prompt resistance to a formal demand, and excludes the notion that Titus had been circumcised.

that the truth of the gospel—not = "the true gospel," but the true teaching of the gospel, i.e., as contrasted with any perversion of it by the admixture of a foreign element, such as Jewish law, here and v. 14, or Gentile philosophy, cp. Colossians 1:5.

might continue—*diamenō*, a stronger form of the verb *menō* = to abide.

with—*pros*, as at 1:18, and see comment on *1 Thessalonians* 3:4; the preposition suggests the active, living power of the gospel.

you.—the apostle knew that he had fought in the interest of all "churches of the Gentiles," and, indeed, of all believers whether Jew or Gentile, not merely of the church at Antioch, in whose behalf the mission to Jerusalem was primarily undertaken, and that freedom for one meant freedom for all.

2:6 But from those who were reputed to be somewhat—as at v. 2 where, as here, the apostle does not speak disparagingly of the leaders themselves, but seems rather to have in view the efforts of his opponents to magnify their authority unduly. See Introductory Note.

(whatsoever they were,—or better, as marg., "what they once were"; for the word, *pote,* which occurs here, is translated "in time past" at 1:13, and "once" at 1:23. Probably the apostle is thinking of the association of the Twelve with the Lord Jesus during His ministry on earth, since it was on this ground that their partisans claimed for them that exclusive authority which he so emphatically repudiates.

it maketh no matter to me:—his direct commission from the Lord, received as already described, 1:12, 15, 16, relieved him of any responsibility to the authority of the apostles. Cp. 2 Corinthians 10:7, 8.

God accepteth not man's person)—*prosōpon,* as at 1:22, see note. This expression is used in the Old Testament, *a,* in the sense of being gracious or kind to anyone, whether of God, Genesis 19:21, or of man, 32:20; *b,* in the sense of being impartial, whether of God, Deuteronomy 10:17, or of man, Leviticus 19:15. In the New Testament it occurs only in the latter sense, and only here and Luke 20:21; in the parallel passages, Matthew 22:16, Mark 12:14, "to look on, to regard," appears; in Jude 16, "to admire the face."||
   The two words, *prosōpon,* "face," and *lambanō,* "accept," are combined *(prosōpolēpsia)* in Romans 2:11; Ephesians 6:9; Colossians 3:25, of the impartiality and justice that characterize all God's dealings with men, and in James 2:1, in an exhortation to Christians not to be influenced in church life by social status.||
   A similar compound *(prosōpolēmptēs),* with the same meaning, is used in Acts 10:34 (noun) and James 2:9 (verb), and, with a negative prefix, in 1 Peter 1:17 (adverb).||
   The apostle's meaning seems to be that expressed in one of his letters concerning ministry generally, "all these worketh the one and the same Spirit, dividing to each one severally even as He will," 1 Corinthians 12:11. They had companied with the Lord; he had been a persecutor of the followers of the Lord; that to him should be committed the full gospel of the grace of God, and that he should become the apostle to the Gentiles, could, therefore, have no merely natural explanation.

they, I say, who were of repute imparted nothing to me:—the apostle was perhaps going to say, "from those who were reputed to be somewhat I received nothing," but on resuming the main thought after his parenthesis, he altered the form of his statement, and instead of "I received nothing," wrote, "they imparted nothing." That is to say, they neither modified his teaching nor added to his authority. "To me" bears the emphasis of the sentence.

2:7 but contrariwise,—here the apostle proceeds to show that, so far from adding anything to his authority, these leaders recognized his apostleship, and expressed their fellowship with him in his work.

when they saw—i.e., as a result of hearing what he had laid before them; see v. 9.

that I had been entrusted with—i.e., by God; this ministry had not been of his own choosing; he speaks of it elsewhere as a "stewardship intrusted" to him, 1 Corinthians 9:17, cp. 1 Thessalonians 2:4; 1 Timothy 1:11, 12; Titus 1:3. The same word is used of the Jews in Romans 3:2, "they were entrusted with the oracles of God," but there it is in the "point" tense, for that trust was of the past; the perfect tense used here implies that the ministry once committed to him by God had not been withdrawn.

The essential qualification for any service is trustworthiness, Matthew 25:21; 1 Corinthians 4:2. It is in the mercy of God that His servants are enabled to be trustworthy, 1 Corinthians 7:25; 2 Corinthians 4:1, and to continue so, Acts 26:22, unto the end, Acts 20:24; 2 Timothy 4:7.

the gospel of the uncircumcision,—the gospel itself is one and the same gospel, whether presented to Jew or Gentile, cp. 1:6-9. The apostle has in mind the sphere in which he was appointed to preach the gospel. By metonymy, "the uncircumcision" = the Gentiles.

even as Peter—see note at 1:18.

with *the gospel* of the circumcision—by metonymy for "the Jews."

Circumcision was enjoined by God upon Abraham, and his male descendants and dependents, as a token of the covenant made with him, Genesis 17; Acts 7:8. Hence it came about that among the Israelites "the uncircumcised" was used as a term for the Gentiles, Judges 15:18; 2 Samuel 1:20. It occurs in the New Testament also in this sense, Romans 2:26; Ephesians 2:11., e.g., but without any trace of the contempt that appears to attach to it in the Old Testament.

Circumcision, however, had a moral as well as a ceremonial significance. Moses, in his reluctance to undertake the leadership of the Israelites, having first without success pleaded physical unfitness, Exodus 4:10, declared his moral unfitness for the task in the words, "I am of uncircumcised lips," 6:12, 30; cp. "I am a man of unclean lips," Isaiah 6:5. So also of the ear, Jeremiah 6:10, and of the heart, which was to be circumcised as well as the flesh in order that God might be loved supremely, Deuteronomy 30:6; Jeremiah 4:4; i.e., all that hindered love to God, such as pride, Leviticus 26:41, and unwillingness to obey the voice of God, Deuteronomy 10:16, cp. Acts 7:51, was to be put away. The condition into which the Israelites ultimately fell was thus described by Jeremiah, "All the nations are uncircumcised, and all the house of Israel are uncircumcised in heart"; hence the word of the Lord, "I will punish all them which are circumcised in their uncircumcision," Jeremiah 9:25, 26. Thus Paul's statement of the significance of circumcision is quite in line with earlier teaching on the subject, "For circumcision indeed profiteth, if thou be a doer of the law: but if thou be a transgressor of the law, thy circumcision is become uncircumcision . . . For he is not a Jew, which is one outwardly; neither is that circumcision, which is outward in the flesh: but he is a Jew, which is one inwardly; and circumcision is that of the heart, in the spirit, not in the letter; whose praise is not of men, but of God," Romans 2:25, 28, 29.

In the economy of grace no account is taken of any ordinance performed on the flesh; the old racial distinction is ignored in the preaching of the gospel, and faith is the sole condition upon which the favor of God in salvation is to be obtained, Romans 10:11–13; 1 Corinthians 7:19.

Shortly after the gospel of grace began to prove itself to be the power of God to the salvation of Gentiles, certain of the Jewish believers became uneasy about the claims of the law, which they feared Paul's gospel, wherein no room was found for circumcision, would make void, Romans 3:31. To them it seemed plain that, except the Gentiles also were "circumcised after the custom of Moses," they could not be saved, Acts 15:1. The party that so taught came to be called "the circumcision," v. 12, Acts 11:2; Titus 1:10. Against their arguments Paul insisted that the logic of the situation forbade any compromise whatever; if any Gentile submitted to circumcision he thereby assumed responsibility to keep the whole law, and so lost his interest in Christ. See 5:3, 4, below.

The importance of the controversy between the two parties lay in this, that had the circumcisionists had their way, the new faith must have remained merely a sect of the Jews, since any Gentile who would attach himself thereto must first become a Jew. The determined repudiation of circumcision, and, consequently, of the Law of Moses, on the part of Paul and his colleagues, and the rapid increase in number of Gentile converts, made directly by the preaching of the gospel apart from Jewish influences, led inevitably to separation between the Jews and the disciples of the Lord Jesus, cp. Acts 19:8–10, and to the acquisition by the latter of a distinctive name, "Christians," which was given to them first at Antioch, 11:26.

The timorous half-gospel of "the circumcision," their attempt to mingle law and grace, which, indeed, so emasculates the gospel that it becomes no gospel at all, 1:6–9 persisted long in spite of Paul's strenuous opposition. Writing perhaps ten years later, he speaks of the "concision," "flesh-cutters," with implied reference, perhaps, to such Scriptures as Leviticus 21:5; 1 Kings 18:28, cp. 5:12, setting them in contrast with the true "circumcision, who worship by the Spirit of God, and glory in Christ Jesus, and have no confidence in the flesh," Philippians 3:2, 3. And in another Epistle of approximate date he declares that the believer has been, in Christ, "circumcised with a circumcision not made with hands, in the putting off of the body of the flesh, in the circumcision of Christ," Colossians 2:11, where, as the immediate reference to His burial and resurrection shows, by the "circumcision of Christ" is intended, not the rite performed on the eighth day, Luke 2:21, but His death on the Cross. The same thought is otherwise expressed in the second clause of 6:14.

2:8 (for he—i.e., God, cp. 1 Corinthians 12:6.

that wrought for Peter—*energeō;* this verb is used again of God at 3:5, "He that . . . worketh miracles among you"; at 1 Corinthians 12:6, "Who worketh all [gifts] in all [persons]; at Ephesians 1:19, 20, "that working of the strength of His might which He wrought in Christ, when He raised Him from the dead"; at Philippians 2:13, "It is God which worketh in you both to will and to work, for His good pleasure." In each of these places the preposition "in," *en,* is present; here it is not; hence the rendering "for," which is usually accepted. The absence of the preposition, however, does not seem to indicate departure from the usual meaning, viz., that God works in the individual in order to make his service effectual.

On the other hand, the words of Proverbs 31:12, LXX, can only be understood as "she worketh good things for" her husband, not "in" him.

Further notes on *energeō* and related words will be found in comments on *1 Thessalonians* 2:13; *2 Thessalonians* 2:9; an analysis of New Testament use of *energeō* is given at 3:5, below.

unto—i.e., with a view to the fulfillment of.

the apostleship of the circumcision—i.e., the ministry of the gospel to the Jewish people. Apostleship is from God, Acts 1:25, through Christ, Romans 1:5; it has its specific sphere here, and is attested by its results, 1 Corinthians 9:2.

wrought for me also—as above, probably = "in me."

unto the Gentiles);—an abbreviation of "unto the apostleship of the Gentiles."

The purpose of this parenthesis is to remind his readers of a fundamental proposition easily forgotten in this controversy. A commission from God requires the power of God for its discharge; and the results of their respective labors testified to the apostleship of both Peter and Paul. After all, the authority for preaching the gospel, v. 7, and the power to make the preaching of it effectual, v. 8, were of God, alike in Paul's case and in that of the Twelve.

2:9 and when they perceived—reverting to the opening of v. 7, lit., "they seeing . . . and perceiving." The first word, *oida,* means that they had grasped the fact, the second, *ginōskō,* that on reflection they had grasped the significance of the fact. On the difference between these words see further comment on *1 Thessalonians* 3:5.

the grace that was given unto me,—a comprehensive expression invariably used by Paul to describe the source of his apostolic commission; see 1 Corinthians 15:10, etc., and 1:15, above.

James—see note at 1:19. The fact that the Judaizers at Antioch, v. 12, professed to "come from James" would give peculiar significance to his support of Paul on this occasion, and would add weight to the argument here.

and Cephas—see note at 1:18. It is noteworthy that where missionary work is in view Peter alone is mentioned, but where church action is described James takes precedence. In this respect the epistle corresponds with Acts 15, for though Peter is mentioned as the first speaker, v. 7, James is evidently the leader of the assembly, v. 13.

and John,—the son of Zebedee and Salome, cp. Matthew 27:56 with Mark 15:40, and brother of the James who was put to death by Herod, Acts 12:2. This is the only mention of John by name in Paul's epistles.

Of the apostolic band John seems to have been most intimate with Christ in the days of His flesh, John 13:23, and with Peter and James (his brother, see above) to have formed an inner circle among them, Mark 9:2, as the apostles formed an inner circle among the disciples, 3:13-19. This assumes that John speaks of himself under the description "one of His disciples whom Jesus loved." It is also probable that he is the unnamed disciple of John the Baptist, John 1:35-40. He was the oldest follower of the Lord Jesus at the time of his death, for, apparently, he outlived all the rest of the first generation of Christians.

The only utterances of John recorded in the gospels are in Mark 10:35, 39; Luke 9:49-54; John 13:25; 21:7. His own gospel, however, contains some of his reflections on the Person, 1:1-18, and works and words of the Lord Jesus, 12:36-43, e.g., and on the mission of the Baptist, 3:31-36. Of the whole New Testament almost a fifth part is from his pen. John is not spokesman in any of the incidents in connection with which his name occurs in the Acts, nor is he mentioned in ch. 15, but the present passage shows that he held a position of recognized responsibility in the church at Jerusalem.

John seems to have been a man of a somewhat hasty and zealous temperament naturally, Luke 9:54, cp. Mark 3:17, and not lacking in courage, Acts 4:13.

they who were reputed—or "are reputed," as in vv. 2-6, where see notes.

to be pillars,—*stulos,* a column upon which the weight of a building is supported, and so, metaphorically, of such as bear responsibility. It was commonly used by the Jews of teachers of the law. The word is found again at 1 Timothy 3:15; Revelation 3:12; 10:1.||

This incidental description of those who extended to him their fellowship is intended to enhance their position and authority, and to forestall any objection that Paul had had the support only of some of the more obscure brethren.

gave to me and Barnabas—see note at v. 1.

the right hands—this custom of shaking hands was in wide use, apparently from very early days, as a pledge binding a person to allegiance to a sovereign, 2 Kings 10:15; 1 Chronicles 29:24, marg., and, but figuratively, Lamentations 5:6, cp. 2 Chronicles 30:8, marg., or to the performance of some undertaking, Ezra 10:19, or the observance of some agreement, Ezekiel 17:18. Josephus, speaking of Artabanus, the king of the Parthians, says, "He gave them his right hand; this is of the greatest force there with all these barbarians, and affords a firm security to those who converse with them" (Antiquities, 18. 9. 3).

Here, however, as the qualifying words "of fellowship" show, the action was the public expression of the approval of the leaders at Jerusalem of the course Paul and Barnabas had taken in their work among the Gentiles.

of—i.e., expressing.

fellowship,—*koinōnia*, "a having in common," "a partnership." "Fellowship" is a general term for the common experiences, interests, and hopes of Christian men, Philippians 2:1, wrought in them by the Holy Spirit, 2 Corinthians 13:14; it had its origin with the apostles at the day of Pentecost, Acts 2:42; it is possible only to such as believe in the Lord Jesus, for the reason that in spiritual things as in physical, light and darkness are mutually incompatible, antagonistic and exclusive, 2 Corinthians 6:14.

The basis of the Christian fellowship is found in the knowledge of the Son of God, 1 Corinthians 1:9, and particularly in the knowledge of His death for our sins, 1 Corinthians 10:16, and in the resurrection, or eternal, life which the Christian possesses in Him, 1 John 1:3. Moreover, knowledge of Christ, His person and character, is the only basis on which fellowship between men and God is possible, 1 John 1:6, 7.

This fellowship with God in His Son, wrought in Christians by the Holy Spirit, enters into every department of the Christian's life, and is to be made effectual by him, Philemon 6. He shares the poverty of the needy among the brethren by giving to them of his substance, Romans 15:26, 2 Corinthians 8:4; 9:13; Hebrews 13:16; and he facilitates the work of the gospel by his gifts, Philippians 1:5; indeed, in these cases the gift which expresses the fellowship is itself called "fellowship." Here the fellowship itself is intended, expressed, not in a gift, but in the shake of the hand.

The ambition of the Christian is to "know the fellowship of the sufferings of Christ," Philippians 3:10, not that he is to desire to suffer what the Lord Jesus suffered at the hands of men when He was on earth, but that whatsoever he suffers may be the consequence only of that devotion to God which involved the Lord Jesus in suffering.||

The corresponding verb, *koinoneō*, occurs at 6:6.

A synonym, *metochē* = "to have together," is translated "fellowship" at 2 Corinthians 6:14.||

that—i.e., in order that. Paul cannot be understood to mean that his labors among the Gentiles depended upon the fellowship of the church at Jerusalem, though, as his journey thither showed, he attached much value thereto. See paraphrase below.

we should go unto the Gentiles, and they unto the circumcision;—there is no verb in orig.; "should go" is supplied in English to complete the sense.

Plainly this mutual recognition of the different spheres in which each was called to preach the gospel does not mean that Paul and Barnabas were precluded from speaking to Jews, or the others to Gentiles. On the contrary, for it was Paul's custom, when he entered a city, to seek out his fellow countrymen first, see Acts 16:13; 17:2; 18:2. The Council at Jerusalem confirmed the existing order of things. Paul and Barnabas were to continue to preach the gospel without any admixture of Judaism, the others to pursue their labors among the Jews, the character of their ministry remaining unaltered also.

The sentence may be paraphrased thus: "They shook hands with us publicly in order that it might be known that in mutual confidence we carried out our commission among the Gentiles, they theirs among the Jews."

2:10 only—i.e., they had but one stipulation to make, and that did not touch the matter of the preaching at all—so little foundation was there for the charge that Paul was indebted to the original apostles, either for the matter of his gospel or for authority to preach it.

they would **that we should remember**—continuous present tense, i.e., "that we should always remember"; beneficent interest is implied, as in Psalm 106:4.

the poor;—i.e., the poor among Christians in Jerusalem and in Judaea generally. The poverty of so many of the saints in these parts was probably due to the persecutions they had suffered, and was rendered more acute by the great famine which affected the whole inhabited earth in the reign of Claudius Caesar, *circa* A.D. 45, say six years before the incident which Paul here recounts. Paul himself, with Barnabas, had at that time carried the gifts of the church at Antioch to the saints in Judaea, Acts 11:28-30. That he had respected the wish of the church at Jerusalem in the matter was well-known to the Galatians, before whom he had recently laid the claims of the Jewish brethren; see 1 Corinthians 16:1 and cp. Romans 15:25-27; 2 Corinthians 8:8, 9, and Acts 24:17.

Ptōchos, = poor, always in New Testament of poverty in material things save in 4:9; Matthew 5:3; Revelation 3:17, and perhaps Luke 6:20.

The belief that a man's life does consist in the abundance of his material possessions is inveterate in fallen human nature, and, in spite of the words of the Lord, Luke 12:15, persists even in the Christian. The inevitable result of this false belief is that men readily cherish base thoughts of the poor and harden themselves against the needy, Deuteronomy 15:7-9, exploiting their labor and even their lives for "dishonest gain," Jeremiah 22:13, 17, marg.

The law of God provided against these natural tendencies by making the prosperity of His people contingent upon their considerate treatment of the poor, Deuteronomy 14:29; 15:10 cp. Proverbs 28:27. For the poor have their rights, and these God has undertaken to maintain, Psalm 140:12, and against those who would take them away He denounces woe, Isaiah 10:2. To oppress the poor is to reproach the Maker of the poor; to show mercy to the needy is to honor Him, Proverbs 14:31, is, indeed, to "know the Lord," Jeremiah 22:16. Therefore blessing is reserved for him "that considereth the poor," Psalm 41:1; and the man that has pity on the poor, and gives practical expression to his pity, makes an investment on the security of God, Proverbs 19:17, cp. Matthew 6:19–21.

That Israel had in heart turned away from God appeared in their treatment of the poor. The deterioration of the character of the people and the consequent decline and fall of the nation was largely due to this cause. Other evidences of declension were not lacking, but in all the burdens of the prophets this is a chief complaint, as a few typical passages will show: "the people of the land . . . have vexed the poor and needy," Ezekiel 22:29; "how manifold are your transgressions and how mighty are your sins . . . ye that turn aside the needy," Amos 5:12; cp. 8:4–8; "thus hath Jehovah of hosts spoken, saying, . . . Oppress not . . . the poor . . . But they refused to hearken, they pulled away the shoulder, . . . they made their hearts as an adamant stone, lest they should hear the law and the words which Jehovah of hosts had sent by His Spirit, . . . therefore came there great wrath from Jehovah of hosts," Zechariah 7:9–12.

The New Testament confirms the teaching of the Old Testament in this respect. It was one of the glories of the Lord Jesus in His own ministry that "the poor had the gospel preached to them," Matthew 11:5, cp., Luke 14:21. It was a laudable thing to sell one's possessions in order that the needs of the poor might be met, Matthew 19:21. The poor, indeed, afford perpetual opportunity to Christians to imitate their Master in doing good, Mark 14:7, and for such as consider them there is a sure reward at "the resurrection of the just," Luke 14:13, 14. The Lord values the gifts of the poor, however meager, 21:1–4, and Christians are to treat them with respect even when they bring no gift at all, James 2:2–6.

Much was said by the Lord, see Matthew 6:19–24; 10:8; Luke 6:38; Acts 20:35, e.g., and by the apostles, see Romans 12:8; 2 Cor. chh. 8 and 9; Ephesians 4:28; James 2:14–16; 1 Peter 4:9, 10; 1 John 3:17, e.g., about the privilege and obligation of remembering the poor. And as under the old economy the Jew was not to allow his giving to be a grief to him, Deuteronomy 15:10, so, under the new, the Christian is to give "not grudgingly, or of necessity, for the Lord loveth a cheerful giver," 2 Corinthians 9:7.

One effect upon the Jews of receiving the Lord Jesus as their Messiah was to revive their interest in the poor. James and his colleagues learned from the history of the nation how intimately the future of the gospel was bound up with the attitude toward the poor of those who accepted it. Hence their exhortation to Paul and his fellow workers among the Gentiles. But Paul had learned the same lesson, alike from history and from the teaching of the Lord Jesus, hence his response.

which very thing I—"I" is not emphatic, so there is no contrast suggested as though Barnabas had not been zealous in the matter. Paul uses the singular here probably to avoid overelaboration of detail in telling his story. He was defending not Barnabas but himself, and hence he refers to Barnabas only when it is necessary to do so for the sake of historical accuracy.

was also zealous to do.—whereas in Greek *kai* ordinarily makes the word that follows it emphatic, in English "also" throws the stress on the word that precedes it; hence the clause may be paraphrased, "which very thing I was not merely willing, but even gave diligence to do."

"Zealous" represents *spoudazō*, elsewhere rendered "give diligence"; it means "to make haste" and so "to exert oneself." The Christian is to exert himself:

to maintain in the bond of peace that unity in Christ of all believers which has been made by the Holy Spirit, Ephesians 4:3;

to gain the approval of God in his understanding of, and use of, the Scriptures, 2 Timothy 2:15;

to obey God in such a way that he may enter into the Sabbath rest that is reserved for the people of God, Hebrews 4:11;

to make sure his calling and election by doing those things commanded, 2 Peter 1:10,

so that when the Lord comes he may be found "in peace, without fault and blameless in His sight," 2 Peter 3:14.

To these may be added 2 Peter 1:5, where the corresponding noun appears: the Christian is to exert himself to supply self-control, patience, godliness, love of the brethren, and love universal.

2:11 But—*de*, introducing a new argument.

The adverb used at 1:18, 21; 2:1, "then," *epeita*, marks a chronological sequence; the events related in that section of the epistle succeeded one the other at longer or shorter intervals. Not so *de*, which is quite consistent with, if indeed it does not actually indicate, a break in that sequence.

Moreover, if the incident about to be related took place after the Council at Jerusalem at all, it must have taken place immediately after it, for Paul and Barnabas separated soon after their return to Antioch, as recorded in Acts 15:36-40, and were never together again. It is hardly conceivable, however, that Peter, and even Barnabas, should have acted as here described within such a brief space after the Council, to which Barnabas was a delegate, and at which the principle of liberty was asserted largely as a consequence of the intervention of Peter. And the difficulty is the greater in view of the fact that it was from Antioch that the mission which procured this decision was dispatched. Could the question have been raised again in this new form immediately after the receipt of the apostolic edict? Here, indeed, the question is not directly of the liberty of the Gentiles, but of their equality with the Jewish believers. The one seems to involve the other, however, for liberty could not long be preserved to those to whom the stigma of inferiority attached.

It is highly probable, then, that the apostle here goes back to the time of strain at Antioch mentioned in Acts 15:1, 2. True, Peter is not referred to there, but neither is there any mention of his presence in Antioch between the breakup of the Council and the departure of Barnabas mentioned in 15:39.

It is possible that the Judaizing teachers may have given to the Galatians an account of this incident in proof that there was a fundamental difference between the gospel preached by Paul and that preached by Peter. In that case it would call for notice, and the relation of the facts afforded the writer an opportunity of confirming this argument by showing that not only was he not dependent on the Twelve for authority to preach, he had, when occasion demanded, opposed and even publicly rebuked their leader for inconsistency in putting the uncircumcised believers at a disadvantage when compared with their Jewish brethren.

when Cephas came to Antioch,—Antioch, now Antakia, the ancient capital of Syria, situated on the river Orontes, was founded by Seleucus Nicator, 300 B.C., and named after Antiochus, his father. It became a city of great importance under the Greeks, who granted full political privileges to the Jews there. Syria became a Roman province under the rule of Pompey, who in 64 B.C. made Antioch a free city.

Christians, men of Cyprus and Cyrene, who had been scattered from Jerusalem through the persecution which arose at the time of Stephen's death, preached the gospel to Gentiles at Antioch, Acts 11:19-26. The church thus formed flourished under the care of Barnabas and Paul, who there received the Divine commission to go on their first missionary journey, 13:1-3.

I resisted him to the face,—i.e., openly, and as an equal; such opposition was, of course, quite inconsistent with a subordinate relationship on the part of Paul. The same expression is used in Acts 25:16, e.g.

because he stood condemned.—*kataginōskō*, "to know something against oneself or another," is used in 1 John 3:20, 21, of the effect of an exercised and enlightened conscience. This is apparently the meaning here, with the further thought, involved in the continuous tense, that the inconsistency of Peter's conduct was plain not only to himself, but to everybody else.||

The word is used in Proverbs 28:11, LXX, of which this incident provides a somewhat apt illustration.

2:12 For—introducing an account of the circumstances under which Paul had resisted Peter.

before—i.e., previous to the arrival of these men.

that certain came from James,—if, as seems probable, this encounter took place previous to the Jerusalem Council, then these may be identified with the "certain men" who "came down from Judaea," mentioned in Acts 15:1. The objection to this identification is that, whereas here Barnabas sides with Peter and the Judaizers, in Acts he is represented as opposing them. The difficulty, however, is not insurmountable, for Barnabas speedily retraced his steps, and, indeed, accompanied Paul to Jerusalem in the interests of freedom. Moreover, Paul does not state that Barnabas actually associated himself with Peter in his action; the words of verse 13 may mean no more than that he gave him countenance.

While it is possible to understand the words as = "certain sent from James," it need not in that case be assumed that he had charged them with a mission to divide the church, or to put a stigma of uncleanness on the Gentile believers, or to expostulate with Peter because he had eaten with them. It is quite conceivable that his emissaries may have exceeded their authority, and have taken a course not anticipated by James. On the other hand, it is possible that, out of sympathy with "the circumcision," and suspicious of the more liberal gospel of Paul, he may have so charged them. Certainly the language of vv. 1–10 suggests that the arguments of Paul prior to the meetings of the Council had affected a change in the minds of James and his colleagues.

he did eat with the Gentiles:—continuous tense, "he used to eat." i.e., "he took meals with," as apparently had been his custom since the vision of Acts 10. While there is no direct injunction in the Mosaic Law forbidding the Israelite to eat with the Gentile, a rabbinic deduction to that effect was rigidly observed by the stricter Jews of the sect of the Pharisees.

but when they came, he drew back—*hupostellō,* continuous tense, "he was drawing back," suggesting a vacillating course. The same word is used of reluctance to proclaim the whole truth, Acts 20:20, 27, and of apostasy from the faith, Hebrews 10:38; the corresponding noun occurs in v. 39. See also comment on *2 Thessalonians* 3:6.||

and separated himself,—*aphorizō,* again the continuous tense, suggesting the same hesitating course. But to that course there could be but one end, viz., division among the Christians involving a stigma of inferiority, or of disloyalty, upon those from whom Peter and the rest separated themselves.

Aphorizō occurs again of:

a, the Divine action in setting men apart for the work of the gospel, 1:15, above, Acts 13:2; Romans 1:1.

b, the Divine judgment upon men, Matthew 13:49; 25:32;

c, the separation of Christians from unbelievers, Acts 19:9; 2 Corinthians 6:17;

d, the separation of unbelievers from Christians, Luke 6:22;

e, the withdrawal of Christians from their brethren, here.

In *c* is described what the Christian must do, in *d* what he must be prepared to suffer, and in *e* what he must avoid.||

fearing them that were of the circumcision.—see note at v. 7. This was not Peter's first experience of the opposition of the Judaizers, see Acts 11:2, 3; it is the less explicable that he should have yielded so readily on this occasion.

2:13 And the rest of the Jews—i.e., those believing Jews who were in the church at Antioch, and who up to that time had eaten with the Gentile Christians.

dissembled likewise with him;—*sunhupokrinomai* = *sun,* "with" and *hupokrinomai,* "to pretend to act from one motive when one's conduct is really actuated by another." In this case Paul charged Peter with pretending that his change of attitude toward the Gentiles was the expression of loyalty to the law of Moses, whereas it was really the outcome of fear of the Judaizers.||

insomuch that even Barnabas—for Barnabas was well-known to the Galatians as the close friend and colleague of the apostle, as one of the chief laborers among the Gentiles, and as one of the party of missionaries who had brought the gospel to their parts. But not even the defection of Barnabas had weakened Paul's purpose to establish the freedom of the new faith.

It is difficult to avoid suspecting that this incident prepared the way for the ultimate separation of these two who had been so long, so honorably and so successfully yoked together in the service of Christ. Even Barnabas, "good man, and full of the Holy Spirit and of faith" though he was, Acts 11:24, failed in this crisis.

was carried away—*sunapagomai,* lit., "to be led along with," and so—to be influenced by, whether of evil things, as here, and 2 Peter 3:17, or of good, Romans 12:16, marg. The former association of Barnabas with the church at Jerusalem rendered him the more amenable to the influence of these brethren.||

with their dissimulation.—*hupokrisis,* whence our word "hypocrisy," originally = the part played by an actor in a theater. See note above on "dissembled."

2:14 But when I saw—having explained how Peter "stood condemned," the apostle proceeds to show how he "resisted him to the face."

that they walked not uprightly—*orthopodeō,* "to walk in a straight path," and so to leave a straight track for others to follow, cp. Hebrews 12:13.|| This metaphor, denoting a course of conduct, is of frequent occurrence in the New Testament, see comment on *1 Thessalonians* 2:12.

according to the truth of the gospel,—Paul charges them with nothing less than robbery of God, for to deny explicitly, or implicitly as Peter and the Judaizers were doing, that men are saved by faith in Christ alone, which is "the truth of the gospel," is to deny to God the glory of His grace, and to rob the Christian of "our liberty which we have in Christ Jesus," 2:4.

I said unto Cephas before *them* all,—probably in a gathering of the church at Antioch. Peter's conduct had been seen by all, and by introducing a caste system into the church it was likely to have far-reaching and mischievous consequences. Hence this public remonstrance, cp. 1 Timothy 5:20.

If—i.e., "if, as is the case."

thou, being a Jew,—*huparchō*, as at 1:14, where see note; i.e., "being a Jew to begin with," "born and bred a Jew."

livest—*zaō*, for which see comment on *1 Thessalonians* 5:10.

Here the tense is present continuous = habit of life. As a matter of fact at the moment Peter was living "as do the Jews," but Paul has in mind what had been Peter's habit before he was influenced by the Judaizers, and what would probably become his habit again when that influence was absent. Thus the use of the present tense adds point to the reproof.

as do the Gentiles,—*ethnikōs*, = "in Gentile fashion."||

and not as do the Jews,—*Ioudaikōs*, = "in Jewish fashion."||

how compellest thou the Gentiles—not necessarily that Peter brought pressure to bear directly on the Gentiles so to do, but the line he had taken was calculated to influence them strongly in this direction. The compulsion thus exercised was not less real because it was indirect.

to live as do the Jews?—*Ioudaizō*, cp. *Ioudaismos*, 1:13, where see note.||

2:15 We—i.e., "we Jews who confessed Christ," Paul thus gives additional force to his expostulation by reminding Peter and the Judaizers that he also was a Jew "born and bred." "We" is expressed in orig. for emphasis, an emphasis which is heightened by repetition and by the addition of "even" in v. 16.

being Jews—the appellation "Jew" is primarily tribal, from "Judah," whereas "Israelite" is national, including all the descendants of Jacob, to whom God gave the name "Israel," Genesis 32:28. The term "Jew" is first found in 2 Kings 16:6, where it is used of those who belonged to the kingdom of Judah, as distinguished from those who belonged to the Northern Kingdom, Israel. Subsequent to the Captivity, however, in general use the name has served to distinguish the people as a race from all the Gentiles. In this sense the apostle uses it here.

by nature,—i.e., not by conversion, but by origin.

and not sinners of the Gentiles,—here, of course, the apostle is taking the Judaizers on their own ground, and in an ironical way reminding them of their claim to moral superiority over "the uncircumcision." That Jews also are sinners he shows plainly as his argument develops; see v. 17.

2:16 yet—*de*, i.e., notwithstanding that we are Jews, and "rest upon, and glory in, the law," Romans 2:17-23.

knowing—*oida*, i.e., perceiving in the very nature of the Christian faith; see note at v. 9.

that a man—*anthrōpos*, a member of the human race, without reference to sex or nationality; cp. Matthew 4:4.

Where the distinction of sex is in view, *anēr* is used of the male, cp. 4:27, "husband," *gunē* of the woman, 4:4, Matthew 1:20, "wife." See further at 3:28.

The apostle's use of the word "man" serves to remind his readers of the solidarity of the race; the Judaizers had too readily forgotten that a common humanity underlies all merely national distinctions.

is not justified—*dikaioō,* = to show, or declare, to be right, Luke 7:29; 10:29; 1 Corinthians 4:4. In the majority of its New Testament occurrences *dikaioō* = "to declare a person to be righteous before God." All doers of the law are justified, Romans 2:13, with this proviso, that if a man "shall keep the whole law, and yet stumble in one point, he is become guilty of all," James 2:10; cp. 3:10 below. As a matter of fact, however, no such doers of law have yet been found among men, and "there is no distinction," i.e., as between Jew and Gentile, "for all have sinned, and fall short of the glory of God," i.e., fail to secure the approval of the sole Lawgiver and Judge. Clearly, then, by works of law shall no flesh be justified, or accounted righteous, in His sight, Romans 3:22, 23, 20, marg., the conclusion here, as in the more extended argument of the Epistle to the Romans, cp. also 3:11 below. And this the converted Jews had themselves acknowledged when they sought justification through Christ.

by the works—i.e., by obedience, by abstaining from the things prohibited and by doing the things prescribed, cp. Hebrews 6:1; 9:14, where such works are described as "dead," i.e., unproductive.

of the law,—*nomos,* the absence of the article here shows that the apostle is asserting a principle, "by obedience to law"; but since speaker and hearers were alike Jews, it is plain that the Mosaic Law is in view. It is, however, the fact that the Mosaic Law is law that is emphasized, and this becomes even more evident where "law" is set in contrast with "grace," as in Romans 6:14, 15, and with "faith," as in 3:28. The Mosaic Law itself is readily divisible into two parts, ceremonial and moral, but such a distinction is never explicitly made in Scripture, neither is it ever assumed. And while the ceremony of circumcision was, apparently, the occasion of the present dispute, Paul himself asserts that submission to the ceremony, or rite, carried with it an obligation to do the whole law, 5:3. Hence throughout this Epistle, and indeed throughout all his writings, the apostle asserts the freedom of the Christian from the Law of Moses in its totality, making no distinction as between ceremonial and moral.

The sentence thus far may be paraphrased: "No one is reckoned righteous by God on the ground that he has done all that which God in His law commands."

save—*ean mē,* lit., "if not," cp. the equivalent grammatical form, *ei mē,* in 1:19; 6:14.

It is plain from the whole argument of the apostle, and see particularly 3:11, 12, that "faith" and "law" are viewed as mutually exclusive; hence it is impossible to understand him here to mean that a man is justified by the works of the law when they are accompanied by faith; indeed this was just the contention of his opponents in the controversy. If, then, the expression here translated "save" is to be read with "by the works of the law," the rendering "but only" is to be preferred as less ambiguous than "save."

It is to be remembered, however, that in the English of the sixteenth and seventeenth centuries, i.e., the English of A.V., "save" meant "but only," whereas now its use is confined to the meaning "except," cp. Luke 4:26, 27, "but he was sent only to Zarephath," "but only Naaman was cleansed," and this sentence from a letter written by Ridley a few days before his martyrdom, A.D. 1555, "I learned without booke almost all . . . the Canonicall epistles, save only the Apocalypse."

It is probable, however, that the apostle intended "save" to be read with "justified," and in that case the sentence may be paraphrased, "a man is not justified by the works of the law, he is not justified except through faith." This has the advantage of retaining the meaning "except," which this expression has everywhere else in Paul's writings.

through—*dia*, when followed by the genitive case of the noun, as here, = by means of.

faith in Jesus Christ,—it is grammatically possible to render "of," as A.V., and to understand the expression in the light of Hebrews 12:2 (where "our" should certainly be omitted), but the faith exercised by the Lord in the days of His flesh does not provide the ground of justification; hence this cannot be the meaning here. For the same reason the meaning cannot be that of Revelation 14:12, where "the faith of Jesus" = the teaching, or doctrine, of which He is the center and which may be summed up in His Name. It would, moreover, be quite possible to translate *pistis* "faithfulness," and it is true that by His faithfulness even unto the death of the Cross, cp. Philippians 2:8, the Lord Jesus became "the author of eternal salvation," Hebrews 5:9, but the words that immediately follow show that faith exercised by men is in the apostle's mind, cp. Romans 3:22, 26, where the context leads to the same conclusion, as also in Ephesians 3:12; Philippians 3:9. In all these places "faith toward our Lord Jesus Christ," Acts 20:21, is to be understood. This conclusion is further strengthened by the parallel evidently intended between "works of law" and "faith in Jesus Christ," for as the "works" are man's work, so "faith" is man's faith.

even we—the pronoun, which is repeated from v. 15, is expressed in orig. for emphasis, = "even we Jews," who glory in the law, and enjoy the privileges of a national covenant relationship with God.

believed—*pistenō*, the verb form of the noun *pistis* used immediately before.

on—*eis* = "into," which is found with "believed" elsewhere in Paul's Epistles only in Romans 10:14*a;* Philippians 1:29; and with "faith" only in Colossians

2:5. The words signify not merely the acceptance of Christ's testimony (as in Rom. 10:14*b,* where there is no preposition), it comprehends also that submission to, that trust in, Him which results from the acceptance of His testimony. Believing His words a man trusts himself to, and so enters into union with, Christ; cp. John 6:29, "believe on [into]" with v. 30, "believe thee."

Christ Jesus,—the significance of the changed order of the name and title may be brought out in a paraphrase, thus: "the condition on which men may be justified is not obedience to law, but faith in Jesus, Whose resurrection has established His claim to be Messiah; and even we who are Jews, finding the law insufficient in this respect, trusted ourselves to Him Who came from glory to humiliation to do for us what obedience to the law never could have accomplished." See comment on *1 Thessalonians* 1:1.

that—"in order that"; this was the very purpose they had in view in believing in Christ at all.

we might be justified by faith—*ek,* lit., "out of." Immediately before the writer had said "by means of"; the two prepositions have a large amount of common ground while each has something distinctive. The use of both secures emphasis, and *ek* is, perhaps, more exclusive than *dia.* The apostle is determined to leave no loophole for escape from the force of his argument, and as he has said "out of works" so now he says "out of faith," lest any subtle reasoner should suggest that "by means of" might mean something less than "out of." Cp. Romans 3:30, and see note thereon at 3:8.

in Christ,—the repetition of the title maintains the emphasis on the fact that the object of faith is a person; indeed it seems as though the apostle intended to suggest the question why, if the law was sufficient for justification, a Messiah must needs be sent at all?

and not by the works of the law:—earlier in the sentence the apostle used these words in the statement of a broad principle concerning mankind generally, now he uses them again in applying that principle to believing Jews specifically.

because—*hoti,* which is frequently used by the apostle to introduce a quotation from the Old Testament in support of a statement made, cp. 3:10, "for it is written"; here, as at 3:11, there is an ellipsis of "it is written," and what follows is rather an adaptation than a quotation of Psalm 143:2.

by the works of the law—the words of the Psalmist are, "enter not into judgment with thy servant," = "do not judge me by Thy law"; the apostle expresses the same idea in a direct categorical statement.

shall no flesh be justified.—lit., "shall not be justified all flesh," with emphasis thrown upon "not." In substituting "all flesh" for "living men" the apostle has recourse to a common Hebraism, cp. Genesis 6:12, and see at 1:16, above. The same passage is adduced, with the same modifications, in Romans 3:20, there to show that by the law all men are condemned, here, that by the law no man is justified.

2:17 But if,—as was the case.

while we sought—lit., "seeking"; the word suggests that they who before "followed after a law of righteousness," but "did not arrive at that law," Romans 9:31, 32, had themselves turned to Christ for the satisfaction which the law had not afforded them.

to be justified in Christ,—not in the law, as would surely have been the case had justification by the law been possible.

we ourselves also—"even we ourselves," Jews though we are; see at v. 16.

were found—i.e., were discovered, or discovered ourselves, to be sinners; suggesting the surprise of the Jew who learned for the first time that before God he had no moral superiority over the Gentiles whom he superciliously dubbed "sinners," while he esteemed himself to be "righteous," see at v. 15, above; cp. Romans 7:10, where the apostle uses the same word to describe his own experience of the law.

sinners,—*hamartōlos,* lit., "one who has missed the mark"; the most general term used in Scripture to describe the condition of the human race since the Fall. In their spiritual arrogancy the Jews applied the word to the Gentiles to express the contempt in which they held them. And now in the light of the life and death of Christ the Jew discovered himself to be in exactly the same case, cp. Romans 3:9.

is Christ a minister—*diakonos;* see comment on *1 Thessalonians* 3:2.

of sin?—i.e., "did Christ make us sinners when through His gospel He revealed to us our sinful condition, and we learned that all our legal righteousnesses were but as a polluted garment?" Cp. Isaiah 64:6, and Romans 6:13, where "sin" is personified; so here, "does Christ further the interests, extend the dominion, of sin?"

God forbid.—lit., "let it not be"; there is no mention of God in orig. Apart from the writings of the apostle Paul, the phrase occurs only in the words of the Jews recorded in Luke 20:16. In all its occurrences, save 1 Corinthians 6:15, it repudiates a wrong inference from right premises, so here.

2:18 For if I—here the apostle uses the singular instead of, as heretofore, the plural, but the pronoun is not expressed in orig., and therefore is not emphatic. The change was, perhaps, made for two reasons. Paul's courtesy does not desert him in the most strenuous controversy; hence he transfers the evident conclusion from Peter's course to himself "in a figure," cp. 1 Corinthians 4:6. But he may also have had in mind the charge of opportunism made against him by some; see 5:11. Thus Peter certainly was a transgressor in the course he actually pursued, and Paul would have been a transgressor had he pursued the course with which his opponents credited him.

built up again—*oikodomeō;* see comment on *1 Thessalonians* 5:11.

those things which I destroyed,—*kataluō,* = to loosen down, used of the demolition of a building, Matthew 24:2, of the death of the body, 2 Corinthians 5:1, of the failure of purposes, Acts 5:38, 39, and of the marring of a person's spiritual well-being, Romans 14:20. The Lord Jesus declared that He came "not to destroy [*kataluo*] the law," Matthew 5:17, that is to say, not to lower the standard of divine righteousness, not to abrogate the least of God's requirements, but, on the contrary, in His own life to "magnify the law and make it honorable," Isaiah 42:21. Here a general principle is stated; "those things" = any things, but the particular application in this case, as the context plainly shows, is to the use of the law as a means of justification.

I prove myself a transgressor.—*parabatēs,* = one who oversteps a prescribed limit; in the New Testament always used of a breach of the law, Romans 2:25, 27; James 2:9, 11.||

Hamartōlos describes sin negatively, and is applicable to all men without distinction; *parabatēs* describes sin positively, and is applicable to those who received the law.

The proposition was true either way: if Peter did right in refusing to eat with the Gentiles he had done wrong in associating himself with them earlier; if he had done right to obey the vision from Heaven, he was doing wrong in disobeying it now. So with himself; if they were right who said he still preached circumcision on occasion, he was indeed a transgressor one way or the other.

What began as a resume of his remonstrance with Peter passes without remark into a statement, addressed directly to the Galatians, of the standing before God of the believer in Christ. The transition seems to be made at this point. Vv. 14–18 is language appropriate, under the circumstances, from one Christian Jew to another, but vv. 19–21 are apparently of wider scope, and are probably to be read as the resumption of his direct address to his readers.

2:19 For—introducing a succinct statement of the conclusive reason why the law must be definitely abandoned as a means of justification.

I—here the pronoun is expressed in orig. not to suggest a contrast with Peter, or with anybody else, but for the sake of impressiveness; what he is about to say will gain in vividness and strength by being expressed in the form of a personal statement. But the words thus introduced describe, not a singular attainment of the apostle's, but what is true of all believers from the moment of conversion. In other words they describe his "standing" in Christ, which is that of all Christians, not his "state," for that is a personal thing which varies with the individual.

through—by means of.

the law—as at v. 16.

died unto the law,—*apothnēskō,* for which see comment on *1 Thessalonians* 4:14; here also the essential meaning, separation, is readily discernible. The law by condemning him, even when his efforts to comply with it were most strenuous, cut him off from hope of justification by its means. In the epistle to the Romans "sin" is said to be the slayer, "sin, finding occasion through the commandment . . . slew me," 7:11; for the law in itself is "holy, righteous, good," but man, being unholy, unrighteous and evil, finds himself, because of his inherent sinfulness, not aided by, but in essential and inevitable opposition to, the law. By the law, then, the knowledge that he is a sinner comes to man, 3:20, and the sinner is "without strength" either to keep the law, 5:6, or to please God, 8:8. Thus, on every hand, "the commandment, which was unto [i.e., which he supposed would prove to be a means of] life, he found to be unto [i.e., to have the effect of revealing to him his actual condition of] death," 7:10; see also 7:6.

that I might live—*zaō,* as in v. 14.
True, it was God's law that "slew" him, but a new element is introduced, grace, v. 21, which discovered to him that this death was the necessary preliminary to the obtaining of life directly from the source of life, God Himself.
"Live" is here = "be justified before," as in 3:12, below, quoted from Leviticus 18:5.

unto God.—his endeavor to live before, i.e., to satisfy the requirements of, the law having proved futile, he appeals from it to God who gave it. God is greater than His law, and is not to be defeated in His purpose by the inadequacy of any particular instrument; what His law cannot accomplish He effects by His grace, cp. Romans 8:3.

2:20 I have been crucified with Christ;—in the original two words only, "with-Christ I-have-been-jointly-crucified." The pronoun is not emphatic, for the apostle is stating something that is true of him, not because he is an apostle, nor because of his spiritual attainments, but because he is a believer, and which is, therefore, true of every believer.
The compound verb, *sustauroō (sus-stauroō)* is used in its literal sense in Matthew 27:44; Mark 15:32; John 19:32, and in a metaphorical sense, as here, in Romans 6:6.||
The apostle now proceeds to explain how he "died unto the law"; he had been, and was still (this is the force of the perfect tense) crucified with Christ. The Judaizers shunned the reproach of the Cross; to them it was a "stumbling block," 5:11; 6:12, cp. 1 Corinthians 1:23; he glorified in it and made it his own, cp. 6:14. Nor is it merely that he had "crucified" the grosser elements in his nature, cp. 5:24; he himself, his virtues and his vices, all that entered

into and made the man, had been nailed to the Cross; henceforth he hoped nothing from the one, feared nothing from the other.

Christ, though He had fully discharged every obligation imposed by the law, endured the extreme penalty prescribed for "transgression and disobedience," Hebrews 2:2. When, therefore, a man believes on Christ, he acknowledges the judgment of God against sin to be just, and accepts the death of Christ as the execution of that judgment upon him for his own guilt. In thus believing the man becomes identified with Christ in His death, and, since death nullifies all claims and all obligations, is "made dead to the law through the body of Christ," Romans 7:4, and ceases, finally, to be under the jurisdiction of the law.

The idea of the believer's death with Christ reappears in Romans 6:7; Colossians 2:11, 12, 20; 3:3, cp. also 1 Peter 2:24; the idea of his crucifixion with Christ appears only here, 6:14, below, and Romans 6:6. The reference to this mode of execution, with its associations of shame, heightens the contrast between the fancied law-keeping of his opponents, and the actual fact of their absolute failure to attain to righteousness thereby. The shame of the Cross was not His Who died upon it, but theirs whose transgressions and disobedience made the Cross necessary.

yet I live;—having explained how he had "died unto the law," he goes on to explain how it is that he "lives unto God."

and *yet* no longer I,—here "I," *ego*, is emphatic, being separately expressed in orig. The pronoun appears here only in the Greek of these two verses, whereas in English it appears six times.

but Christ liveth in me:—i.e., by His Spirit, cp. "if any man hath not the Spirit of Christ, he is none of His. And if Christ is in you," Romans 8:9, 10. Christ in person, i.e., in His glorified human body is in Heaven at the right hand of God, but He is represented here by the Holy Spirit, see John 14:17, and Romans 8:11, last clause, and what is said to be done now by Christ is done by Him through the agency of the Holy Spirit. There is no exactly parallel statement in New Testament, but cp. Ephesians 3:17; 1 John 5:12; Colossians 1:27 (which should probably be read "Christ among you"), and this of course would also be by His Spirit. When Paul "sought to establish his own righteousness," Romans 10:3, everything depended upon his vigilance and energy, but when he realized the futility of his best efforts and trusted in another than himself, i.e., in Christ, he became conscious of a new power working in him for righteousness.

and that *life* which I—live—or, simply, "in that I live," cp. Romans 6:10, marg.

In other passages in which the believer is said to have died with Christ, he is said also to be "raised together with Christ," Colossians 3:1, cp. Romans 6:5, 11, 13. It is to this life of the spirit in association with Christ in resurrection that the apostle here refers.

now—i.e., as a Christian, since his conversion.

in the flesh—by metonymy for "the body"; in the earthly environment and in the body suited thereto.

I live in faith,—there was no outward change, the new life made no appeal to the senses, because it was received in response to faith and was maintained by the exercise of faith. Faith is, indeed, the characteristic function of the new life.

the faith **which is in**—as at v. 16, where see note. The Christian cannot be said to live by the faith which was manifested by the Lord Jesus when He was on earth. Neither is the Son of God here presented as an example to be followed, as that the believer is to trust God as Christ trusted God, Psalm 22:9, and trusts Him, Hebrews 2:13, but as being Himself the proper object of the believer's confidence.

Again, through *pistis* may be translated "faithfulness," and though the faithfulness of Christ is the ground of the Christian's confidence that He will complete the work He has begun, this meaning does not harmonize with the context; cp. the end of the note on the same words at v. 16. Moreover the statements that follow are reasons for trusting Him rather than proofs of His faithfulness; they declare what He did, not what He is doing or has undertaken to do. The two ideas are, however, very intimately related, the proofs of His faithfulness are the reasons for trusting Him; what He has done is the guarantee of His will and of His power to continue and to complete the work of salvation. The Christian's faith rests on the faithfulness of God. But it is the former, not the latter, that is in the mind of the apostle here.

the Son of God,—this title occurs again in Paul's writings only in Romans 1:4; 2 Corinthians 1:19; Ephesians 4:13, but the shorter form "His [i.e., God's] Son," is much more frequent; see 1:16; Romans 8:3; Colossians 1:13, etc., and comment on *1 Thessalonians* 1:10.

The word "son," *huios,* is used in Scripture in two senses, *a,* of the relation of offspring to parent, as in 4:30, and *b,* of the expression of character, as in 3:7; see further at comment on *1 Thessalonians* 5:5. In the title "Son of God," "Son" is used sometimes in one, sometimes in the other, of these meanings. Thus, e.g., when the disciples so addressed Him, Matthew 14:33; 16:16; John 1:49, when the centurion so spoke of Him, Matthew 27:54, they probably meant that He was a manifestation of God in human form. But in such passages as Luke 1:32, 35, Acts 13:33, which refer to the humanity of the Lord Jesus, the body prepared for Him by God, Hebrews 10:5, the word is used in sense *a* above.

The Lord Jesus Himself used the full title on occasion, John 5:25; 9:35; 10:36; 11:4, and on the more frequent occasions on which He spoke of Himself as "the Son," the words are to be understood as an abbreviation of "the Son of God," not of "the Son of Man"; this latter He always expressed in full; see Luke 10:22, John 5:19, etc.

John uses both the longer and shorter forms of the title in his gospel, see 3:16-18; 20:31, e.g., and in his epistles, and cp. Revelation 2:18. So does the writer of the Epistle to Hebrews 1:2; 4:14; 6:6, etc. In these writers, as well as in the epistles of the apostle Paul, the word "Son" is to be taken in the sense *b* above. An eternal relation subsisting between the Son and the Father in the Godhead is to be understood. That is to say, the Son of God, in His eternal relationship with the Father, is not so entitled because He at any time began to derive His being from the Father (in which case he could not be coeternal with the Father), but because He is and ever has been the expression of what the Father is; cp. John 14:9, "he that hath seen Me hath seen the Father." The words of Hebrews 1:3, "Who being the effulgence of His [God's] glory, and the very image of His [God's] substance" are a definition of what is meant by "Son of God."

Thus absolute Godhead, not Godhead in a secondary or derived sense, is intended in the title. And the apostle uses it here at the climax of his testimony because God alone is the proper object of human faith, Jeremiah 17:5, 7, and because only as the true dignity of the Lord Jesus is apprehended is it possible to realize the grace of the love and the value of the gift which he declares to be the sole ground of the salvation of men. Human effort is excluded in the very nature of the case, since He by Whom we are justified is the Son of God.

who loved me,—point tense, as in 2 Thessalonians 2:16, where it is used of the love of God, as here of the love of the Son; love in each case seen in its eternal aspect, timeless, immutable; so also in Romans 8:37; Ephesians 5:2, 25.

Whereas in New Testament the world is frequently said to be the object of the love of God, as in John 3:16, Romans 5:8, e.g., it is never said to be the object of the love of Christ. Save in the incident recorded in Mark 10:21, His love is always mentioned as having for its object those who believe, whether individually, or collectively, the local church, Revelation 3:9, and the church which is His body, Ephesians 5:25.

and gave Himself up—*paradidōmi;* see note at 1:4, above. This word also is in the point tense because it refers to the "one act of righteousness," Romans 5:18, in which the eternal love of God found its highest expression, and by which the salvation of believers was secured.

Paradidōmi is used again of the act of the Lord Jesus in submitting to death in Ephesians 5:2, 25; and of the act of God in sending Him with that purpose in view, Romans 8:32, cp. 4:25. It is also used of the actions of men by means of which the Divine purpose was accomplished. It is used of the treachery of Judas Iscariot, Matthew 10:4, where it is translated "betray"; of the handing over of their prisoner to the Roman authorities by the rulers of the Jews, Matthew 27:2; Acts 3:13; and of His final delivery by Pilate to the soldiers for execution, Matthew 27:26.

Complete comprehension of "the mystery of God, even Christ" lies beyond the capacity of the human mind. The more closely it is considered the greater grows the wonder of its unfathomable depths. Not only was God in Christ during His life on earth, John 14:10, God was in Christ in His reconciling death, 2 Corinthians 5:19. This ground is holy, yet is it to be approached, albeit with "reverence and awe," for all that God has been pleased to reveal is proper subject for the worshipful consideration of His children. Two cautions are needful here, however. We may not go beyond what is written, and we may not expect to eliminate mystery from the Divine sacrifice or to reconcile all that is revealed concerning it; the human point of view is far too low, the human outlook far too limited, to admit of that.

The variety in the use of the same word, *paradidōmi*, to describe the part taken in the tragedy of the Cross by men by God, and by Christ Himself, is in harmony with the general testimony of Scripture. Plainly, men were responsible for the death of Jesus of Nazareth. He Himself declared that He would be killed by Gentiles at the instigation of the Jews, Mark 10:33, 34, and in due time "they crucified Him," 15:25. In his first sermon Peter charged the Jews with His murder, "Him, . . . ye by the hand of lawless men [i.e., of Gentiles] did crucify and slay," Acts 2:23; "ye . . . killed the Prince of life," 3:14, 15; "Jesus, Whom ye slew, hanging Him on a tree," 5:30. Judas, the Jewish authorities, Pilate, these were the links in the chain by which the "determinate counsel and foreknowledge of God," 2:23, was carried out. Each delivered Him to the other, and thus each became equally responsible for His death, though the actual nails of crucifixion were driven by the hands of Roman soldiers. Since the death of Christ was to be vicarious, the consequence of the assumption by Him of the sins of men, the prophets ascribe it to the act of God, Lawgiver and Judge. The language of Isaiah 53, e.g., is so frequently used of the Lord Jesus in the New Testament as to preclude any doubt that His experiences are described therein, and indeed that this is so is explicitly stated by one of the evangelists, John 12:38–41. And the words of v. 10 are, "it pleased Jehovah to bruise Him; He hath put Him to grief . . . Thou shalt make His soul an offering for sin."

Zechariah had a similar vision concerning the Messiah; he heard the words, "Awake, O sword, against My Shepherd, against the man that is My fellow, saith Jehovah of Hosts; smite the Shepherd," 13:7. And these words the Lord Jesus modified in such a way as to make the stroke of the sword the act of Jehovah Himself. "It is written," He said, "I will smite the Shepherd," Matthew 26:31. And in the actual experience of the desolations of the Cross He asked, in the language of Psalm 22:1, "My God, My God, why hast Thou forsaken Me?" This is death in its essential element, the aversion of the face of God. God had forsaken Him. The experience thus described was not subjective, it was real, actual. It was not at all that the Sufferer in His distress and agony thought or feared that God had turned away from Him, for that would mean that His faith in God had failed. These words expressed not His fear but the stern and awful fact. God had brought the Sinbearer, albeit He was the Holy and

Beloved One, "into the dust of death," v. 15. Thus He "spared not His own Son, but delivered Him up for us all," Romans 8:32.

There is yet another aspect under which the death of Christ is presented to us, "He poured out His soul unto death," Isaiah 53:12. It was a purely voluntary act of His own, carried out in obedience to His Father, cp. Philippians 2:8, but under no other constraint. On one of the occasions on which He declared the end toward which He steadfastly moved, He was explicit on this point. "I lay down My life," He said, "no one taketh it away from Me, but I lay it down of Myself. I have authority to lay it down, and I have authority to take it again. This commandment received I from My Father," John 10:18. Accordingly, when the officers came to arrest Him, He made it clear, by His action in causing them to fall backward to the ground, that only as He willed it could they lay hands upon Him at all, John 18:3-12.

The language in which the actual death is described demands careful consideration. Crucifixion may be called an indirect method of execution. No mortal stroke is dealt; the victim is simply put into a position in which life is impossible and death inevitable. Vitality ebbs slowly away, so slowly that ordinarily the impatient soldiers hastened the end; see John 19:32. But the narrative of the evangelists plainly indicates that the death of the Lord Jesus did not take place in the way normal under the circumstances. For one thing He died much earlier than was usual, see Mark 15:44; John 19:32, 33, nor did His life ebb slowly from Him, "Jesus . . . cried with a loud voice, . . . and . . . He gave up the ghost," Luke 23:46. Ordinarily when men die the head droops, but of the Lord Jesus it is said "He bowed His head, and gave up His Spirit," John 19:30. Each of these statements is significant. The words translated, "bowed His head," occur again but twice in New Testament, in Matthew 8:20 and its parallel Luke 9:58, where they are rendered "lay His head." They mean more than the mere physical act; they mean that the rest denied him on earth He found, His work completed, on His Father's bosom.

But the full price must be paid, He must pass completely under the dominion of death, so "He gave up His spirit." Again, the word is *paradidōmi*, often used in connection with this death, and always denoting a conscious, deliberate act, and so here. He had voluntarily assumed the body prepared for Him, that in it He might do the will of God; He voluntarily left it, that by so doing He might fulfill that will to the uttermost, Hebrews 2:14; 10:5, 7. "Christ . . . through the eternal Spirit offered Himself to God," 9:14; to that end He submitted to crucifixion at the hands of men, He "bare our sins in His own body upon the tree," He bowed under the stroke of divine justice, He laid down His life, He gave up His spirit, He experienced the separation of the spirit and soul from the body, for a brief space He remained under the dominion of death, cp. Romans 6:9. He endured the penalty of sin to the uttermost, but each act that went to make up the whole of that absolute obedience, the price of our redemption, was His own.

for me.—*huper,* = "on my behalf," "for my salvation." See comment on *1 Thessalonians* 5:10. for a list of the prepositions used in New Testament in connection with the death of Christ.

The singular pronoun here is in keeping with the rest of the section, but there is no other instance of its use in this connection in New Testament. In His love for the church, Ephesians 5:25, Christ does not lose sight of the individual believer. Each member of His body is the direct object of His love, and it is as true that He died for each as it is that He died for all. Hence the individual believer appropriates to himself that which is the possession of all.

2:21 *I* do not make void—*atheteō,* = "to reject"; see comment on *1 Thessalonians* 4:8.

the grace of God:—see 1:6, above, and note. The teaching of the Judaizers certainly did set it aside, for if salvation is by grace it is no more of works, and, conversely, if it is of works it is no more of grace; works and grace are incompatibles, they are mutually exclusive; see Romans 11:6.

for—introducing the proof of the apostle's proposition that to add circumcision, or law-keeping in any form, to the death of Christ, is to set at naught the grace of God.

if righteousness—*dikaiosunē,* i.e., justification; see at v. 16, above, and 5:5, below.

is through the law, then—the inevitable conclusion, the obvious inference, is—

Christ died for nought.—*dōrean,* from *dōrea,* = "a gift," something bestowed freely, without price, or compensation, as in John 4:10; Acts 2:38; 2 Corinthians 9:15, e.g. Hence *dōrean* also means "freely," "gratuitously," as in Matthew 10:8; Romans 3:24; 2 Corinthians 11:7; 2 Thessalonians 3:8; Revelation 21:6; 22:17. But it also = "gratuitously" in the sense of causelessly, as in John 15:25, of the hatred of the Jews for the Lord Jesus, and "vainly," or without either purpose or result, as here.||

GALATIANS

CHAPTER THREE

Verses 1–29

3:1 O foolish Galatians,—the meaning is, not that the Galatians were naturally stupid, senseless, but that they had not used their senses, else they would never have allowed themselves to be led into the absurd position in which they were found. The tone is certainly not that of contempt, nor is it so much that of indignation as of reproach, as in the Lord's words on the way to Emmaus, Luke 24:25.

Up to this point the apostle had dealt only indirectly with the difficulty in the Galatian churches. Now he begins to reason with them directly, first from their own experience, vv. 1–5, and then from Scripture, vv. 6–29—4:17, then from their experience, 4:8–20, and from Scripture again, 4:21–31, concerning their defection, threatened or actual, from the true gospel.

who did bewitch you,—*baskaino,* = "to subject a person to an occult evil influence," popularly called "the evil eye."‖

before whose eyes Jesus Christ was openly set forth crucified?—*prographō,* lit., "to write before," as of Old Testament, Romans 15:4, cp. Jude 4, and of a previous letter, Ephesians 3:3.‖

Here, however, it is probably used in another sense, unexampled in the Scriptures but not uncommon in the language of the day, = "proclaimed," "placarded," as a magistrate proclaimed the fact that an execution had been carried out, placarding his proclamation in a public place. The apostle carries on his metaphor of the "evil eye"; as a preventative of such mischief it was common to post up charms on the walls of houses, a glance at which was supposed to counteract any evil influence to which a person may have been subjected. "Notwithstanding," he says in effect, "that the fact that Christ had been crucified was placarded before your very eyes in our preaching, you have allowed yourselves to be 'overlooked,' you have been fascinated by the enemies of the Cross of Christ, when you had only to look at Him to escape their malignant influence"; cp. the interesting and instructive parallel in Numbers 21:9.

3:2 This only would I learn from you,—a crucial question, the answer to which would settle the whole matter in dispute. There is, perhaps, a tinge of irony in the query, consistent with the word "foolish" which he applies to them. If they were sagacious enough to revise the gospel by which they had been saved, surely they had not allowed such an evident consideration as this to escape them.

Received ye the Spirit—point, or momentary tense; the Holy Spirit had been given to, and received by, each of them, individually, at a definite time in his spiritual history. Two questions arise here, *a*, On what condition is the Holy Spirit imparted to men? and, *b*, After the fulfillment of the condition, at what interval, if any, does He begin His operations?

The first of these questions is answered in Acts 5:32; the condition is obedience, not to God in His law, but to God in His gospel concerning His Son; and in John 7:39, where the condition is faith, of which obedience is the outward expression; see at 5:7, below. The second is answered in Ephesians 1:13, "in whom, having also believed, ye were sealed with the Holy Spirit of promise." Cp. Romans 13:11, where the same tense is translated "when we first believed"; it would be equally appropriate to insert "first"; in Ephesians 1:13, "in whom, when ye first believed, ye were sealed," or the word might be rendered "when ye believed," as it is in Acts 19:2, see below.

These words of the apostle are in complete harmony with those of the Lord Jesus spoken to Nicodemus. A man, in order to enter the Kingdom of God, must be born of the Spirit, John 3:3. Replying to the question, "How can these things be?" v. 9, the Lord declared that "the Son of man must be lifted up: that whosoever believeth may in Him have eternal life," v. 15. The new birth is the inception of eternal life; eternal life is the sequence to the new birth. The new birth ushers the man into eternal life, eternal life is entered upon in the new birth; to be born anew is to have eternal life. Thus the Lord Jesus Himself made it plain that when a man believes in Him he is born of the Holy Spirit, and to this the teaching of the apostles is conformed, cp., e.g., Romans 8:9. A man born anew is "not in the flesh"; but he is "not in the flesh" just for this reason, that the Spirit of God dwells in him. On the other hand, "if any man hath not the Spirit of Christ" (Who is the Spirit of God, as the preceding words show) "he is none of His," i.e., he is not born anew at all. It is when a man believes that he becomes a child of God, cp. John 1:12 with 1 John 5:1, and to this relationship the indwelling Spirit Himself bears witness, Romans 8:16.

The imposition of the apostle's hands in the case of John's disciples, Acts 19:6, may be compared with the imposition of the hands of Peter and John in the case of the Samaritans, and of the hands of Ananias in the case of Paul himself, Acts 8:17; 9:17; but the records in Acts 2:37-42; 10:44-48, show that the laying on of hands was not a necessary condition of the receiving of the Spirit, not even when an apostle was actually present, for in each case the Spirit was given, but there is no reference in either case to the laying on of hands.

This is the first mention of the Holy Spirit in the Epistle; henceforth His part in the salvation of the believer is referred to frequently.

by the works of the law,—as at 2:16.

or by the hearing—*akoē* is used by the apostle in three ways, *a*, by metonymy, for the organ of hearing, the ear, 1 Corinthians 12:17; 2 Timothy 4:3, 4; *b*, for the receiving of a message, Romans 10:17; c, for the message itself, Romans 10:16; 1 Thessalonians 2:13, cp. Hebrews 4:2.

While something may be said in favor of c here, on the whole it seems better to understand the word in sense b.

of faith?—thus read the words = "the receiving of the message by faith," as in Romans 10:17, "faith cometh by hearing." Plainly the answer must be "by the hearing of faith," for law demands but has nothing to give, and, as a matter of universal experience, no one ever had "received the Spirit" by obedience to law.

3:3 Are ye so foolish?—i.e., so reluctant to exercise your senses that you have not seen an inconsistency so glaring as this. The same word as in v. 1.

having begun—*enarchomai*, point tense, referring them back to the moment at which by faith they responded to the message of the gospel. In Philippians 1:6 the same word is used of the operations of God in the soul; the two beginnings are one in time.||

in the Spirit,—i.e., "in the sphere of the spirit"; the contrast with the "flesh" seems to fix the reference to the inner man. The absence of the article in orig. is in favor of this view, but that in itself would not determine the interpretation, for the article is sometimes absent where the Holy Spirit is certainly intended. See further comment on *1 Thessalonians 5:1; 2 Thessalonians 2:13.*

Since there are no initial capital letters in the more ancient Greek MSS. (the "uncials"), their use in the English versions is interpretation rather than translation. Evidently the Revisers understood the word here to refer to the Spirit of God. It may be remarked here that in this Epistle the word *pneuma*, = spirit, occurs eighteen times; of these A.V. has "spirit" eleven times, "Spirit" seven times, whereas R.V. has "spirit" only thrice, but "Spirit" fifteen times.* See note in each case.

are ye now perfected—*epiteleō*, = "to complete," as in Zechariah 4:9, LXX. The tense is continuous, for while a beginning is made at a definite point, perfecting is a process. It is probable, too, that the middle voice is to be understood = "are ye now perfecting yourselves?"

in the flesh?—with reference to ordinances, such as circumcision, and keeping of laws. The order of the sentence in orig. forms a chiasm, thus:

  a, having begun
  b, in spirit
  b, in flesh
  a, are ye perfected?

_____

*As printed in *The Parallel New Testament, Greek and English.* Oxford Press.

Having appealed to the fact that He had come into their lives at the outset of their Christian experience, the apostle now approaches the subject from the other side, and asks whether they expect themselves to complete by rites and ceremonies the work the Holy Spirit began within them. The idea is preposterous that a work begun in the higher sphere, the spirit, should be perfected in the lower, the flesh, that they who with the gift of the Holy Spirit had received the righteousness that is of God by faith, should now seek to establish their own righteousness by works of law.

In Old Testament the word "flesh" is used to translate several Hebrew words which need not be particularized here. It is ordinarily = "the physical frame," whether of beasts, Leviticus 8:31; Isaiah 31:3, e.g., or of men, Genesis 2:21. "All flesh" is of frequent occurrence, and is used sometimes of that part of the animal kingdom which inhabits the land, including man, Genesis 6:17, or excluding man, 6:19; sometimes of the human race alone, 6:12, cp., Deuteronomy 5:26.

Inasmuch as "flesh" is subject to disease and pain, and finally to corruption, the frailty of man is emphasized where it is used of him, cp. 2 Chronicles 32:8; Psalm 78:39; Daniel 2:11, e.g. Inasmuch as it is soft and impressionable, it is used metaphorically of the new heart given to those who turn to God. And inasmuch as it is an integral element in manhood, desire for God is declared to dwell in the flesh as well as in the heart, Psalm 63:1; 84:2. Throughout the Old Testament "flesh" does not appear to be anywhere used in a bad sense.

The Old Testament meanings of "flesh" are, with no exception, that of Psalm 63:1; 84:2, found again in New Testament, but in New Testament "flesh" (which, save in Rom. 14:21; 1 Cor. 8:13, is always the translation of the one Greek word, *sarx*) has a wider range of meaning. Its uses there may be analyzed as follows:

a, the substance of the body whether of beasts or of men, 1 Corinthians 15:39;

b, the human body, 2 Corinthians 10:3*a;* Galatians 2:20; Philippians 1:22;

c, by synecdoche (see Index), of mankind, in the totality of all that is essential to manhood, i.e., spirit, soul, and body, Matthew 24:22; John 1:13; Romans 3:20;

d, by synecdoche, of the holy humanity of the Lord Jesus, in the totality of all that is essential to manhood, i.e., spirit, soul, and body, John 1:14; 1 Timothy 3:16; 1 John 4:2; 2 John 7; in Hebrews 5:7, "the days of His flesh" = His past life on earth in distinction from His present life in resurrection;

e, by synecdoche, for the complete person, John 6:51–57; 2 Corinthians 7:5; James 5:3;

f, the weaker element in human nature, Matthew 26:41; Romans 6:19; 8:3*a;*

g, the unregenerate state of men, Romans 7:5; 8:8, 9;

h, the seat of sin in man (but this is not the same thing as in the body), 2 Peter 2:18; 1 John 2:16;

i, the lower and temporary element in the Christian, Galatians 3:3; 6:8, and in religious ordinances, Hebrews 9:10;

j, the natural attainments of men, 1 Corinthians 1:26; 2 Corinthians 10:2, 3*b;*

k, circumstances, 1 Corinthians 7:28, the externals of life, 2 Corinthians 7:1; Ephesians 6:5; Hebrews 9:13;

l, by metonymy (see Index), the outward and seeming, as contrasted with the spirit, the inward and real, John 6:63; 2 Corinthians 5:16;

m, natural relationship, consanguine, 1 Corinthians 10:18; Galatians 4:23, or marital, Matthew 19:5.

For analysis of New Testament usage of "spirit," "soul," and "body," see comment on *1 Thessalonians* 5:23. For "flesh and blood" see at 1:16, above.

3:4 Did ye suffer so many things—see the history in Acts 14:1-7.

in vain?—i.e., to no purpose, as at 4:11; was it all a mistake, and such a costly one? Persecution at the instigation of the Jews had failed to move them from the faith. Would they succumb before the subtler methods of the Judaizers?

if it be indeed in vain.—through all his argument and expostulation the apostle assumes the genuineness of the Galatians' faith. So here in this word, spoken aside as it were, he shows that he is unwilling to believe that they had actually turned away, that he hopes they will yet shake themselves free from the trammels of this false teaching, cp. Hebrews 6:9; 10:39.

3:5 He—that supplieth to you the Spirit,—i.e., God, as in 2 Corinthians 9:10*a*, cp. Luke 11:13; Acts 5:32; lit., "the Supplier," the tense is present continuous. Verses 2-4 are retrospective; in them the apostle appeals to the past experience of the Galatians; here he appeals to an experience they were then enjoying.

The function of the Holy Spirit is to maintain the Christian in fellowship with God, 2 Corinthians 13:14, to strengthen him, Ephesians 3:16, to secure to him the victory over the inveterate tendencies of his fallen nature, Gal. 5:17, and to bear fruit unto holiness in him, 22; in fact, to meet all the needs of the new life by keeping him in instant and vital communion with God. There is, moreover, the continual need of the assembled believers, the churches of the saints, which also is met by the Spirit; see 1 Corinthians 12:4-11. This ministry of the Spirit, as the apostle tacitly acknowledges by his question, was then in actual operation among them.

In addition to the two passages just mentioned, *epichoregeo*, the word of the text, occurs again in Colossians 2:19, of Christ as the Head of the body and the source of its supplies, and in 2 Peter 1:11, of the reward of present faithfulness to be given by God at the setting up of the eternal kingdom. Only in 2 Peter 1:5 is it used of the active agency of the Christian himself.||

The corresponding noun, *epichoregia,* occurs in Ephesians 4:16; Philippians 1:19.||

The simple form of the verb, *chorēgeō*, occurs in 2 Corinthians 9:10*b*, and in 1 Peter 4:11, in both places of the divine supplies. ||

The prefix strengthens the word and emphasizes the idea of fullness and sufficiency. God, Who bountifully supplies all that His people need to enable them to live worthily of their calling, will also liberally reward their faithfulness in the day of Christ.

In 2 Corinthians 9:10*a*, where the character of God, by Whose bounty every living thing is sustained, Psalm 145:15, is declared, the stronger form of the verb is used, but in the latter part of the verse, where the will and capacity to receive are in view, the simple form is used.

That the source of the Christian's supplies is said, here and in 2 Corinthians 9:10*a*, to be God, and in Colossians 2:19 to be Christ, is an incidental testimony to the Deity of the latter.

therefore—resuming the subject of v. 2; vv. 3, 4 are parenthetic.

and worketh—as at 2:8, where see note. This word also is in the present continuous tense, lit., "He who is working," from which it appears that the gift of "miracles" was still operative in the Galatian churches.

The New Testament usage of *energeō* makes it clear that the apostle does not here refer to himself or to any human agent, for that word is never used of men, save in Philippians 2:13*b*, in which as it is used immediately before of God, and of the Christian only as the result of the working of God in him, it is not really an exception. In the New Testament *energeō* is used of:

a, God 2:8, and here, 1 Corinthians 12:6; Ephesians 1:11, 20; 3:20; 2:13*a*; Colossians 1:29;

b, the Holy Spirit, 1 Corinthians 12:11; James 5:16, cp. Romans 8:26, and see comment on *1 Thessalonians* 5:17;

c, the Word of God, 1 Thessalonians 2:13;

d, supernatural power, undefined, Matthew 14:2, Mark 6:14;

e, faith, as the energizer of love, Galatians 5:6;

f, the example of patience in suffering, 2 Corinthians 1:6;

g, death (physical) and life (spiritual), 2 Corinthians 4:12;

h, sinful passions, Romans 7:5;

i, the spirit of the Evil One, Ephesians 2:2;

j. the mystery of iniquity, 2 Thessalonians 2:7.

These, then, are the powers that work in the human heart, regenerate and unregenerate. ||

For an analysis of the corresponding noun, *energeia*, see comment on *2 Thessalonians* 2:9.

miracles—lit., "powers," i.e., works of a supernatural origin and character, such as could not be produced by natural agents and means. For the distinction between "powers," "signs," and "wonders," see comment on *2 Thessalonians* 2:9.

There is no means of learning whether these miracles were physical or moral, or, as may well have been the case, both. Elsewhere the apostle distinguishes miracles from gifts of healing on the one hand, and from prophecy and tongues on the other; see 1 Corinthians 12:10, 28. Manifestation of power in the name of Christ in any sphere is evidence of the presence of God. Here it seems best to understand the word in the widest sense.

This association of the Holy Spirit with the power of God is common in the New Testament; see Luke 4:14; Acts 1:8; 10:38; Romans 15:13; 1 Thessalonians 1:5, et al.

among you,—these words may be understood either as = "within you individually," cp. Matt. 14:2, or as = "among you as churches," cp. 1 Corinthians 12:6, "God who worketh all [things] in all [persons or communities]." The latter is probably intended. Of course, every individual experience of the power of God, and every manifestation of the power of God through an individual, would be included in the things that happened "among them."

doeth he it **by the works of the law,**—i.e., in response to obedience to commandments and observance of ordinances.

or by the hearing of faith?—the answer to this question was inevitable; from the beginning of the gospel among them its blessings were imparted to those who "had faith to be made whole," Acts 14:9.

3:6 Even as—so plain is this that the apostle does not wait to supply the answer, but assuming it to be "by faith," he goes on to adduce as illustration the well-known case of Abraham, to whose circumcision the Judaizers had probably referred when they urged the Galatians to submit to that rite. Paul, however, shows that not even Abraham was justified by his circumcision, but by his preexisting faith. He thus confirms their spiritual experiences by an appeal to the Scriptures.

Abraham—an ellipsis is to be supplied, such as "even as was the case with Abraham who . . ."

believed God,—i.e., he accounted that God was able to fulfill His promise, and this he did, not ignoring the natural impossibility, but looking it squarely in the face; see Romans 4:19.

and it—i.e., the fact that he believed God; faith, which, though it is not specifically mentioned here, is mentioned at Romans 4:9, cp. v. 5.

was reckoned unto him—plainly whatever is "reckoned" to belong to a person cannot have been his originally and naturally, cp. Romans 2:26, e.g. Abraham in common with all the descendants of Adam, Romans 5:12, was a sinner, i.e., he was, viewed from the divine standpoint, destitute of personal righteousness. Hence if his relationship with God was to be rectified, and this is what is meant by justification in such a case, it must be accomplished otherwise than by his own meritorious deeds.

for—*eis* = "unto," as in Romans 10:10, "believeth unto righteousness," e.g.; hence "for" here cannot be understood as = "as" or "instead of." The act of believing is not viewed as a meritorious act taking the place of righteousness; for the apostle has already shown, 2:15:17, and he shows more fully in Romans 3, that men, whether Jews or Gentiles, are incapable of any act or work on account of which God can accept them. Not even Abraham, by whom the foundation of the Jewish faith was laid, so to speak, nor David, who gave it such expression in his Psalms, were exceptions to this absolute and universal rule; see Romans 4:1–8.

righteousness.—*dikaiosunē,* as at 2:21, i.e., by his implicit acceptance of the assurance of God that he should have a numerous posterity, Abraham was justified; he entered upon a new relationship with God. Adam hearkened to Eve, and determined to live his own life in his own wisdom and strength. This was the Fall of Man. Abraham, hearkening to God, determined to live by His promise, took God's word against all human experience, and shaped his course by it. But the man who trusts God has really put himself in the right attitude toward God; hence God can accept him, justify him.

The words are quoted from the LXX of Genesis 15:6, which differs slightly from the Hebrew, as comparison with the English version of the passage in Genesis shows; the latter is of course made from the Hebrew. It is noteworthy that the words translated, "believe," "reckon," "righteousness," appear in this passage for the first time in the Bible.

Genesis 15:6 is quoted again in Romans 4:3, in support of the same contention, namely, that God accepts men not on the ground of works, but of faith, a doctrine which is there more fully elaborated. James also quotes it, 2:23, in a connection in which he seems to argue in favor of the principle condemned and dismissed by the apostle Paul. But the contradiction is only seeming, and disappears when the passages are carefully compared. Paul has in mind the attitude of Abraham toward God, his acceptance of God's word, a purely subjective mental act, in itself quite incapable of verification by man, and such as, in the nature of the case, could be known only to God. He is concerned only with the effect of this attitude of mind upon the relations between God and Abraham, not with its effect upon Abraham's character, nor with its influence upon his subsequent actions. He knows but one kind of faith, and that is real; the contrast he draws is always that between faith and the lack of it, unbelief, Romans 11:20.

With James it is different. There is, he declares, faith and faith—faith that is real, and faith that is false, barren faith, which is not faith at all. And the difference appears in this, that true faith is attested by appropriate works done in obedience to the Word of God, as in the case of Abraham, who was "justified by works." So saying, James does not contradict the apostle of the Gentiles. Each writer is thinking of a different epoch in Abraham's life; Paul of the event recorded in Genesis 15, James of that recorded in Genesis 22, which occurred some forty years later. In Abraham's obedience to God in the matter of Isaac the Word of God recorded in Genesis 15:6 was "fulfilled," or confirmed; his response to the command of God attested the reality of the faith professed so many years before. In 15:6, moreover, the word is "believed," in 22:18 "obeyed" is used.

Moreover, the two writers do not use the words "faith" and "works" in quite the same sense. Faith with Paul is acceptance of God's Word, resulting in trusting oneself to God. With James faith is the acceptance as true of certain statements about God (v. 19), and this may not affect one's conduct at all. The former faith Paul declares to result in acceptance with God, i.e., justification; concerning the latter James significantly asks, "Can that faith save him?" (v. 14). Works with Paul are ritual observances and external obedience to the precepts of the moral law. With James the ceremonial idea is excluded, the moral law only is in his mind, together with obedience to any specific command of God to an individual, as in the cases of Abraham and Rahab. The works of which Paul speaks could be performed quite independently of faith; the works to which James refers are possible only where faith is real, and where faith is real such works will certainly be present to attest that reality.

And so with righteousness, or justification; Paul thinks of a rectified relationship with God, James of right conduct. In Paul's sense the sinner, the ungodly, can be justified, accounted righteous; in James' sense the right doer only is justified, as in Romans 2:13. Paul indeed uses the word "righteousness" on occasion in James' meaning, but neither James, nor apparently any other of the Biblical writers (but see Heb. 11:7) ever uses it in Paul's meaning. With Paul, to repeat, it describes a right relationship with God, which, however, always results in right conduct; with the others it describes right conduct alone, which, however, is always the result of a right relationship with God, cp., e.g., 1 John 3:7. See further at 5:5, below.

3:7 Know—ginōskō, as in 2:9, where see note. The translations of the text = "know ye," a command or exhortation, and of the margin, "ye perceive," a statement, are equally possible grammatically. In the latter case the meaning would be, "you are aware that these words are on record concerning Abraham's faith, and now you perceive what is implied in them." But, on the whole, it is probable that the text represents the writer's meaning. The Judaizers were of those who "compass sea and land to make one proselyte," Matthew 23:15. They had been persuading the Galatians that only by circumcision could they become "sons of Abraham"; but now the apostle shows that because of his faith, not because he had been circumcised, Abraham was accepted by God, entered into covenant relation with Him and received all his privileges and blessings, and this he impresses upon them by the imperative "know ye."

therefore—what he is about to say is plainly implied in the fact that Abraham was justified by faith.

that they which be of [*ek* = out of] **faith,**—i.e., those, be they Jews or Gentiles, who seek justification not by works but by faith, those whose spiritual life is derived from, and whose spiritual character is formed by, faith. Such, of course, acknowledge that they are without resources in themselves, and that they depend solely upon God. To them faith is not a merit by which they might be commended to God, it is the expression of realized need, and of submission to, and dependence upon, God for its supply. Cp. "him that is of faith in Jesus," Romans 3:26, and ct., concerning the Jews, "they which are of the law," 4:14, and concerning Gentiles, "they that are of faction" (so lit.), 2:8.

the same—lit., "these," i.e., these and no others; neither natural descent nor adhesion to the law could make a man sharer in the character, privileges, and dignity of Abraham; the position of the word in the sentence makes it emphatic as in Romans 8:14.

are sons of Abraham.—*huios,* as in 2:20, where see note.

The principle thus defined and stated by the apostle was latent in the actions and in the words of the Lord Jesus. Zacchaeus, Luke 19, was, apparently, a Jew by birth, but his course of life had been such as to alienate him from his country-men, v. 7, as his own words acknowledge, v. 8, and as indeed the comment of the Lord Jesus on the incident implies, v. 10. The Savior came to him "forasmuch as he also was a son of Abraham," v. 9; which obviously does not mean because of his natural descent, for in that all the Jews shared, nor because of his adhesion to the law of Moses, for at best he was "a Jew outwardly," Romans 2:28, 29, but because he tacitly acknowledged the claim of the Lord Jesus to regulate his life, i.e., because of his faith in Him as the One sent by God. Cp. also John 8:39, where, however, *teknon* = child, a more general term, is used.

The words of the Lord recorded in John 6:29 are also to the point here; the only "work" that God recognizes is a right attitude of heart toward His Son, and whatever proceeds therefrom; see comment on *1 Thessalonians* 1:3.

3:8 And—perhaps better "moreover," for what follows does not merely explain what goes before, it strengthens the argument by adding something to it.

the Scripture,—*graphē,* lit., "writing," "document"; in New Testament used of Old Testament, sometimes in a general sense of the whole collection, when the plural form is used, "the Scriptures," Matthew 21:42, e.g.; sometimes of a particular passage, when the singular is used, "the Scripture," here, and James 4:5, "this Scripture," Mark 12:10, "another Scripture," John 19:37, "in Scripture," or "in a Scripture," 1 Peter 2:6, text and marg., e.g. The full title, "the Holy Scriptures," is found only in Romans 1:2. In 2 Peter 3:16 the words "the other Scriptures" imply that Paul's epistles were counted in the same category as the Old Testament.

The second of the two quotations in 1 Timothy 5:18 occurs only in Luke 10:7; since the apostle thus includes a word from Deuteronomy with a word from Luke's Gospel, it seems a fair deduction that he intended to include the latter with the former in the common designation "Scripture." In 2 Timothy 3:16 the inspiration of God is said to be the characteristic of every document that had already been admitted as canonical by the Jews, i.e., the Old Testament, and of every document, in addition thereto, that was to be accepted as authoritative by Christians, i.e., what in due course came to be the New Testament. The facts of the gospel as preached by Paul and his colleagues in Galatia, Acts 16:1 ff, is the subject of v. 14; the Old Testament is the subject of v. 15; the completed canon of scripture, the Old Testament, together with the writings of the apostolic age, which in course of time came to be known as the New Testament, is the subject of v. 16. It is implied in v. 17 that with these the man of God would be in possession of the complete revelation of the mind of God for him, and fully provided against every spiritual need.

The New Testament writers, like the Jews generally, John 7:42, not infrequently personify the Scriptures (personification is a figure of speech in which inanimate things are credited with the qualities and powers of sentient beings), representing them as saying the things recorded in them; see John 19:37; Romans 4:3; James 4:5, e.g., and cp. Romans 9:17, where the message sent by God to Pharaoh through Moses, and recorded by him in Exodus 9:16, is quoted as what "the Scripture saith unto Pharaoh." In the present passage Scripture is credited with more pronouncedly sentient qualities, "foreseeing," and with active powers, "preached." Cp. also v. 22, below, "The Scripture hath shut up all things under sin." "In such cases *hē graphē* stands obviously for the Author of the Scriptures—God, by whose inspiration they were written" (Ellicott). That this is the case is plain from the obvious fact that the book of Genesis, in which "the Scripture" referred to is found, was written by Moses more than four centuries after the words were spoken. Cp. Matthew 11:13, "the law prophesied," and see further at v. 10, below.

Another word, *gramma,* lit., "a letter," i.e., of the alphabet, is by the Lord Jesus used of the Pentateuch, John 5:47, and by the apostle Paul of the complete Old Testament, 2 Timothy 3:15, "the sacred writings" (where "sacred" is *hieros,* which occurs again in New Testament in 1 Corinthians 9:13, and in LXX in Joshua 6:8, where, however, it does not appear in the Hebrew text nor in the English version||).

foreseeing—*proeideō,* used in Acts 2:31 of David's prophetic vision of Christ recorded in Psalm 16. "What does the Scripture see?" seems to have been a common formula among the rabbis.||

that God would justify—lit., "that God justifies"; the present tense is used because this is the sole ground upon which God accepts any person at any time, and hence when He came to deal with the Gentiles for their salvation He would take no other. Alternatively the words may be paraphrased thus: "Moreover, the Scripture, foreseeing what is now taking place, namely, that God is justifying the Gentiles."

the Gentiles by faith,—see at 2:16. From Scripture the apostle has shown that Abraham had been justified by faith, and if Abraham, their "forefather according to the flesh," then surely the Jews likewise. But what of the Gentiles? He quotes Scripture again to show that the Gentiles are to be accepted in the same way, cp. Romans 3:30, "He shall justify the circumcision by, *ek*, lit., "out of," faith, and the uncircumcision through, *dia*, lit., "by means of, [the] faith." The change in the prepositions is made to suit the different relation in which Jew and Gentile stood with God. The Jew had the divine law; if he could not be justified on the ground of his obedience to that, on what ground could he be justified? On the ground of faith; by a personal appropriation of the promises of God. The Gentiles, on the other hand, had no point of contact with God save in conscience and in nature, and these had long ceased to speak to them of God. By what means, then, could the Gentiles be justified? By means of faith, for in due time the gospel would be preached to them also.

preached the gospel beforehand—*proeuangelizomai,* one word only, i.e., the words that follow, spoken to Abraham by God, anticipated the gospel, which is now preached as an accomplished fact, cp. Romans 1:2.||

unto Abraham, *saying,* In thee—in Abraham the family and nation were founded from which the promised Deliverer came; in Abraham also began a line of spiritual men whose characteristic is faith in God, and who are drawn from "every tribe, and tongue, and people, and nation." These latter, and not those who merely trace to him their descent "after the flesh," are the true "sons of Abraham."

shall all the nations—i.e., Gentiles as well as Jews, cp. Matthew 8:11; John 12:20 and 32. The quotation is from Genesis 12:3, cp. 18:18; where the former has "families" the latter has "nations"; the meaning is unchanged.

be blessed.—*eneulogeō,* as in Acts 3:25. The blessing is salvation.||
When this declaration of the purpose of God to bless mankind was first made in the form of a promise to Abraham the human race had but recently begun to be divided into separate groups, tribal and national, and the nation Israel had as yet no existence. The developments among men described in Genesis 11:1–9 were part of the purpose of God, see Deuteronomy 32:8; along these lines He had designed that the world should be prepared for the coming of His Son, and for its own salvation. To Abraham God imparted a knowledge of His purpose, and, indeed, of the Agent in its accomplishment, John 8:56. When, at length, the nation Israel was brought into being, it became possible for Him to reveal His mind to them with increasing definiteness. To Israel were the promises given, and to them were committed "the oracles of God," in which the promises were enshrined, Romans 3:2. But that "all nations," and not Israel only, were in the mind of God for salvation is plain from each section of the Scriptures, the Law, the Prophets, and the Psalms, as Paul shows in the epistle to the Romans; see 9:25–27; 10:18–21; 15:9–12.

3:9 So then they which be of (*ek* = out of) **faith are blessed**—*eulogeō,* the simple form of the word used immediately before, and with the same meaning. Comparison of v. 7 with v. 9 shows that by the "sons of Abraham" is meant those who qualify for receiving the blessing of Abraham in the same manner as Abraham. Not all Gentiles are to be saved, but only such Gentiles as put their trust in God.

with—i.e., in fellowship with; sharing his faith in God they share also what his faith received from God.

the faithful Abraham.—not with Abraham because he was circumcised, but with Abraham because he believed God.

Just as the blessing is not withheld from the Jews because they are Jews, so it is not extended to the Gentiles because they are Gentiles; it is for those who, whether Jews or Gentiles, like Abraham, believe God.

The article makes the word that follows emphatic, and signalizes faith as the essential feature in Abraham's character, his exercise of faith in the bare Word of God as the vital fact in his history.

Pistos ordinarily conveys the idea of faithful in the sense of trustworthy, as in 1 Thessalonians 5:24 (where see note); but it is also = "believing," as in Acts 16:1; 2 Corinthians 6:15, e.g. Here it is best understood in the latter sense. The note on "the faith" at 1:23, above, may be consulted.

3:10 For—so far the argument has been that justification is by faith, always and only. Now the apostle turns to show that it is not merely vain to seek justification by works; to do so, and to fail to comply with every demand of the law, is to incur the penalty prescribed for any breach of it.

as many as are of (*ek* = out of) **the works of the law**—i.e., those, whether Jews or Gentiles, who depend in whole or in part upon obedience to the Law for justification. The assumption that complete obedience to the law lies beyond the power of man underlies the whole of this argument. This is not an assumption likely to be disputed, cp. James 2:10, 11.

are under a curse:—*katara* = a malediction, whether pronounced by man out of his malevolence and hatred, as in James 3:10, cp. 2 Peter 2:14, or by God in His righteous judgment, as here and v. 13, cp. Hebrews 6:8.||

The corresponding verb, *kataraomai,* is used in the same way, of the imprecations of men, in Luke 6:28; Romans 12:14; James 3:9. The fig tree that disappointed its Creator in failing to fulfill the end of its existence, and was condemned therefore by the Lord Jesus to perpetual barrenness, was said by Peter to have been "cursed" by Him, Mark 11:21. Men who because of their alienation from God fail to fulfill the end of their being, and so disappoint their Creator, are finally to be pronounced "cursed," i.e., they are to be rejected from the eternal kingdom and to be judged worthy of, and sent into, the eternal fire, Matthew 25:41. The blessing and the curse are set in contrast in Deuteronomy 30:19, as they are in Matthew 25:34, 41. The former includes the ideas of nearness to God and consequent fruitfulness, or usefulness; in the latter the dominant ideas are rejection by God, cp. Hebrews 6:8, distance from Him, cp. Matthew 25:41, and consequent barrenness and uselessness, cp. Mark 11:21.||

for it is written,—(the perfect tense, signifying the abiding effect of what was written) a form of words frequently used by the apostle, as by the Lord Jesus, to introduce a quotation from the Old Testament It is the recognition of the authority of the Scriptures. In His disputes, whether with Satan, Matthew 4:4, 7, 10, or with men, 22:31, 43, e.g., the Lord Jesus appealed to these Scriptures, and while there was no submission to them in any case recorded, on the other hand the fact of their authority was not questioned, it was at least tacitly acknowledged. The passage here quoted is Deuteronomy 27:26, though neither the Hebrew, which has "cursed is he that confirmeth not the words of this law to do them," nor the LXX, which has "cursed is every man that continueth not in all the words of this law to do them," is followed exactly.

Cursed—*epikataratos,* a strengthened form of the word as it ordinarily appears; see note above, cp. v. 13 and John 7:49.||

is every one which continueth not—*emmenō,* a strengthened form of the word ordinarily translated "abide"; used of Paul's residence through two years in Rome, Acts 28:30, and of continuing in the faith of the gospel, 14:22, and of continuing in the law or covenant, here and in Hebrews 8:9.||

in all things that are written in the book of the law,—these words do not occur in either the Heb. or LXX of Deuteronomy 27:26; see, however, 31:26, where they do occur, as also in Joshua 1:8, et al. They are probably added here to emphasize the wide scope of the demand of the law; not only must its ordinances be carried out to the letter and its moral precepts be punctiliously observed, "the law" must be understood in the most comprehensive sense of which the word is capable.

"The book of the law" in the strict sense would refer to the Pentateuch alone, for the law is the law of Moses, and in this passage the narrower sense is apparently intended. In some other passages, however, "the law" is used in a wider way to include other parts of the Old Testament. Thus it is used of the Psalms in John 10:34; 15:25; of the Psalms, Isaiah, Ezekiel, and Daniel in John 12:34; of the Psalms and Isaiah in Romans 3:10–18; of Isaiah in 1 Corinthians 14:21. It seems from these instances that "the law" was an alternative title to "The Scriptures" for the whole book.

to do them.—the apostle was well aware that the Galatians had not seen what is involved in submission to the Law of Moses; they had not realized that failure to do all, always and everywhere, just as it is written, involves the professed lawkeeper in eternal disaster. Law is unbending, it yields nothing to weakness, its standard is never lowered, not even by a hairbreadth; law makes no compromise, and finds no room for mercy; "a man that hath set at nought Moses' law dieth without compassion," Hebrews 10:28.

3:11 Now—or, "but further," "then again," introducing a new argument based upon another Scripture. If what had been said seemed to leave any loophole for escape from the conclusion of v. 10, what is now added makes plain that even should a man, in his own estimation or that of his fellows, "continue in all things to do them," he would not on that account escape the curse or receive the blessing.

that no man—lit., "no one," cp. "a man is not," and "all flesh is not," in 2:16; the expressions are varied, perhaps, to emphasize the impossibility of justification on the ground of relation to law.

is justified by the law—*en*, which may be understood as = "by means of," or as = "under," see Romans 2:12; 3:19, where it is so rendered. The effect is the same whichever way the words are taken, cp. "by the works of the law," 2:16.

in the sight of God,—lit., "before," i.e., as God judges, cp. 1 Corinthians 3:19; Ephesians 6:9; 2 Thessalonians 1:6. There is a contrast implied between the possibly favorable verdict of man and the certainly adverse judgment of God. What a man thinks of himself or of others in such matters is of no moment; it is the judgment of God that counts.

is evident:—*dēlos*, as in 1 Corinthians 15:27, and Matthew 26:73, "bewray-eth," lit., "makes evident."||

for,—i.e., "for it is written" as in v. 10.

The righteous—*dikaios,* i.e., the well-behaved person who, judged by ordinary human standards, does right; see, e.g., Matthew 1:19 and Mark 2:17. The superlative degree of such excellence of character is described in the phrase "righteous before God," Luke 1:6.

The apostle Paul uses the word "righteous" of men only here, in 1 Timothy 1:9, and in Romans. In the latter Epistle 1:17 is the same as the present passage, 2:13 refers to lawkeeping, 5:7 to right conduct generally, 3:10 condemns men, when judged by the Divine standard, denying righteousness to them absolutely and universally.

In Romans 5:19 the expression "made righteous" occurs, and it occurs there only in Scripture. The meaning of "righteous" in this case is fixed by the context. By one act of disobedience on the part of Adam, all who should thereafter be born of him were constituted, or put into the place and condition of, sinners, and this, of course, apart from any acts of their own. So also, by His one act of obedience in His death, Christ put all who should thereafter believe on Him into the place and condition of righteous persons, constituted them righteous. Thus the words "made righteous" do not refer to conduct or to character, but to relationship with God, and into that relationship men are brought only by faith in Christ. Cp. note at v. 6, above.

shall live—*zaō,* as in 2:19, above, see comment on *2 Thessalonians* 5:2. Spiritual life, life in communion with God, is meant.

by, *ek* = out of, **faith;**—see at 2:16, above.

The words may be understood in one of two ways, either as, "he who is righteous by faith [not he who is righteous by works] shall live," or as, "he who is righteous [i.e., well-behaved] shall live by faith [i.e., not by his well-doing]." The latter seems to accord best with the context, and to provide the more direct contrast with the words quoted in the following verse. Thus the meaning will be, the righteous man, the well-behaved person, the lawkeeper, the doer of good, does not live before God because of his conduct, but because he puts his trust in Him. Hence it is not merely that the man ignorant of the law, the Gentile, or the lawbreaker, the wicked Jew, may be justified by faith. The argument of the apostle goes much further than that; it is that even the righteous Jew can have life in no other way.

The quotation is from Habakkuk 2:4, which should be read as in margin, "Behold, his soul is puffed up, it is not upright in him, but the just [or righteous, the words are equivalent] shall live in his faithfulness." In their original setting the words do not seem to bear the meaning attached to them by the apostle. The prophet is drawing a contrast between the waverer and the steadfast person; the one shall perish in the troubles of the times, the other shall be preserved. But the apostle reads the Scriptures by a new light since he knew Christ and was taught by the Spirit. He goes below the surface meaning; faith lies at the root of faithfulness (cp. note on "faith in Jesus Christ" at 2:16). A man is faithful to God just because he has faith in God. And if faith in God preserves a man in temporal danger, faith in God will surely preserve him from spiritual disaster also. And for this reason, faith establishes a vital union between the soul that exercises it and the God in Whom it is exercised.

The quotation appears again in Romans 1:17 and Hebrews 10:38. In the former the apostle uses it to justify his association of the two ideas "righteousness" and "faith" by showing that they are found together in the Holy Scriptures. The latter follows the LXX, but reverses its clauses, while the LXX itself differs considerably from the Heb., as may be seen by comparing the quotation with the English translation of the text in Habakkuk.

3:12 and—*de,* better rendered "but" to mark the contrast; the passage may be paraphrased "the righteous shall live by faith, but that is entirely different from living by the law."

the law is not of [*ek* = out of] **faith;**—i.e., law and faith differ essentially; they are antagonistic one to the other, they have no point in common, they are mutually exclusive in principle, they cannot cooperate to the same end.

but,—*alla* = "on the contrary." Here again "it is written" is to be supplied.

He that doeth them—lit., "he that hath done them"; the standpoint is that of the Judgment at which the life as a whole is reviewed. The Heb. of the original of the citation is "he that shall do," i.e., "he that shall have been found to do them." Clearly, then, the doing is to be lifelong, unintermittent, and is never to fall by so much as a hairbreadth below the Divine standard. "Doeth" is the emphatic word in the sentence.

shall live in them.—i.e., the "statutes and judgments of God"; quoted from Leviticus 18:5, cp. Ezekiel 20:11,and see Romans 10:5 where the same passage is quoted in a somewhat different form.

The conclusion to be drawn from these Scriptures though it is not expressed is sufficiently evident. If a godly Jew were to keep the law so as to satisfy the requirements of God, such a one would in his doing find life. There are none such. Abraham at the beginning found justification not in his obedience, but in his faith. Habakkuk, centuries later, declared that the just (i.e., before men) lives (i.e., before God) by faith. The evidence, then, is varied and conclusive, that not by works of law but by faith in God the double blessing, justification and life, is received. And since the gospel came faith in God is faith in the Lord Jesus Christ, see 2:16, above.

The alternation of the words "justification" and "live" in this section shows that the effect of faith is justification and regeneration simultaneously. Hence all who are justified are also born anew, all who have been born anew are also justified. Cp. "justification of life," Romans 5:18.

3:13 Christ redeemed—*exagorazō* = "to purchase," but especially to purchase a slave with a view to his freedom. Here and at 4:5 it is used of the deliverance of Christian Jews from the law and its curse.

Exagorazō has also the meaning "to buy up," as in Ephesians 5:16; Colossians 4:5, "buying up the opportunity," see marg. and cp. Daniel 2:8.||

The simple form, *agorazō* = "to purchase," directs the mind to the fact that a price has been paid; see Matthew 13:44; 1 Corinthians 7:30, e.g. In 1 Corinthians 6:20; 7:23; 2 Peter 2:1; Revelation 5:9; 14:3, 4, it refers to the death of Christ as the price paid by God, or Christ, for the possession of men, whether Jews or Gentiles. This figure is not fully developed anywhere in Scripture; it is not said to whom the price was paid; all the suggestions that have been made to supply this lack are speculative and vain.

A synonym of these words, *lutroō*, = "to deliver," is also translated "redeem" in New Testament. In Luke 24:21 it means to set Israel free from the Roman yoke; in Titus 2:14 it means to set men free from the yoke of self-will, and in 1 Peter 1:18 from a vain manner of life, i.e., from bondage to tradition.||

The corresponding noun, *lutrōsis,* occurs in Luke 1:68, 2:38, where national deliverance is meant, as in Luke 24:21; and in Hebrews 9:12 where deliverance from the guilt and power of sin is meant.||

A strengthened form of *lutrōsis, apolutrōsis,* also occurs of:

a, deliverance from physical torture, Hebrews 11:35;

b, the deliverance of the people of God at the coming of the Son of Man, Luke 21:28.

c, forgiveness, i.e., deliverance from the guilt of sins, Romans 3:24; Ephesians 1:7; Colossians 1:14; Hebrews 9:15;

d, the deliverance of the believer from the power of sin, and of his body from bondage to curruption, at the coming of the Lord Jesus, Romans 8:23; 1 Corinthians 1:30; Ephesians 1:14; 4:30.||

Another noun, formed from the same verb, should be added here for the sake of completeness, *lutron,* found in Matthew 20:28; Mark 10:45, of the life of the Lord Jesus as the ransom price to be paid for the deliverance of men.||

Cp. 1 Timothy 2:6 where *antilutron,* = an equivalent, or adequate, ransom price, occurs.||

us—i.e., the Jewish believers; as occasionally in his writings the apostle here associates himself with his nationals, cp. Ephesians 1:11, 12 with 13, e.g. The Gentiles were not under the law; indeed the law was itself the "middle wall" that divided them from the Jews; see Ephesians 2:14, 15.

from the curse of the law, having become a curse—i.e., by becoming; the words describe the means taken for the accomplishment of the redemption. The curse attaches to all under the law, inasmuch as all have failed to meet its requirements, with one exception, Christ, Who was "born under the law," 4:4, below, but Who did not Himself incur the curse, because He was "the Righteous One," Acts 3:14, not in the sight of men, indeed, for they crucified Him as a blasphemer, but in the sight of God Who raised Him from the dead. So being Himself free from the curse, He passed under it voluntarily, that those under it by inheritance and desert might escape.

By the death of Christ the unbending rigor of the law is confirmed and illustrated. The law of God makes no exceptions, but demands always the full penalty from all who come within its jurisdiction. In view of that awful exhibition of its terrors, how could the Galatians suppose that their efforts to keep it would result other than disastrously for themselves?

The Son of God did not "become a curse for us" in His Incarnation. From before His birth He was called "holy"; He "advanced in . . . favor with God," Luke 1:35; 2:52; and at the close of thirty years of life in the flesh God spoke of Him from heaven in the words, "This is My beloved Son, in Whom I am well pleased," and later repeated the testimony, Matthew 3:17; 17:5. There is no statement made in Scripture that He became the sin-bearer in His baptism, or in Gethsemane, or at any juncture in His life previous to the Crucifixion. With the Cross alone, then, must these words of the apostle be associated, and this the quotation of Deuteronomy 21:23 confirms.

The language of 2 Corinthians 5:21, "made to be sin," should be compared with this, "became a curse." In each case the reality of the association of the

Lord Jesus with the sins of His people, and the completeness of the satisfaction He offered to the law in His death upon the Cross, is vividly set forth.

There is another aspect of the Cross that stands in marked contrast to that which the apostle here presents. In Ephesians 5:2 Christ in His death is said to have given Himself "an offering and a sacrifice to God for an odor of a sweet smell," and in Hebrews 9:14 it is written "through the Eternal Spirit [He] offered Himself without blemish unto God."

for us:—*huper,* = "on behalf of," as at 1:4; 2:20. For this and the other prepositions used in New Testament to describe the relation of the death of Christ to sin and sinners; see comment on *1 Thessalonians* 5:10.

for it is written, Cursed is every one that hangeth on a tree:—from LXX of Deuteronomy 21:23, where, however, both Heb. and Greek have "accursed of God." Of course the curse throughout this section is "of God," but the apostle, with the delicacy that becomes the Christian, refrains from emphasizing that fact when he speaks of the Son of God as Himself the bearer of the curse.

Since crucifixion was a Roman, not a Jewish, method of execution, the hanging to which the law of Moses refers was apparently the exposure of the body of a person already executed by another method, such as stoning, cp. Deuteronomy 21:21, 22.

Crucifixion was equally abhorrent to the Roman and to the Jew; thus Cicero, "the very name should be excluded . . . from the thought, eyes, and ears of a Roman citizen . . . It is a crime to bind a Roman citizen . . . But what shall I say about lifting him on a cross? No word can adequately describe such a nefarious thing."

It is this solemn fact that the Holy and Righteous Son of God was exposed on a gibbet that constitutes "the stumblingblock of the Cross," 5:11. Human nature whether religious, as in the case of the Jew, or philosophic, as in the case of the Gentiles, recoils from the thought of seeking salvation through a crucified Messiah, 1 Corinthians 1:23, cp. 1 Peter 2:8. Apart from the illumination of the Holy Spirit, John 16:8, 9, "the word of the Cross" must remain foolishness to men, 1 Corinthians 1:18.

Xulon, "tree," is used once only of living wood in the New Testament, Luke 23:31; cp. the figurative expression "tree of life." It is rendered "staff," i.e., a bludgeon, in Matthew 26:47, "stocks" in Acts 16:24, and "wood" in 1 Corinthians 3:12. The Heb. word which it represents here is rendered "tree" in Genesis 2:9, "timber" in Ezekiel 26:12, and "gallows" in Esther 5:14.

3:14 that—i.e., "in order that."

upon—*eis,* better "unto"; the sequence is "Christ became a curse on behalf of the Jews, in order that the blessing of God might extend to the Gentiles."

the Gentiles might come the blessing of Abraham—i.e., salvation, whether viewed as justification or as life.

Since the Jews were shut out from blessing by the very law in which they gloried, Gentiles could not hope to obtain it by putting themselves under that law. But if to the Jews the blessing was secured by the death of Christ, and in response to faith, then on the same ground, and on the same condition, the blessing would extend to the Gentiles also.

Eulogia, blessing, = that favorable attitude of mind, whether in God or in man, which expresses itself in kind words and kind acts. In the New Testament it is used of:

a, "fair speech," as in Romans 16:18 (this is the literal meaning of the word, and this is the only passage in which it is used in a bad sense);

b, the favor of God shown to the earth in making it fruitful, Hebrews 6:7

c, the sum of the favor shown by God to men in Christ, Romans 15:29; 1 Corinthians 10:16; Ephesians 1:3; 1 Peter 3:9b, and here;

d, the acknowledgment of the favor of God, i.e., thanksgiving, James 3:10; Revelation 5:12, 13; 7:12 (that "to bless" = "to give thanks," cp. Matt. 26:26 with Luke 22:19, and see 1 Cor. 14:16);

e, kindness shown to others whether in word or deed, specifically of a freely offered gift in relief of another's need, 2 Corinthians 9:5, 6;

f, a birthright, Hebrews 12:17.||

in Christ Jesus;—An entirely new dispensation, or manner of dealing with men on the part of God, was ushered in by the redemption accomplished at the Cross; henceforth the blessing of Abraham was available to Jews solely through faith in Christ, and it was equally available to Gentiles on the same terms.

The order of the name and title corresponds with the context, connoting that He came down in order to accomplish this redemption, and to secure to men this blessing. See notes at 1:12; 2:4.

that—"in order that," introducing another result of the redemptive work of Christ.

we—as the pronoun is not separately expressed in orig., and hence is quite unemphatic, "we" can hardly = "we Jews." Moreover, the apostle now reverts to v. 2, where he speaks of the Galatians as receiving the Spirit; hence "we" must here be understood as = "we who believe, whether Jew or Gentile."

might receive—i.e., might receive the fulfillment of the promise formerly made, cp. Acts 1:4. The disciples were to "wait for [the fulfillment of] the promise of the Father," the promise the Father had given through the Son, both before His death, John 14:26, and after His resurrection, Luke 24:49.

the promise—*epangelia* = an undertaking to do, or give, something; in the New Testament, with the exception of Acts 23:21, it is used only of the promises of God, and describes "a gift graciously bestowed, not a pledge obtained by negotiation" (Lightfoot).

of the Spirit through faith.—i.e., "the promised Spirit," v. 2; cp. "the promise of My Father," i.e., the Holy Spirit, Luke 24:49, and "the Holy Spirit of promise," Ephesians 1:13. For a similar idiom see Hebrews 9:15, "the promise of the eternal inheritance," i.e., "the promised eternal inheritance."

There is no Old Testament record of any promise to Abraham of the gift of the Spirit, nor do the words of the apostle necessarily imply that there was. In the message to Abraham the comprehensive word "blessing" is used; later revelation of the purposes of God specified the gift of the Holy Spirit as included in this, cp. Isaiah 32:15; Ezekiel 36:27; Joel 2:28, e.g. Two things are to be kept in mind in connection with these prophetic utterances: *a,* read in the light of the New Testament it is plain that the personal Holy Spirit was intended, and not merely a holy influence from God; *b,* that while these prophecies still await their fulfillment, yet He Who is promised in them to renewed Israel has been given to the Christian in accordance with the words of the Lord Jesus; see John 14—16, e.g. See further at 4:6, below.

3:15 Brethren,—the tension under which the apostle has been writing now relaxes, and persuasion replaces argument, but the earnest reasoning and the tender appeal have the same source, loyalty to the Lord and His truth, love to the Lord and His people.

I speak after the manner of men:—lit., "according to [a] man." The phrase is found in the New Testament only in Paul's writings and occurs, as under, of:

    a, the practices of fallen humanity, 1 Corinthians 3:3;

    b, anything of human origin, Galatians 1:11;

    c, the laws that govern the administration of justice among men, Romans 3:5;

    d, the standard generally accepted among men, here;

    e, an illustration not drawn from Scripture, 1 Corinthians 9:8;

    f, probably = "to use a figurative expression," i.e., to speak of the evil men with whom he had contended at Ephesus as "beasts" (cp. 1 Cor. 4:6 and *e,* above), 1 Corinthians 15:32.

Lightfoot prefers "from worldly motives"; but the other *(d)* interpretation seems to make better sense.‖

See also Romans 6:19, where, however, the Greek is slightly different, *anthrōpinos,* = "pertaining to mankind"; the meaning is as *e, f,* above.

Though it be but a man's covenant, yet when it hath been confirmed, no one maketh it void, or addeth thereto.—cp. Hebrews 6:16; and if this is the case in human affairs, how much more will a covenant made by God prove inviolable?

The Lord Jesus Himself taught His disciples to reason thus from the ways of men to the ways of God; see Matthew 7:7-12; Luke 15; 18:1-8, e.g.

"Confirmed," *kuroō,* see 2 Corinthians 2:8.‖ LXX has the same word in Genesis 23:20.

"Make void," *atheteō,* as in 2:21.

"Addeth," *epidiatasso,* = "appointed" or "commanded beside."‖

The Judaizers, by adding conditions to the covenant which it did not contain, violated this fundamental principle of honorable dealing; and not only so, for, since they claimed Divine authority for these conditions, they were actually crediting God with a breach of faith which even men would condemn in their ordinary dealings one with another. God gave the law, indeed, but neither in place of the promise nor in addition to it; His object in giving it is explained in v. 19.

3:16 Now—*de,* "but"; the apostle does not further pursue the suggestion of the closing words of the preceding verse. Imputation of unfaithfulness to God is only one of many vicious things latent in the doctrine of salvation by works.

to Abraham were the promises spoken,—"promises" because the one promise was repeated in a variety of forms, see Genesis 12:1-3; 13:14-17; 15:18; 17:1-14; 22:15-18, and because it contained the germ of all subsequent promises, cp. Romans 9:4. The statement that the promise was made to Abraham is repeated from v. 8, though in a different form. The repetition is made in order to emphasize the superior antiquity of the promise when compared with the law, and in order to introduce the following words, which contain the idea now to be developed.

and to his seed.—*sperma,* which is used in the New Testament of:
   a, that which, having life in itself, under suitable conditions reproduces that from which it came, as of crops, Matthew 13:24;
   b, and, for the same reason, of children, Matthew 22:24, and descendants however remote, John 7:42; 8:33;
   c, figuratively, such as are born of God, and so enter His Kingdom (John 3:3-5), and manifest its characteristics, Matthew 13:38;
   d, the Divine nature implanted in the believer in the new birth, in virtue of which he becomes a child of God, 1 John 3:9;
   e, those who share the spiritual characteristics of Abraham, Galatians 3:29, cp. Romans 9:29;
   f, Christ, here.

He saith not,—cp. v. 8, where "the Scripture . . . preached the gospel beforehand" is used with reference to this promise. Since it was God Who gave the promise, and Who alone could give it, "He" must be understood of God. Cp. Romans 15:9, 10; Ephesians 4:8; 5:14, where "it is written" and "He saith," are alternative ways of referring to Old Testament Scripture. Cp. also 1 Corinthians 6:16; Hebrews 8:5.

And to seeds, as of many; but as of one, And to thy seed, which is Christ.—the quotation is, word for word, from LXX of Genesis 13:15; 17:7, 8. The word "seed" is a collective noun, and though singular in form is ordinarily (but not always, it is used of an individual in Gen. 4:25, e.g.) used for a number of persons viewed collectively. Thus Paul himself uses it of "many nations," Romans 4:18; 9:7, as well as of Israel, 9:8, and of Christians, v. 29, below. Moreover, the plural form "seeds" is not anywhere used in Scripture of human progeny; indeed the only place of its occurrence is 1 Samuel 8:15, where it = "crops."

The apostle's emphasis on the fact that the word "seed" was used to Abraham, not "seeds," and his deduction that an individual was intended, not a nation, presents a difficulty. Now a difficulty in Scripture is a call to more careful consideration of the passages concerned.

It is not plain, e.g., even to the careful reader, that Exodus 3:6 contains a cogent argument for the present existence and the future resurrection of those who have departed this life. Yet the Lord Jesus found this in the words, and the implication becomes quite evident when they are read in the light of what He had to say about them, Mark 12:26,27; see comment on *1 Thessalonians* 4:13. So also the use of a singular noun in the promise to Abraham held an unexpected significance.

It is true that the use of "seeds" would have been unnatural and meaningless, in Hebrew and Greek as in English, but had it been the intention of God to refer only to the natural descendants of Abraham, another word could have been chosen, one with a plural in ordinary use, such, e.g., as "children." But all such words were passed over in favor of one that could be used only in the singular. Was this accidental? No, the apostle declares, it was designed, the seed intended was Messiah. Indeed, some of the rabbis had recognized this, and understood "seed" in such passages as Genesis 4:25; Isaiah 53:10, to refer to the Coming One.

Abraham was called, and descendants were given to him other than by the way of nature, only that through him Messiah might come. The earth was to be blessed through Abraham's seed, not through his descendants in the mass, but through One among them. And, moreover, that the Messiah Himself was the true Israel is now plain from such passages as Isaiah 49:3 and Hosea 11:1, cp. Matthew 2:15.

Thus, the apostle argues, if Christ is the person to whom the fulfillment of the promises of God is secured, then only such as are "in Christ" can receive them. And this he affirms particularly in v. 29, "If ye are Christ's, then are ye Abraham's seed, heirs according to promise."

This verse is a parenthesis introduced in order to strengthen the argument subsequently developed; for if Christ is the person to whom the promise was to be fulfilled finally, then it becomes more manifest still that the law could not have annulled it. There seems to be an ellipsis after "seed" in the earlier part of the verse, thus: "Now to Abraham were the promises spoken, and to his seed [they are to be fulfilled]," cp. note on "receive," v. 14, above.

3:17 Now this I say;—the same words are rendered "Now this I mean" in 1 Corinthians 1:12, and are to be understood here in the same sense; they introduce the application of the statements of vv. 15, 16, to the matter in hand.

A covenant—etymologically considered the word "covenant" is formed from two others meaning "coming together," and thus describes a mutual undertaking between two or more parties who severally make themselves responsible for the discharge of certain obligations. But the Greek word *diathēkē,* from which it is translated, does not in itself contain the idea of joint obligation, it means rather an obligation undertaken by one alone. Accordingly it is used interchangeably with "promise," see v. 16, above, and v. 18, below. There was no condition attached to the promises or covenant of which the apostle is here speaking; Abraham and his descendants were to observe the ordinance of circumcision as a token that they accepted and remembered the promise of God, indeed, but the fulfillment of that promise was not made to depend on the observance of circumcision, although a penalty was attached to its nonobservance; see Genesis 17:14.

The New Testament uses of the word "covenant" may be analyzed as follows:

a, a promise or undertaking, human or divine, v. 15, above;

b, a promise or undertaking on the part of God, Luke 1:72; Acts 3:25; Romans 9:4; 11:27, here, Ephesians 2:12; Hebrews 7:22; 8:6, 8, 10; 10:16;

c, an agreement, a mutual undertaking, between God and Israel, see Deuteronomy 27—30 (this covenant is also described as a "commandment," 7:18, cp. v. 22), Hebrews 8:9; 9:20;

d, by metonymy, the token of the covenant, or promise, made to Abraham, Acts 7:8;

e, by metonymy, the record of the covenant, see Exodus 25:16; 2 Corinthians 3:14; Hebrews 9:4, cp. Revelation 11:19.

These passages all refer to the dealings of God with Israel; and these covenants are included under the designation "first," Hebrews 9:15, cp. "old," 2 Corinthians 3:14.

f, the basis, established by the death of Christ, on which the salvation of men is secured, Matthew 26:28; Mark 14:24; Luke 22:20; 1 Corinthians 11:25; 2 Corinthians 3:6; Hebrews 10:29, 12:24, 13:20.

This covenant is called the "new," Hebrews 9:15, the "second," 8:7, and the "better," 7:22. Both covenants are intended in 4:24, below.

There remain two passages in which *diathēkē* occurs, and in which the translation is much disputed, Hebrews 9:16, 17. There does not seem to be any sufficient reason for departing in these verses from the word which is used everywhere else.||

The Greek titles of the Scriptures are "Old Covenant" and "New Covenant"; the English word "Testament" is taken from the titles prefixed to the Latin versions.

confirmed beforehand by God,—the promise was originally given as recorded in Genesis 12, and was confirmed by the vision of the furnace and the torch, Genesis 15, by the birth of Isaac, ch. 21, and by the oath of God, ch. 22; cp. Hebrews 6:13-17.

the law, which came four hundred and thirty years after,—Paul is not concerned here with the exact duration of the interval between the intimation to Abraham of God's purpose to bless the world through him, and the giving of the law at Sinai immediately after the Exodus. The Hebrew text of Exodus 12:40 reads as in the English Version; the LXX reads: "And the sojourning of the children of Israel, while they sojourned in the land of Egypt and the land of Chanaan, was four hundred and thirty years." The number of years cannot have been less than four hundred and thirty in either case. That the period was a considerable one is all the argument requires.

doth not disannul,—*akuroō,* as in Matthew 15:6; Mark 7:13, where it is rendered "make void" with reference to the Word of God. It is the word translated "confirmed" in the context, but with a negative prefix attached, and is stronger than that rendered "make void" in v. 15.||

so as to—lit., "with a view to," i.e., the intention of God in giving the law was not to abrogate the promise given centuries before, and which was still unfulfilled. What that purpose was is declared in v. 19, below.

make the promise of none effect.—*katargeō,* = "to render ineffective or useless," as the barren fig tree did the ground it occupied, Luke 13:7, and as the death of Christ makes ineffective, prospectively, the power of the devil, Hebrews 2:14.

For *katargeō,* see comment on *2 Thessalonians* 2:8.

3:18 For—The apostle now proceeds to justify his use of such strong words as "disannul" and "abrogate" in this connection.

if the inheritance—the inheritance promised to Abraham was the land of Canaan, but that land was given, and a numerous posterity promised to people it, only as a means to an end, namely, that the purposes of God expressed in the original promise, "in thee shall all the families of the earth be blessed," Genesis 12:3, might in due time be fulfilled. In Romans 4:13 the apostle speaks of Abraham as "[the] heir of the world," intending, apparently, to sum up in that phrase the promises made to him and to his immediate descendants, and to give them the widest conceivable scope, cp. particularly Genesis 17:4. In the present passage he uses "inheritance" in the same comprehensive way, but apparently without any reference to the earthly elements in the promises, and having in mind only those spiritual and heavenly blessings of which Canaan was intended to be a type.

There is an ellipsis here which may be supplied thus, "if the title to the inheritance is of the law————."

The word rendered "inheritance" is *klēronomia,* lit., "what is obtained by lot," what is allotted to one, a portion. It is always rendered "inheritance" in the New Testament, but only in a few cases in the Gospels has it the meaning ordinarily attached to that word in English, i.e., that into possession of which the heir enters only on the death of the owner. The New Testament usage of *klēronomia* may be set out as under:

a, that property in real estate which in ordinary course passes from father to son on the death of the former, Matthew 21:38; Mark 12:7; Luke 12:13; 20:14;

b, a portion of real estate made the substance of a gift, Acts 7:5; Hebrews 11:8;

c, the prospective condition and possessions of the believer in the new order of things to be ushered in at the return of Christ, Acts 20:32; Ephesians 1:14; 5:5; Colossians 3:24; Hebrews 9:15; 1 Peter 1:4;

d, what the believer will be to God in that age, Ephesians 1:18.

In the present passage *b* and *c* are blended, and the word has its most comprehensive sense. Not a present but a prospective possession is always in view in the word.||

The simple form *klēros,* = a lot, which is "given" or "cast," a method of seeking Divine direction (see Prov. 16:33; Matt. 27:35; Mark 15:24; Luke 23:34; John 19:24; Acts 1:26). It is also used of a person's share in anything, Acts 1:17; 8:21. In Acts 26:18; Colossians 1:12 it is used interchangeably with *klēronomia, c,* above. In his First Epistle, 5:3, the apostle Peter uses *klēros* of the churches when he addresses the elders, lit., "the charges allotted [to you]," cp. Acts 20:28.||*

is of the law,—lit., "law," i.e., law in the abstract, law as a principle.

it is no more of promise:—once more the fundamental antagonism between law and grace, works and faith, is emphasized. "Once allow that the ground of the inheritance is law and the obedience that law demands, then," the apostle declares, "that inheritance cannot be obtained by anyone merely on the ground that it was promised as a gift."

but God hath granted it to Abraham by promise.—three things demand attention in this verse: first, a new word is introduced, *charizomai,* the verb corresponding to the noun *charis,* "grace." This is well rendered "granted" = "given by an act of grace." Second, the verb is in the perfect tense = "has freely given," indicating that the grant is still in force. And, third, the place of emphasis is given to the word "God"; it is His character that is at stake, for if the law had abrogated the promise then the word and the oath of God had failed.

The word *charizomai,* = "to bestow a favor unconditionally," is used in the New Testament as under:

a, of the release of a prisoner under sentence, as an act of clemency, Acts 3:14;

b, of the delivery for punishment of an innocent prisoner, Acts 25:11, 16;

c, of the gift of sight to the blind, by the Lord Jesus, Luke 7:21;

d, of the free, unconditioned promise made to Abraham by God, here;

e, of the act of forgiveness, divine, Ephesians 4:32; Colossians 2:13; 3:13, or human, Luke 7:42, 43; 2 Corinthians 2:7, 10; 12:13;

f, of the provision made for the believer in and with Christ, Romans 8:32; 1 Corinthians 2:12;

g, of the privilege of believing on, and of suffering with, Christ, Philippians 1:29;

h, of the exaltation by God of the self-humbled Son, Philippians 2:9.

---

*From *kleros* the word "clergy" is derived; the Rheims or Douay version renders "lording it over the clergy," thus assuming the superior rank of a "bishop," and suggesting a difference between "clergy" and "laity." But this is clearly wrong, for the "charge" of the beginning of the verse is the "flock" of the end of it.

In each case the idea of a free, unconditioned act is involved, and in all save one or two cases this is the dominant thought, cp. Acts 27:24; Philemon 22.||

3:19 What then is the law?—if the law cannot procure the gift of the Spirit, v. 2, if it does not give evidence of possessing any inherent power, v. 5, if no man is justified by it, if no man obtains life by its means, if no one is brought into the enjoyment of blessing by it, vv. 11, 12, 14, cp. v. 21, then what purpose was it intended to serve? with what object was it given? The question arises here naturally, for it cannot be supposed that God gave this law gratuitously, purposelessly, and yet the apostle had denied to the law every advantage claimed for it, or that might be claimed, and left it without any ostensible reason for its existence.

It was added—the use of the same English word here and in v. 15 does not involve any contradiction, for the Greek word there used conveys the idea of supplementing an agreement already made. Here the word is *prostithēmi* = "placed beside," the meaning of which may be seen in its use in such passages as Acts 2:41; 13:36; the apostle does not use it elsewhere in his Epistles. Hence the meaning here is not that something had been added to the promise by way of completing it, as in v. 15, but that something had been given as well as the promise, cp. "the law came in beside," Romans 5:20.

because of—*charin*, which has two distinct meanings, *a*, "on account of," pointing to the ground on which something is done, as in Ephesians 3:1, 14, see also Luke 7:47; 1 John 3:12; in these cases it is retrospective, it points back. But, *b*, it may also be prospective, pointing forward, as in 1 Timothy 5:14; Titus 1:5, 11; Jude 16, and here; in these passages the purpose with which something is done is intended. 1 Timothy 5:14 is probably the closest parallel to the present passage, "give none occasion to the adversary for reviling," i.e., "do nothing to provoke the adversary to speak evil of the Lord." Accordingly the words may be paraphrased "the law was added in order to provoke transgressions," see *c*, below, and cp. Romans 7:8.

transgressions,—*parabasis*, see note at 2:18, above; it is always used of a breach of law, Romans 4:15, and particularly of the Mosaic Law, Romans 2:23; Hebrews 2:2; 9:15, but also of the prohibition in Eden, Romans 5:14; 1 Timothy 2:14.||

Three interpretations of the sentence seem possible: *a*, that the law was given because the conditions of the covenant had been transgressed; but the covenant did not depend upon the fulfillment of conditions, it was a promise made by God and to be redeemed by Him in His own time and way; *b*, to restrain transgressions; but this, as a matter of fact, the law did not do; on the contrary, c, the law created transgressions, for though "until the law sin was in the world" yet "where there is no law, neither is there transgression," "and the law came in . . . that the trespass might abound," Romans 5:13; 4:15; 5:20. The law does not make men sinners, but it does make them transgressors. That is to say, the sinfulness of mankind was not brought home to them by the promise, so the law was given in order that sin might reveal itself under a form in which it could neither be mistaken nor excused. Men "had not known sin, except through the law," for "through the law is the knowledge of sin," and "through the commandment sin" becomes "exceeding sinful," Romans 7:7; 3:20; 7:13. The law was added to the promise, then, that conscience might have a standard external to itself, and that under the unmistakable and inexorable demands of the law men might learn their own powerlessness to discharge their obligations to God of a Savior.

till the seed should come to whom the promise hath been made;—i.e., Christ; see v. 16. Not only was the purpose of the law entirely different from the purpose of the covenant, or promise, they differed also in this, that whereas the fulfillment of the latter was the abiding purpose of God, the former was imposed only until a certain stage in the development of His counsels had been reached.

and it was **ordained**—*diatassō*, i.e., commanded, or administered.

through angels—in the Pentateuch the only reference to angels in connection with the giving of the law is Deuteronomy 33:2 (which in LXX reads, "His angels with Him on [lit. "from"] His right hand"), cp. Psalm 68:17. In the New Testament there are also Acts 7:53 and Hebrews 2:2, but whereas Stephen mentions the agency of the angels in order to emphasize the majesty of the law, the writer of the epistle to the Hebrews, like the apostle here, mentions it in order to show the inferiority of the law to the gospel, because of the inferiority of the agents by whom it was administered.

by the hand—an idiomatic expression = "by the agency of"; see Leviticus 26:46.

of a mediator.—i.e., Moses, for though that title is not given to him in the Old Testament, yet it is made plain that at the giving of the law he discharged the functions of a mediator; see Exodus 20:19; Deuteronomy 5:5.
   Mesitēs, apart from v. 20, is used elsewhere only of Christ, 1 Timothy 2:5; Hebrews 8:6; 9:15; 12:24. In the Old Testament it appears only in Job 9:33, "daysman."||
   The object of this section of the apostle's argument seems to be to demonstrate the inferiority of the old economy, glorious though it was, to the new, and to this end he enumerates four points of difference:
   a, the law was given in order to justify God in His condemnation of men;
   b, it was a temporary expedient;
   c, it was given through the agency of angels;
   d, it was received by a human mediator.

Whereas:

a, the gospel of grace, wherein the promise is embodied and potentially fulfilled, is given for the salvation of men;

b, it is final and permanent;

c, it is ministered directly by God Himself, apart from angelic agency;

d, it is received by men, apart from human mediation.

Thus the words of the apostle, written in another connection, are true also in this: "If the ministration of condemnation is glory, much rather doth the ministration of righteousness exceed in glory," 2 Corinthians 3:9.

The argument of the apostle, *d,* assumes the Deity of Christ, for had He been a man in the same sense that Moses was a man, He must have been a mediator in the same sense that Moses was a mediator, and in that case the contrast loses its point. When Paul elsewhere speaks of Christ as "mediator" he assumes His Deity and asserts His humanity, for had Christ not been divine it would have been superfluous to say of Him "Himself man" as the apostle does; see 1 Timothy 2:5.

3:20 Now—lit., "but," introducing an argument directed against the assumption that mediatorship in itself adds weight or importance to a covenant. The apostle seems to make this suggestion as against the excessive honor paid to Moses by the Jews on account of his part in the receiving and giving of the law, and their consequent unwillingness to receive the Lord Jesus and His gospel of grace.

a mediator is not a *mediator* **of one;**—i.e., of one party: mediatorship is necessary, and possible, only in cases in which two parties undertake mutual obligations. The article appears before "mediator" in orig., and "the mediator" would be an accurate rendering, for the sense is generic, as, e.g., in the sentence "the helmsman is in a responsible position." for this is true not merely of a particular helmsman but of every helmsman. So here, that "the mediator is not a mediator of one" is true of every mediator. It is, perhaps, best rendered by the indefinite article in English, to make it quite clear that the statement is not made of any particular mediator, Moses or Christ, but is true of any and every mediator and in every case.

but God is one.—i.e., in this case all the obligations were assumed by one of the parties to the covenant, God. And this is the reason why this covenant to Abraham, differing in this respect from other covenants, alike such as are made among men and those made between God and men, is also called "a promise."

Many interpretations of this verse have been offered, but the key to its meaning lies in this, that it arises out of the closing words of the preceding verse, and is intended to support the contention underlying them, viz., that the presence of a mediator in a covenant makes that covenant, on that account, inferior in dignity to one in which a mediator has no place. Lightfoot's note here is very much to the point: "The very idea of mediation supposes two persons at least between whom the mediation is carried on. The law, then, is of the nature of a contract between two parties, God on the one hand, and the Jewish people on the other. It is valid only so long as both parties fulfill the terms of the contract. It is therefore contingent, and not absolute . . . Unlike the law, the promise is absolute and unconditional. It depends on the sole decree of God. There are not two contracting parties. There is nothing of the nature of a *stipulation*. The giver is everything, the recipient nothing."

That part of Lightfoot's note which refers to the words "but God is one" is also worth transcribing: "This proposition is quite unconnected with the fundamental statement of the Mosaic Law, "The Lord thy God is one God," though resembling it in form." For the apostle is not here concerned with the Unity of God, he is declaring that on God alone rested the whole responsibility for the discharge of the obligations of the covenant He made with Abraham.

3:21 Is the law then against the promises of God?—the law was later than, and inferior to, the promise, and did not annul it. Was there, then, any necessary antagonism between the law and the promise, both of which had their origin in God?

God forbid:—as at 2:17. It is inconceivable that these two things, albeit each was instituted with a distinct purpose, could be in themselves inconsistent one with the other. They represent different elements in the character of God. One, the law, is the expression of His righteousness; the other, the promise, is the expression of His grace. Now God is not at war with Himself. Had not grace and truth been in God, essential elements in His character, they could not have come by Jesus Christ; see John 1:17, and cp. Psalm 89:14. It is the glory of the gospel that in it these two great principles find their highest and entirely harmonious expression; it is the gospel of the grace of God, and therein He has shown His righteousness; see Acts 20:24, and Romans 3:25.

for if there had been . . . given—i.e., by God, at any time.

a law . . . which could make alive,—lit., "a law with the power of imparting life." *Zōopoieō*, a compound formed of the two words "alive" and "make," occurs as under:

a, of God as the Bestower of every kind of life in the universe, 1 Timothy 6:13, and, particularly, of resurrection life, John 5:21; Romans 4:17;

b, of Christ, Who also is the Bestower of resurrection life, John 5:21b, 1 Corinthians 15:45, cp. v. 22;

c, of the resurrection of Christ in "the body of His glory," 1 Peter 3:18;

d, of the power of reproduction inherent in seed, which presents a certain analogy with resurrection, 1 Corinthians 15:36;

e, of the "changing," or "fashioning anew," of the bodies of the living which corresponds with, and takes place at the same time as, the resurrection of the dead in Christ, Romans 8:11;

f, of the impartation of spiritual life, and the communication of spiritual sustenance generally, John 6:63; 2 Corinthians 3:6, and here.||

verily—*ontōs,* = what is actual, and not merely nominal; "real" as opposed to "seeming," "pretended." Thus the centurion was impressed that the Lord Jesus must be a righteous man in more than a merely formal sense, Luke 23:47, and the Jews held John to be a true prophet, not a false one, Mark 11:32.

The disciples testified that the Lord had actually risen from the dead, not in appearance merely, as though He had not really died, or as though what they had seen was only a vision, Luke 24:34.

The Jews fancied themselves free, the Lord offered them real freedom, John 8:36.

The exercise of the prophetic gift would constrain strangers to declare that the claim of the church that God is present is good, He actually is present, 1 Corinthians 14:25.

The really needy are to be distinguished from those who are only apparently so, 1 Timothy 5:3; 5:16.

Some under the glamor of material things mistake the shadow for the substance; let such turn from their delusion to lay hold on the life which is life indeed, 1 Timothy 6:19.

So here. The difference between the promise and the law was not merely nominal but fundamental. Had it been nominal merely and not fundamental, then the law also would have availed for righteousness and life.||

righteousness—lit., "the righteousness," i.e., the righteousness after which the Jews sought, the means of attaining to which was the subject of discussion, and which is here = life, cp. note at v. 12, above; both words are used to sum up and express succinctly all the blessings latent in the promise to Abraham and secured to faith.

would have been of the law.—*ek,* see note at v. 7, above. This the apostle had shown to be impossible, vv. 3–10, above.

An inviolable principle in the dealings of God with men, the principle of the continuity of His providence, is involved in the rhetorical question with which this verse opens. A change in God's methods does not argue a change in His plans. Neither does the adoption of a new way of dealing imply any defect or imperfection in that which preceded it. God's purpose develops, and the means He uses to further it increase in number and variety. It is not possible to anticipate God's steps. Something quite unexpected happens, something essential to the development of the completed plan, and yet something different from, but not incongruous with, what has gone before. This principle is illustrated, for example, in Romans 8:3, 4: "What the law could not do, in that it was weak through the flesh, God, sending His own Son in the likeness of sinful flesh and as an offering for sin, condemned sin in the flesh, that the ordinance of the law might be fulfilled in us"; and, again, in 4:9, below, in a description of the law given by way of contrast with the gospel, for in itself "the law is holy, and the commandment holy, and righteous, and good," Romans 7:12. Similarly the Levitical priesthood was complete and perfect in itself, although perfection in

worship was not attainable through it, Hebrews 7:11, 12, 18, 19. But it was typical of that priesthood through which perfection would be attained, and, being typical, it was bound to be temporary. As with the priesthood, so with the tabernacle and the sacrifices, 9:10; 10:1, 2. So again in regard to the "first covenant," 8:7, the words "if that first covenant had been faultless" do not indicate inherent imperfection in that covenant itself. The failure was on the part of those with whom it was made; with them it was that God "found fault," v. 8. And the first covenant, notwithstanding that in due course it "became old and waxed aged and vanished away," v. 13, had its place in the development of the Divine purposes and was perfectly adapted to play its part therein. In the same manner the law was not "against the promises of God"; on the contrary, it also served to bring about their fulfillment.

This principle is important from another point of view. In His acts and ways God revealed Himself. Only from what He said and did could men learn what He is. Thus each new method of dealing adopted by God was a fresh manifestation of His character. But while no single act, no one of His ways, could manifest that character in its entirety, no act or way was inconsistent with it, or misrepresented it. And this is indeed the reason why the providence of God is continuous, because His providence, His actings, are true, though partial, expressions of what He is.

3:22 Howbeit—"but," "on the contrary"; what actually happened was the very opposite of the supposition at the close of v. 21.

the scripture—see at v. 8, above; the reference is probably to Deuteronomy 27:26, quoted in v. 10. In the parallel and much more extended passage, Romans 3:9–20, several texts are adduced in support of the same proposition, the universality of sin.

hath shut up—*sunkleiō,* = to shut up with, as fish are enclosed in a net, Luke 5:6, i.e., completely, and without possibility of escape. It occurs again in v. 23, and in Romans 11:32; what is here said to be done by the Scriptures is there said to be done by God. Cp. also Psalm 31:8; 78:62, LXX.||

all things—*ta panta,* neuter, but as only persons are capable of sinning, only persons are intended. Cp. John 6:37, "all that which [neuter] the Father giveth Me shall come unto Me; and him that cometh [masculine] to Me I will in no wise cast out." In Romans 11:32, "all" is masculine, though, of course, all persons, male and female, are included. There is no "common" gender in Greek, as there is in English, consequently when a statement is made concerning mankind generally, the masculine is usually employed, though the neuter is sometimes used, as in the passages referred to above. Cp. the equivalent expressions "all men," "mankind," "the human race."

under sin,—i.e., "under the dominion of"; see Romans 6:14; in Romans 11:32 "unto disobedience." The proved impossibility of keeping the law of God was the evidence of the sinful condition of mankind; from this conclusion there is no escape, and to this rule (that all men are sinners) there is no exception. It was necessary, however, that the truth about their state should be brought home to men, if for no other reason than this, that only those that are conscious of guilt will seek justification. Cp. the words of the Lord Jesus, Luke 5:32.

that—"in order that"; what follows declares the object of God in shutting up all under sin and to disobedience, and, once more, the relation between the law and the promise. Again cp. Romans 11:32, "[in order] that He might have mercy upon all."

the promise—i.e., the things promised, righteousness, life, the inheritance, and cp. Hebrews 10:36; 11:39. See note at v. 18.

by faith in Jesus Christ—an ellipsis must be supplied here, "the promise [the fulfillment of which is secured] by faith in Jesus Christ."

might be given—see note on "might receive," v. 14, above.

to them that believe.—lit., "the believers." These words are not merely a repetition of "by faith." It was common ground between the apostle and his opponents that believers received the promises; the Judaizers held that they received the blessings on the ground of their works, Paul that they received them on the ground of their faith in Christ. There was no dispute whether men are justified by faith, the dispute was whether they are justified by faith alone. The Judaizer in apostolic days, and his successors since, have contended that believing men are justified by their works, but not, of course, that unbelieving men are justified by their works. On the contrary, the apostle contends that believing men are justified by their faith alone, cp. Romans 3:22.

3:23 But before faith came,—i.e., before the death and resurrection of Christ and the descent of the Holy Spirit, before the new dispensation was thus ushered in. This verse and the following provide a further answer to the question of v. 19, "What then is the law?"

The article stands before "faith" in orig., "the faith," as at 1:23; but this does not justify the conclusion that faith is here = "the gospel." The article more probably points back to "faith" in v. 22 ("the article of renewed mention").

we—i.e., we Jews, for, of course, the Galatians, being Gentiles, never had been under the law.

were kept in ward under the law,—*phroureō,* a military term, used, *a,* of blocking up every way of escape, as in a siege; *b,* of providing protection against the enemy, as a garrison does; see 2 Corinthians 11:32, "guarded," i.e., kept the city with a garrison. It is used of the security of the Christian until the end, 1 Peter 1:5, and of the sense of that security that is his when he puts all his matters into the hand of God, Philippians 4:7. In these passages the idea is that of protection; here, as the following words show, it means rather imprisonment, bondage. A prison, however, is not merely a place of durance, it is also a place of protection; law the jailer is also law the protector. The "middle wall of partition," Ephesians 2:14, preserved the Jews from the contamination of heathen vices. The law was thus what the Lord Himself called it, a "fold," John 10:1.||

shut up—as in v. 22, lit., "being shut up," not "having been shut up." The latter, the perfect participle, would describe a continuous state resulting from an initial act, = "were shut up and remained so." The former, the present participle, is a more vivid picture of the vigilant bondage of the law. As the efforts of the Jews to obtain justification by their works were constant, so, and as constantly, was every way of escape from condemnation closed up. Sin had dominion over them because they were under the law; see Romans 6:14.

unto the faith which should afterwards—*mellō*, to be about to be; this word is of fairly frequent occurrence in the New Testament, and connotes more than mere futurity, though this fact is not always made evident in the English versions. Its meaning may be learned from a consideration of its use in a few passages. Thus in Matthew 2:13, it was not merely that Herod would, at some indefinite time, attempt the destruction of the Child, he was about to seek it; the case was urgent, Joseph and Mary must fly at once. In Luke 7:2 the centurion's servant was said to be "at the point of death," so also in John 4:47. In Matthew 17:22 the Lord spake of His death not merely as certain but as imminent; so also in Mark 10:32, the end of His earthly course was at hand. The disciples were sent to certain places immediately before the Lord visited them, Luke 10:1. The Lord knew what He was about to do for the multitude, there would be no need to go to find and bring the necessary material, John 6:6. Peter and John were at the gate about to enter the Temple at the moment the lame man asked an alms, Acts 3:3. It was when Moses was about to begin work on the Tabernacle that God instructed him how it was to be made, Hebrews 8:5. The apostle had warned the converts at Thessalonica that persecution would not be long delayed, 1 Thessalonians 3:4.

Other passages might be adduced to illustrate the meaning of *mellō*, but these will serve to introduce an inquiry into its significance in the passage under consideration and in others more or less related thereto.

Mellō appears in certain New Testament passages with reference to the old dispensation in its relation to the new dispensation while the latter was as yet still future. Thus the apostle Paul speaks of "Adam, who is a figure [lit., "type," the only person spoken of in Scripture as a type of Christ] of Him that was about to come," Romans 5:14. Again, the observances of the old covenant were "a shadow of the things that were about to come," Colossians 2:17. So here, the Jews "were kept in ward under the law, shut up to the faith which was about to be revealed."

The significance of these passages is plain. During the age that preceded the Incarnation, from the primal promise given in Eden, the advent of Messiah was presented to the people of God as imminent. The time for that advent, however, was set within the authority of the Father, it was not communicated to men. Considered from the point of view of those to whom the promise was made, its fulfillment might have taken place at any time. Hence the coming of Messiah and the inauguration of the new age were always imminent, impending, hanging over each generation, and stimulating the godly to inquire when the time of that coming would be, or even what its characteristics would be, 1 Peter 1:11; but all such inquiry was fruitless in information, though no doubt most fruitful in the inquirers' communion with God in His Word. Thus the people of God were kept in expectancy, and when the object of hope is God, and Christ, an expectant mind produces a holy life, cp. 1 John 3:3. See also such passages as Genesis 49:18; Psalm 119:166, 174; Isaiah 25:9; 26:8; Micah 7:7; Luke 2:25, 38; 23:51 (noting that "salvation" = "Savior," cp. Luke 2:30; John 4:22).

Mellō, moreover, is used in a similar way in a number of passages which refer to the age that is to be ushered in by the return of the Lord Jesus. Thus in Matthew 12:32 the Lord speaks of "the impending age," so does the apostle in Ephesians 1:21, cp. Hebrews 2:5, "the inhabited earth," and 6:5, "the age," "which is about to come." Again, where the latter speaks of judgment, he describes it as not merely certain but imminent; see Acts 17:31; 24:25; 2 Timothy 4:1, so also James 2:12; cp. the testimony of John the Baptist concerning "the impending wrath," Matthew 3:7.

Resurrection, too, is imminent, Acts 24:15, and the Judgment Seat of Christ is probably in Paul's mind when he speaks of "that which is impending" in 1 Timothy 6:19, where "time" is an addition to the English versions. In 1 Timothy 4:8 the apostle sets in contrast "the life which now is" and "that which is [about to] come"; for in the latter an incomparable glory "is about to be revealed" to us, Romans 8:18; cp. 1 Peter 5:1, where the words recur.

As in the earlier age, so also in this. The consummation of God's plans is not said to belong to some necessarily distant time, but merely to a time undefined, but always imminent, impending. The attitude toward that age of the believer of this age is, therefore, to be one of expectancy; he is to wait for the Lord Jesus from heaven, 1 Thessalonians 1:10.

be revealed.—until that revelation was made there was no way of escape from the strict surveillance and the unrelenting condemnation of the law. But when Christ came He led out from that fold all who heard His voice and followed Him, and to them He gave eternal life, John 10:28, as a free, unearned gift.

3:24 So that the law hath been our tutor—*paidagōgos,* lit., "a child-leader," "a leader of children"; in 1 Corinthians 4:15, though the idea of instruction may not be altogether absent, the apostle refers rather to the pastor than to the teacher, to those who cared for the saints rather than to those who taught them; here and in v. 25 the idea of instruction is altogether absent. Indeed, in this and allied words the idea is that of training, discipline, not of the impartation of knowledge. The *paidagōgos* was not the instructor of the child; he exercised a general supervision over him and was responsible for his moral and physical well-being. Thus understood, *paidagōgos* is appropriately used with "kept in ward" and "shut up," whereas to understand it as = "teacher" introduces an idea entirely foreign to the passage, and throws the apostle's argument into confusion, cp. "guardians and stewards," 4:2, below.||

The use of the word is shown in the following dialogue freely translated from Plato's "Lysis":

"Do your parents allow you to do as you please?" I asked. "Why, how could they permit that?" he replied. "Well, who has charge of you?" "My paedagogue here," said he. "What! though he's a slave? It's shameful that a freeman should be governed by a slave. . . . And what does this paedagogue do in governing you?" "Oh, he takes me to school." "And your teachers, do they govern you?" "Yes, certainly." "A fine lot of masters and governors your father sets over you."

Lightfoot says that in Numbers 11:12 the Jerusalem Targum (an ancient paraphrase of the Old Testament in Aramaic, or colloquial Hebrew) translates the Heb. word rendered in English "nursing father" by *paidagōgos*, written in Heb. letters. He adds, "As well in his inferior rank, as in his recognized duty of enforcing discipline, this person was a fit emblem of the Mosaic Law."

A synonym, *paideutēs*, found in Romans 2:20 and Hebrews 12:9, also refers to training, not to teaching; in the former passage the discipline of the school is in view (cp. Acts 22:3, where for "instructed" read "trained"); in the latter the discipline of the family.||

The corresponding noun, *paideia*, likewise refers to discipline, as may be seen in Ephesians 6:4; Hebrews 12:5, 7, 8, 11. In 2 Timothy 3:16 the marg. is to be preferred, that the Holy Scripture is profitable for teaching has already been stated: the impartation of the knowledge of the will of God ("teaching") produces conviction of mistaken ways ("reproof") and leads to restoration to a right state of mind and to right ways ("correction"), and so to that "discipline . . . in righteousness" which is essential to the well-being and to the efficiency of the man of God.||

The verb, *paideuō*, also means to train, whether in the schools of men, Acts 7:22; 22:3, or in the school of God, Titus 2:12, cp. 2 Timothy 2:25. And it is used of the family discipline, as in Hebrews 12:6, 7, 10, and cp. 1 Corinthians 11:32; 2 Corinthians 6:9; Revelation 3:19. In 1 Timothy 1:20 *paideuō* is translated "teach," but, however the passage is to be understood, it is clear that not the impartation of knowledge but severe discipline is intended. In Luke 23:16, 22, Pilate, since he had declared the Lord guiltless of the charge brought against Him, and hence could not punish Him, weakly offered, as a concession to the Jews, to "chastise, *paideuō*, Him and let Him go."||

to bring us unto [*eis*] Christ,—two popular interpretations of these words must be dismissed: *a*, that which understands them to mean that the law was the "paedagogue" until Christ came, for in that case a different Greek preposition (*achri* = until, as in 4:2, or *heōs*, as in 2 Thessalonians 2:7, or *mechri*, as in Luke 16:16) must have been used; *b*, that which understands them to mean that as the "paedagogue" brought the boy to the teacher, so the law brought men to Christ, for here Christ is not set forth as teacher but as Savior.

The meaning may be expressed in a paraphrase: "We were kept in ward under law, . . . with the coming of Christ in view." The "shutting up" was not an end in itself, it was necessary that they should know and feel the constraints of the taskmaster in order that they might welcome the Deliverer when He appeared.

that—"in order that," with this end in view.

we might be justified by faith.—not to come under the control of a new "paedagogue," not to be instructed by a new teacher, but that by Christ we might be delivered from intolerable bondage, and enter upon the enjoyment of the promised blessings, justification, life, the Holy Spirit, and that not by works but by faith.

3:25 But now that [the] faith is come, we are no longer under a tutor—"We," i.e., "we [Jewish] Christians," Cp. Romans 7:6, "we have been discharged from the law," and 1 Corinthians 9:20, "not being myself under the law"; this latter categorical statement of the believer's relation to the law was omitted from A.V., but has been restored to the English reader by the Revisers.

3:26 For—introducing the reason for the statement that the believer is not under the paedagogue, law. The status of sonship carried with it freedom from such bondage; cp. Romans 8:15 with 5:1, below.

ye are all—the last word carries the emphasis of the sentence, and is directed against the distinction made by the Judaizers between those believers who had received circumcision and those who had not.

In vv. 23-25, where the apostle's statements were true only of Jews, he uses "we" and "our"; in vv. 26-29, where his statements are true of all converts, Jews and Gentiles, he substitutes the second personal pronoun, "ye," thus applying directly to the Galatians the conclusion to which his argument had brought them. Israel stood in covenant relation with God before Christ came, the Gentiles did not; but, whatever their former condition, now all who had trusted in Christ had been brought into a relationship with God incomparably superior even to that of Israel before Christ came.

Here, and throughout the epistle, the apostle assumes the sincerity of the Galatian converts' faith in Christ. They had received "The Spirit of adoption," Who prompted them to cry, "Abba" (the Aramaic word), "Father" (the Greek word), and Who "Himself bare witness with their spirits that they were children of God"; cp. v. 3 with Romans 8:15, 16, They were his brethren, then, see v. 15, above, objects of his love and care, and to be protected from every assault, subtle or fierce, on their faith. This inclusive statement does not, of course, commit the apostle to a judgment on the spiritual condition of any individual among them, he takes them on the ground of their profession; as to what is within only God knows any man's heart. Behind his indignation with those who sought to lead them astray, and with their folly in paying any heed to such teachers, lay a conviction of the reality of the work of God among the Galatians, and a tender desire for the spiritual welfare of those who had responded to the gospel message; see 4:12–20.

sons of God—in Christ Jesus.—*huios,* which is used in New Testament of:
  a, male offspring, 4:30, below;
  b, legitimate, as opposed to illegitimate, offspring, Hebrews 12:8;
  c, descendants, without reference to sex, Romans 9:27;
  d, friends attending a wedding, Matthew 9:15;
  e, those who enjoy certain privileges, Acts 3:25;
  f, those who act in a certain way, whether evil, Matthew 23:31, or good, v. 7, above;
  g, those who manifest a certain character, whether evil, Acts 13:10; Ephesians 2:2, or good, Luke 6:35; Acts 4:36; Romans 8:14;
  h, the destiny that corresponds with the character, whether evil, Matthew 23:15; John 17:12; 2 Thess. 2, 3, or good, Luke 20:36;
  i, the dignity of the relationship with God whereinto men are brought by the Holy Spirit when they believe on the Lord Jesus Christ, Romans 8:19, here, and 4:6, 7, below.

For another analysis of the New Testament use of this word, see comment on *1 Thessalonians* 5:5.

A synonym of *huios, teknon,* = child, occurs frequently both in the natural sense and in a figurative one. In *teknon* the fact of birth is prominent (it is derived from *tiktō,* to bring forth), in *huios* the dignity of the position into which the child is born and the character consonant therewith. Cp. the expressions "the child of his father" and "the son of his father"; the first is relationship, the second character.

Both words occur in Ephesians 2:2, 3; men are "children of wrath," i.e., by natural descent; whether Jew or Gentile, all are born in a state of alienation from God; by practice and in character they inevitably become "sons of disobedience." See a similar distinction in Ephesians 5:6, 8.

Teknon is noticed in comment on *1 Thessalonians* 5:5, and *teknion* at 4:19, below.

The difference between believers as "children of God" and as "sons of God" may be studied in Romans 8:14–21. Believers, as such, are children of God, and being children are heirs of God, and enjoy the liberty proper to their relationship, a liberty which they do not as yet fully enjoy, but which they will one day experience even to the extent of deliverance from corruption and death. Romans 9:8; Ephesians 5:1, and Philippians 2:15 are the only other passages in which the apostle speaks of "the children of God."

"As many as are led by the Spirit of God, these are sons of God," i.e., these and no other. For all who become children of God attest the reality of their confession by yielding themselves to the guiding and enabling of the Spirit of God; thus by becoming sons of God, i.e., by manifesting in their conduct the character of God, they give evidence that they are indeed the children of God. As to his "standing" the believer is a child of God, as to his "state" he ought to be a son of God, and it is a vain thing for anyone to be a child of God unless he is giving evidence that he is a son of God. But full conformity to the "image of His Son" will be attained only when the Lord comes, cp. Romans 8:29 with 1 John 3:2; for that consummation the groaning creation waits, Romans 8:19.

The apostle John does not use *huios*, "son," of the believer, he reserves that title for the Lord; but he does use *teknon*, "child," as in his Gospel 1:12; 1 John 3:1, 2; Revelation 21:7 is a quotation from 2 Samuel 7:14.

The Lord Jesus used *huios* in a very significant way, as in Matthew 5:9, "Blessed are the peacemakers, for they shall be called the sons of God," and vv. 44, 45, "Love your enemies, and pray for them that persecute you; that ye may be [become] sons of your Father which is in heaven." The disciples were to do these things, not in order that they might become children of God, but that, being children (note "your Father" throughout), they might make the fact manifest in their character, might "become sons." See also 2 Corinthians 6:17, 18.

Here the contrast is between the Jewish state of pupilage under the law and the believer's state of sonship in Christ. It is noteworthy, too, that the apostle does not now call the converts sons of Abraham, as in v. 7, above, but much more and higher than that, they were sons of God.

through faith—these words may be taken with those that follow "through faith in Christ Jesus," and in favor of this Colossians 1:4; 2 Timothy 3:15 may be quoted, and cp. v. 22. Or they may be taken parenthetically, i.e., as a reiteration of the point the apostle is seeking to establish, and in that case the idea is "sons of God in Christ Jesus, and made such not by circumcision but by faith." The latter interpretation is, on the whole, to be preferred, in view of the use of the phrases "into Christ," "in Christ," in vv. 27, 28.

3:27 For—introducing the ground for the statement that "all" were sons of God in Christ Jesus. This ground is twofold, the first reason is adduced in this verse, the second in v. 28.

as many of you—*hosos*, i.e., "all of you," as in v. 10, above, and 6:12, 16, below, and in John 1:12; Romans 8:14, et al. The same word is used in the same connection in Romans 6:3, "all we who were baptized"; neither in that passage nor in this is the language capable of the interpretation that some of those to whom the apostle wrote had been baptized, others not. The normal order in apostolic days is stated in Acts 18:8, "and many of the Corinthians hearing believed, and were baptized"; no other order is discernible, nor is any exceptional case recorded. What is written in Acts and the epistles abundantly justifies the conclusion that all who believed were baptized, and all who were baptized were baptized on profession of faith. While Acts 8:37, see margin, is without adequate testimony as part of the original text, it is undoubtedly a very ancient addition thereto, and as such is a valuable witness to the practice of the early evangelists.

The two cases recorded in Acts 16 present little or no difficulty. That Lydia was baptized is evidence that she had believed, though that fact is not stated; so also with her household, the fact that baptism was administered to them testifies to their faith. The apostle spoke the Word not only to the jailer, but to all his house, and that Word was an amplification and enforcement of "Believe on the Lord Jesus, and thou shalt be saved, thou and thy house," words which must not be taken as though they ran, "Believe on the Lord Jesus, and thou and thy house shall be saved." Thereupon the jailer was baptized, "he and all his," but the only reason suggested by the context for administering baptism to him or to them is that they had all responded to the apostlic message, and that they had all believed on the Lord Jesus. The words "with all his house," v. 34, are to be taken both with what precedes them, "rejoiced greatly," and with what follows them, "having believed God." Obviously if all the members of his household were capable of rejoicing for such a cause, they were also capable of believing. And if "all his house" had not believed why should they rejoice that the jailer had done so?

Of the citizens of Corinth who were baptized in consequence of the testimony of Paul, the apostle himself actually administered the rite to very few persons; see 1 Corinthians 1:14–16. Like Peter, who commanded others to baptize Cornelius and "his kinsmen and his near friends," Acts 10:24, 48, Paul delegated that duty, reserving his own strength for the higher service of preaching the gospel, 1 Corinthians 1:17. In making his comparison between baptizing and evangelizing, however, the apostle is certainly not depreciating the former; some time after he wrote these words, he wrote an exposition of the meaning of baptism in the epistle to the Romans, ch. 6, and in one of his latest letters, his language assumes that the believers at Colossae had been baptized, 2:12. Moreover, the same considerations, among others, show that he is not suggesting a contrast between his own ministry and that of Peter, as though baptism had no place in the former whereas it was characteristic of the latter. On the contrary, both men followed the same course; while they did not actually baptize the converts themselves, they saw to it that the commandment of the Lord was obeyed. Cp. also John 4:1, 2. The verse under consideration is, of course, sufficient testimony that the Galatian converts also had been baptized.

as were baptized—*baptizō,* which the Eng. translators perhaps did well to leave untranslated, since there is no exact equivalent in the language; "immerse" expresses only part of the idea, i.e., to put into (water); *baptizō* means to put into (water) and to take out again. Drs. W. Sanday and A. C. Headlam thus define Christian baptism (International Critical Commentary, *Romans,* 5th Ed.): "Baptism—expresses symbolically a series of acts—

Immersion = Death.

Submersion = Burial (the ratification of death).

Emergence = Resurrection."

The same writers thus paraphrase the words of Romans 6:3, "When the water closed over our heads, that meant that we lay buried with Him, in proof that our death to sin, like His death, was real."

The late Dr. H. P. Liddon (*Explanatory Analysis of St. Paul's Epistle to the Romans*, 4th Ed.) remarks, "The baptism for adults by immersion is present to the apostle's mind. The (i) descent into the water . . . and the (ii) rising from it . . . were the two striking features of the rite, corresponding to (1) the Death, and (2) the Resurrection, of Christ; and so to the Christian's (1) "Death unto sin," and (2) "New Birth unto righteousness." Between the two comes the moment during which (the person being baptized) is beneath the water; it corresponds to Christ's Burial, and in the Christian life to the permanent effect of his (having died to sin) . . ."

Dr. James Denney, writing on the same passage (Expositor's Greek Testament, *Romans*) has "Therefore we were buried with Him (in the act of immersion) . . . baptism, inasmuch as one emerges from the water after being immersed. . . ."

Commenting on Colossians 2:12 Dr. A. S. Peake says: "The rite of baptism, in which the person baptized was first buried beneath the water and then raised from it, . . . baptism is not the mere plunging into water, but the immersion from it too . . ."

Baptism in water was appointed by the Lord, Matthew 28:19; it was the regulated public confession of faith in Him on the part of those who responded to the gospel, and was practiced by the apostles from the outset, Acts 2:41. It is mentioned by the apostle Paul in one of his earlier epistles, 1 Corinthians, and in one of his latest, Colossians, and as already noted, an exposition of the meaning of the ordinance forms a section of the epistle to the Romans.

into Christ—ideally the moment of believing is the moment of baptism, for in the act of being baptized the believer sets forth in symbol what happened when he first trusted in Christ. But in actual experience the baptizing takes place at a time later, by more or less, than the moment of believing. The mention of baptism was probably intended to remind the Galatians that they had themselves declared their identification with Christ in His burial, whereas the new teaching was a practical denial thereof. For of believers on the Lord Jesus it is said that they:

died with Christ, Colossians 2:20;

were buried with Christ, Colossians 2:12;

were quickened with Christ, Ephesians 2:5;

were raised with Christ, Colossians 3:1;

are seated with Christ in the heavenlies, Ephesians 2:6;

are to be manifested with Christ in glory, Colossians 3:4.

All this is said of the believer at the present time, as he is "in Christ Jesus," for these words, which appear at the end of Ephesians 2:6, are to be read with each separate statement of that and the preceding verse. But mere submission to a rite in the flesh, such as circumcision, and obedience to the law, did not contemplate such a result.

The practical import of baptism is expressed in Romans 6:11: the believer is to reckon himself to be dead unto sin, but alive unto God in Christ Jesus.

did put on Christ.—*enduō,* = "to clothe oneself with," a word which, beside its frequent use for literal garments, Acts 12:21, e.g., is also used of the incorruptible body, wherein the dead in Christ shall be raised, and of the immortal body, which is to swallow up the mortal body of those who are alive at the Parousia, 1 Corinthians 15:53; 2 Corinthians 5:3.

It is the word used by the Lord Jesus to express the relationship between the promised Holy Spirit and those who were to receive Him, Luke 24:49.

The believer is said to have put on "the new man," Ephesians 4:24; Colossians 3:10; and "therefore," he is exhorted to "put on a heart of compassion, kindness, humility, meekness, longsuffering, . . . and love," vv. 12, 14. Such is to be the ordinary apparel of the Christian; in this character he is to appear daily in the world. The same thought is expressed in the words, "put ye on the Lord Jesus Christ," Romans 13:14.

The believer, however, is "enrolled—as a soldier," 2 Timothy 2:4, and as such has suitable armor provided for him, and with this he is exhorted to clothe himself, Romans 13:12, Ephesians 6:11; 1 Thessalonians 5:8.

The whole is summed up in Romans 13:14, for the man who "puts on the Lord Jesus Christ" stands both in the Christian's dress and in the Christian's panoply.

Enduō occurs in Job 29:14, LXX, "I put on righteousness, and it clothed me," and in Judges 6:34, "the Spirit of the Lord clothed itself with Gideon"; in the latter passage at least the idea is not dissimilar to that of this passage.

The apostle may also have had in mind the Roman custom whereby on attaining to manhood the youth discarded the garments of childhood and put on the *toga virilis,* the garment of manhood, and became a citizen, enjoying the freedom and privileges of citizenship, and discharging its responsibilities, and at the same time taking his place in the councils of his family.

In this sense the words "put on Christ" are without exact parallel elsewhere, though they suggest Paul's characteristic expression "in Christ," for it is by putting on Christ that a man comes to be in Christ, and at His Parousia will be found in Him, Philippians 3:9. The intimacy of the relationship thus described stands in vivid contrast with the relationship between God and the believers contemplated by the Judaizer, who wished to bring them again under the bondage of the law.

3:28 There can be—*eni,* = "there is in," i.e., "there exists," does not merely state the fact, it asserts the impossibility of the contrary. Thus James declares that "partiality cannot exist with the Father of Lights," 1:17; and Paul asks "could it be possible that there did not exist one wise man in the Church at Corinth?" 1 Corinthians 6:5. See also Colossians 3:11.||

neither Jew nor Greek,—i.e., national distinctions do not obtain in Christ; the world, men of "every tribe, and tongue, and people, and nation," is the object of the love of God and the proper sphere of the gospel. Cp. "there is no distinction between Jew and Greek," "for the same Lord is Lord of all," Romans 10:12.

there can be neither bond nor free,—i.e., social distinctions do not obtain in Christ; the rich and the poor, the master and the servant, the wise and the simple, princes and such as are of low degree, meet together in the gospel to share a "common salvation."

there can be no male and female:—i.e., distinction of sex does not obtain in Christ; woman, no less than man, finds in Him her Savior and her Example. The change from "neither-nor" to "no-and" may be due to the fact that these words are quoted from Genesis 1:27, LXX; or it may be intended to indicate that, whereas national and social distinctions are conditions not fixed in the nature of man by any law of God, but arose subsequent to the Fall, the distinction of sex is the primal ordinance of the Creator and belongs to the constitution of the race; see Matthew 19:4. Even so, sex is not a barrier to salvation, nor is it a hindrance to the development of the graces of the Christian life.

for ye all—"all" is emphatic again, as at v. 26; the apostle now supplies the reason why the distinctions just mentioned, with their attendant privileges, are lost in the new relationship with each other into which they had been brought when they "put on" Christ.

are one *man* in Christ Jesus.—"man" is added in accordance with Ephesians 2:15, where the apostle speaks of Jew and Gentile becoming "one new man" in Christ. The figure is closely analogous to that of "the body," under which the mutual relation of believers is set forth in 1 Corinthians 12:12–26; Ephesians 4:4, et al.

In John 10:16, where the Lord speaks of gathering His sheep from the different "folds" into "one flock," the final gathering is in view, "they that are Christ's at His Parousia," 1 Corinthians 15:23. In John 17, where the Lord asks the Father for those who believe on Him (and who are thus already incorporated into the "one [new] man in Christ Jesus") that they "may be one," spiritual progress is in view. Hence this unity is moral; oneness of life is already theirs, then let them all have one ideal, one ambition—to be like the Son, that so they might please the Father and confirm their testimony to the world, vv. 11, 21. In vv. 22, 23 the consummation at the coming of the Lord seems to be in view, for whereas "believe" is the word that answers to present testimony, "know" is the word that answers to the revelation of that day.

Here and in Ephesians 2:15 "one" is masculine in gender, i.e., "one person"; in John 17 "one" is neuter, i.e., "one thing," as in 1 Corinthians 3:8; 11:5. In the first case vital union is in view; in the second moral. The first is present, an already accomplished fact in Christ—life; the second is a process in course of accomplishment in the power of the Holy Spirit—character.

3:29 And—*de*, "but," "once more"; as so often before in the course of the epistle, the apostle carries his readers to the conclusion that all the privileges contemplated by the Jews belong to those who are "of faith" in Christ; see v. 7 above; v. 28 is a digression, v. 29 follows on and completes the argument of v. 27.

if ye are Christ's,—i.e., if ye belong to Christ, not merely if ye are His property, but if ye are "members of His body" Ephesians 5:30.

then are ye Abraham's seed,—see at v. 16, above.

heirs—*klēronomos;* see note on "inheritance," v. 18, above: the same general remarks apply in both cases.

New Testament usage of *klēronomos* may be analyzed as under:

a, the person to whom property is to pass on the death of the owner, Matthew 21:38; Mark 12:7; Luke 20:14; Galatians 4:1;

b, one to whom something has been assigned by God, on possession of which, however, he has not yet entered, as Abraham, Romans 4:13, 14; Hebrews 6:17; Christ, Hebrews 1:2; the poor saints, James 2:5;

c, believers, inasmuch as they share in the new order of things to be ushered in at the return of Christ, here and 4:7, below, Romans 8:17; Titus 3:7;

d, one who receives something other than by merit, as Noah, Hebrews 11:7.||

Sunklēronomos, a joint heir, is used of Isaac and Jacob as participants with Abraham in the promises of God, Hebrews 11:9; of husband and wife who are also united in Christ, 1 Peter 3:7; of Gentiles who believe, as participants in the gospel with Jews who believe, Ephesians 3:6; and of all believers as prospective participants with Christ in His glory, as recompense for their participation in His sufferings, Romans 8:17.||

The article is omitted before both "seed" and "heirs," for the Galatian believers were not the only seed, the only heirs, though they shared these privileges.

according to promise.—these are the emphatic words of the sentence, "of Abraham, seed—according to promise—heirs." Thus the apostle sums up and applies the argument developed in the section 15-22, above.

The argument of vv. 27-29 may be thus outlined: "you were baptized into Christ, therefore you put on Christ, and so you are one in Christ; you are Christ's [members], therefore you are Abraham's seed and heirs of the promises of God."

GALATIANS

CHAPTER FOUR

Verses 1–31

4:1 But I say—as at 5:16. The argument throughout has acknowledged the divine origin and the obligation of the Law. Ideally the Jews were heirs, i.e., insofar as they were Jews in spirit, children of Abraham in faith as well as children of Jacob in nationality, for "he is not a Jew, which is one outwardly; . . . but he is a Jew, which is one inwardly," Romans 2:28, 29. But there is a difference, and that difference the apostle proceeds to explain.

that so long as the heir—i.e., any heir, every heir; see note on "mediator," 3:20, above. Here also the indefinite article is, perhaps, to be preferred.

is a child,—*nēpios,* "a minor"; in the New Testament immaturity is always intended by this word. It is used of the young in years in Matthew 21:16; of those of whatever years who are unsophisticated in mind and who are of trustful disposition, Matthew 11:25; Luke 10:21; Romans 2:20; 1 Corinthians 13:11, and of the spiritually immature in 1 Corinthians 3:1; Ephesians 4:14; Hebrews 5:13. Here and in v. 3 it is used of the condition of Israel under the law.||

The corresponding verb appears in 1 Corinthians 14:20, "be not [little] children, *paidion,* in mind: howbeit in malice be ye [act as] babes, *nēpiazō,* but in mind be men" [become mature].||

he differeth nothing from a bondservant,—during the period of nonage the privileges and responsibilities of the heir are in abeyance.

though he is lord of all;—i.e., of all that has been bequeathed to him, if the father is dead, or of all that has been apportioned to him, or is intended for him, if the father is still alive. In either case the lordship is prospective, not actual yet.

4:2 but is under guardians—*epitropos,* as in Matthew 20:8; Luke 8:3, "steward," lit., "one to whose care something is committed."||

The corresponding verb, *epitropō,* is translated "permit," "give leave," "suffer"; see 1 Corinthians 14:34; 16:7; 1 Timothy 2:12, e.g., the only places of its occurrence in the Epistles of Paul. An allied noun, *epitropē,* is translated "commission" in Acts 26:12 (||), and refers to delegated authority over persons. This usage of cognate words suggests that the *epitropos* was a superior servant responsible for the persons composing the household, whether children or slaves.

and stewards—*oikonomos,* which refers rather to responsibility in things and affairs. So in Luke 16:1, 3, 8; Romans 16:23, in temporalities, and in 1 Corinthians 4:1, 2; Titus 1:7; 1 Peter 4:10, in spiritualities. A hard and fast distinction cannot always be maintained, however, since one person might exercise the functions of both the "guardian" and the "steward"; see Luke 12:42. Here, where the words are used together, the distinction is probably intended; the heir, during his minority, was in subjection both as to his person and as to his property.||

until the term appointed—*prothesmia,* = "a stipulated date."||

of the father.—two questions arise here, first, whether the apostle has in mind the Roman law of inheritance or some other; and, second, whether he contemplates the heir of a father already deceased, or the apparent heir of a father still alive. In answer to the former, it is better to suppose that the apostle had not any particular legal system in mind, that his illustration is general; and this is attested by two things, namely, that the terms he uses are not the appropriate legal terms, and that the plural "guardians and stewards" seems to be used to suggest that specific persons are not intended. In answer to the second question, there are difficulties either way; but these are largely consequent on pushing the analogy too far. If the father is assumed to be still alive, why should a term appointed to the minority be mentioned? And if he be assumed to be dead, how can he, in figure, set forth God who does not die? It is best then to read the illustration on the assumption that the father is dead, but that the analogy ceases before this point is reached.

4:3 So we also,—i.e., "we Jews," as the context, both before and after, requires the pronoun to be understood. With the condition of the Gentiles the apostle deals later, vv. 8–11, below.

when we were children,—*nēpios;* here the apostle states, in so many words, what he has implied from 3:23 onward, i.e., that while the law was in force the Jews were in a state corresponding to the state of childhood, or minority, among men; cp. "infant," used of a minor in English law.

were held in bondage—*douloō,* for which see comment on *1 Thessalonians 1:9.*

under the rudiments—*stoicheion,* which is used in the New Testament of:
   a, the substance of the material world, 2 Peter 3:10, 12;
   b, the elementary principles of religion, whether Jewish, here, or Gentile, Colossians 2:8, 20, or both, v. 9, below;
   c, the elementary principles (the "A B C") of the Old Testament as a revelation from God, Hebrews 5:12.||
   See further at v. 9.

of the world:—*kosmos,* which originally meant that which is orderly, regular, and hence, an adornment, a meaning which it retains in 1 Peter 3:3. In the New Testament *kosmos* is used of:

a, the globe, the planet earth (the Greeks used it of the universe, because of "the order observable in it"), Matthew 13:35; John 21:25;

b, the earth in contrast with heaven, 1 John 3:17, and perhaps Romans 4:13;

c, the human race, mankind, Matthew 5:14; John 7:4; 2 Peter 2:5; 3:6;

d, the Gentiles as distinguished from the Jews, Romans 11:12, 15;

e, the sum of the temporal possessions possible to man, Matthew 16:26;

f, the present order of human affairs, which is in opposition to God, John 8:23; 14:30; 1 Corinthians 2:12; Galatians 6:14; James 1:27; 1 John 5:19; the present passage and Colossians 2:8 are to be included here;

g, an expression of magnitude and variety, James 3:6.

The corresponding verb, *kosmeō,* is translated "trim" in Matthew 25:7; it appears also in Luke 21:5, of the adorning of the temple, in 1 Timothy 2:9; 1 Peter 3:5, of the adorning of the person, and in Titus 2:10 of the Christian's life as adorning the gospel.

The adverb, *kosmiōs,* is rendered "modest" in 1 Timothy 2:9, and "orderly" in 3:2, the first of women, the second of men.||

The adjective, *kosmikos,* is used in Titus 2:12 with the sense of *f,* above, "worldly lusts," and in Hebrews 9:1 with a sense approximating to that of *b,* above, "a sanctuary of this world."||

4:4 but when the fullness—*plērōma,* that which fills anything up; it is used in the New Testament of:

a, a patch on a rent, Matthew 9:16; Mark 2:21; the contents of a basket (lit., "the fullnesses of how many baskets"), Mark 8:20;

b, the plenteous harvest of the fruits of the earth, 1 Corinthians 10:26;

c, the restoration of the Jews to spiritual and national prosperity, Romans 11:12;

d, the full number, Romans 11:25;

e, that which satisfies every claim and which accomplishes every purpose, Romans 13:10 (and see 5:14, below);

f, the set time, the end of an appointed period, here, and Ephesians 1:10 (cp. Mark 1:15; Luke 1:23);

g, that which is complete, having no part omitted, Romans 15:29;

h, the grace and truth of which Christ was "full" (*plērēs,* v. 14), John 1:16; see also Ephesians 4:13;

i, God, in the completeness of His being, Colossians 1:19 (see marg.); 2:9; Ephesians 3:19;

j, the Church, which is the complement of Christ as the body is the complement of the head, Ephesians 1:23.||

of the time came,—*chronos* = time in duration, as distinguished from *kairos* (a season, v. 10, below) = time viewed in its characteristics, see comment on *1 Thessalonians* 5:1; cp. also the phrase "the consummation of the ages" in Hebrews 9:26, margin, which refers to the Cross as this refers to the Incarnation.

This moment in history (the verb is in the "point" sense) corresponds with "the term appointed" in the illustration, v. 2. That Messiah would come God had promised through the prophets, the time of that coming He had not declared; as in the new so in the old dispensation, "times and seasons the Father had set within His own authority," Acts 1:7, cp. 1 Peter 1:11. On the one hand the time fixed in the counsels of God had arrived; on the other the season was ripe, and the law had done its work among the Jews in shutting up all under sin; see Romans 3:9; 11:32, and, as profane history testifies, the Gentile world also was ripe for the coming of Him who was to be not only the Messiah of the Jews but the Savior of the world.

God sent forth His Son,—i.e., that One Who was, and from eternity had been, the Son of God. The words may not be read as though "God sent forth One Who, in His birth, became His Son" were intended; see note at 2:20, above; they declare the preexistence, the Eternal Sonship, and the essential Deity of the Lord Jesus.

born—*ginomai,* as in John 1:14, "the Word became flesh," and Philippians 2:7, "becoming (marg.) in the likeness of men." Its original meaning is "to come into a new state of being," and its earliest use in Greek writings is with reference to birth. An ancient papyrus has this sentence "she gave birth to a boy who as soon as he was born, *ginomai,* was bathed with water from the spring." In the New Testament however, the only other places where *ginoma*i = "to be born" are John 8:58 and Romans 1:3. In Matthew 11:11, as in Job 14:1, LXX, a different Greek word is used, *gennaō;* see 4:23, below.

of a woman,—these words declare the method of the Incarnation, and attest the real humanity of the Lord Jesus; while they suggest the means whereby that humanity was made free from the taint of sin consequent upon the Fall, viz., that He was not born through the natural process or ordinary generation, but was conceived by the power of the Holy Spirit.

Though the virgin birth of the Lord Jesus is not necessarily involved in the statement of the apostle here, the exclusive reference to His mother harmonizes with the records in Matthew and Luke; and see Genesis 3:15. The humanity, not the Deity, of the Lord Jesus is the subject immediately before the apostle's mind, therefore to have written "of a virgin" would have given a wrong emphasis, would have carried the argument in a wrong direction, and would not have suited his purpose so well as the word he actually uses. On the other hand, had it been possible, it would certainly have been much more effective to refer to His father in this connection, because that would have made His relation to the law quite unmistakable, and indeed would have been the natural thing to do. Hence the reference here to the mother of the Lord alone, without any reference to His father, is a not unimportant, even if it is still a subsidiary, contribution to the Biblical evidence that the virgin birth of Christ was part of "the faith once for all delivered to the saints."

The Hebrew text of Psalm 40 runs, "ears hast Thou digged for Me," as in margin of R.V., but the LXX has "a body didst Thou prepare for Me," and in this form the passage is quoted in Hebrews 10:5. The thought is the same in either case, though it is differently expressed, for whereas in the Hebrew text the part is put for the whole; i.e., if there is an ear there is, of course, a body of which that ear forms a part, in the Greek translation and in the New Testament quotation, the whole is put for the part; i.e., if there is a body it must, of course, include an ear as part thereof. The figure is synecdoche.

Since that man is of woman born is universal fact, the statement of the text would be superfluous if the Lord Jesus were no more than man. He already existed in another nature, "in the form of God," Philippians 2:6, and hence was, in a sense entirely unique, "the Son of God." Possessing this inalienable nature, He assumed, in His birth, the nature of man, "a true body and a reasonable soul," of which He is still possessed and which also is inalienable; see, e.g., such passages as 1 Timothy 2:5; 2 Timothy 2:8.

born under the law,—lit., "under law," see note on "law" at 2:16. The preceding words bring the Lord into relation with the human race, these bring Him into relation with the Jewish nation; cp. Romans 15:8, and Hebrews 2:14-18. He thus took upon Himself all the general obligations imposed by God upon mankind in the Law written in their hearts; see Romans 2:15, and the particular obligations imposed by God upon the Jews in the Law given at Sinai. The fulfillment of this Law by the Lord was the outward and evident token of His acceptance by God, and of His competence for the work He had undertaken to do.

4:5 that He might redeem—as at 3:13, above. Neither the Incarnation of the Son of God, nor His keeping of the Law in the days of His flesh availed, in whole or in part, for the redemption of men. Apart from the Incarnation death would have been impossible for Him; hence this was the condition necessary for the accomplishment of the redemption, but was itself no part of that redemption. His redemptive work proper began and ended on the Cross; accordingly the statement of the Savior's relation to sin is invariably made in terms that confine that relationship to His death. Hence it is nowhere said in the New Testament that Christ kept the law for us. Only His death is vicarious, or substitutionary. He is not said to have borne sin during any part of His life; it was at the Cross that He became the sin-bearer, 1 Peter 2:24.

The first part of Isaiah 53:4 is interpreted in Matthew 8:17, where the context in which these words are quoted makes it plain that they are to be understood not of the death of the Lord Jesus, nor of any vicarious suffering endured by Him, but of His sympathy with suffering humanity and the expression of that sympathy in the alleviation of distress wherever He came in contact with it. Some parts of Isaiah 53 do undoubtedly describe the vicarious sufferings of the Cross, as the closing part of verse 5, e.g., which is quoted in 1 Peter 2:24. These are typical illustrations of the principle that the New Testament is the only guide to the understanding of the Old Testament In the first part of Mark 10:45, e.g., the Lord declares the purpose of His life "not to be served but to serve," and of His death, "to give His life a ransom for many." His death was in harmony with His life, and was its fitting climax, but the two are here distinguished by the Lord Himself, and this distinction is observed by each of the New Testament writers.

them which were under the law,—i.e., the Jews. And if it was necessary that the Jews might be redeemed from under the law, how much more must the Gentiles not allow themselves to be brought under it when they become believers on Him Who died to accomplish that redemption! The death of Christ secures for the believer at once freedom from the curse, 3:13, and from the bondage of the law, v. 3, cp. Romans 6:14.

that—"in order that," repeated here as in 3:14, which is closely parallel with the present passage. There the consequence of the redemption accomplished by Christ is said to be blessing first for the Gentiles, and then for all; here the blessing is first said to be for the Jews, then for all.

we—i.e., "we who believe," Jews and Gentiles.

might receive the adoption of sons.—the idea of adoption is here preferred to that of birth, which has served hitherto, in order to distinguish the sonship of the believer from that of the Lord Jesus, and to remind the reader that the relationship in the former case is the result of an act of God in grace. Adoption is thus "the assumption into sonship by an act of God's grace, as distinct from the sonship that results from birth."

Huiothesia, "adoption," is a compound of two words, *huios,* "son," and *tithēmi,* "to place," and thus = "the place and condition of a son given to one to whom it does not belong by natural descent." It is used only by the apostle Paul in the New Testament. In Romans 9:4 he speaks of Israel having "the adoption as sons," with probable reference to Exodus 4:22; Hosea 11:1; but the arguments of the apostle, alike in this epistle and in that to the Romans, make it plain that the adoption of Israel was of a transient character, different from, and inferior to, the adoption of the believer in Christ. In Ephesians 1:5 he declares that the "adoption of sons" had its origin in the counsels of God, which were formed in eternity according to His own will, working uninfluenced by anything external to Himself, and that it has for its object the manifestation of His grace to the universe. Romans 8:15 is parallel with v. 6, below. Romans 8:23 represents the "adoption" of the believer as still future, and identifies it with "the redemption of the body," i.e., with the change of the living and the resurrection of the dead at the coming of the Lord; see note at 3:13*d*.||

It is significant, however, that in the New Testament the Lord is not said to have kept the law. That would be an understatement of the character of His life, for He not merely "kept the commandments of God," He always did "the things that are well pleasing in His sight," 1 John 3:22, cp. John 5:30.

There is a figure of speech (a "chiasm," see at 1:1, above) involved in vv. 4 and 5 which may be displayed thus:

a, born of a woman,

b, born under the law,

b, that He might redeem them which were under the law,

a, that we might receive the adoption of sons.

The first and fourth lines refer to mankind, without distinction of nation or race, the second and third to the Jews alone.

The parallel between v. 5 and Hebrews 9:15 is noteworthy:

a, that He might redeem

b, them which were under the law;

c, that we might receive the adoption of sons.

a, that a death having taken place for the redemption

b, of the transgressions that were under the first covenant,

c, they that have been called may receive the promise of the eternal inheritance.

The purpose of God in sending His Son is elsewhere said to be:

that the world might be saved through Him, John 3:17;

that He might give life to the world, John 6:32, 33;

that He might be an offering for sin, Romans 8:3;

that men might live through Him, 1 John 4:9;

that He might be the propitiation for our sins, 1 John 4:10;

that He might be the Savior of the world, 1 John 4:14.

In a few passages the phrase "He was manifested" is found: to put away sin by the sacrifice of Himself, Hebrews 9:26; as the Lamb of God, 1 Peter 1:19, 20; to take away sins, 1 John 3:5.

Other direct and categorical statements of the objects before the Lord Jesus in His coming into the world found in the New Testament are:

to call sinners, Matthew 9:13;

to seek and to save that which was lost, Luke 19:10;

to do the will of the Father, John 6:38, cp. Hebrews 10:7, 9;

for judgment, that they which see not may see; and that they which see might become blind, John 9:39;

that they [the sheep] might have abundant life, John 10:10;

in order to die, John 12:27, cp. Hebrews 2:9;

that whosoever believeth on Him may not abide in the darkness, John 12:46;

to bear witness to the truth, John 18:37;

to save sinners, 1 Timothy 1:15;

to die, and through death to destroy the devil, Hebrews 2:14;

to deliver those who were in fear of death, Hebrews 2:15;

to be a high priest, and so to make propitiation for sins, Hebrews 2:17.

4:6 And because ye are sons,—ordinarily the verb "to be" is not expressed in Greek, its presence here shows that the apostle intends to emphasize the fact of the present sonship of those to whom he wrote. Once more he assumes the reality of the profession of the Galatians; see note at 3:26, above. Before the question of circumcision had been raised among them they had had a certain definite experience, they had called God "Father"; but the correlative of fatherhood is sonship; only if they were actually sons of God could they address Him by this title. Plainly if the gospel as preached by Paul had brought them into the closest relationship with God, and secured for them the highest conceivable dignity, on the sole condition of faith, nothing that they could do themselves in the way of lawkeeping, and nothing that others could do for them, such as circumcision (and, of course, the same thing is true of baptism or of other religious acts) could enhance the blessings of which they were already partakers through grace.

Hoti, here rendered "because," may be taken in one or other of two senses, either, *a,* as indicating the reason why God had given His Spirit to them, or, *b,* as indicating the proof of their sonship. That the latter is the apostle's meaning is evident from two considerations. First, because the impartation of the Spirit and the introduction into sonship are alike said to be the immediate consequence of believing on Christ; see notes at 3:2, 3. And, second, because this is the meaning of Romans 8:14, where the thought is expanded into "the Spirit Himself beareth witness with our spirit, that we are children of God," v. 16. A further consideration, confirmatory of this exegesis of the apostle's words, is that his immediate purpose was not to instruct them concerning the gift and operation of the Holy Spirit, but to convince them that they were sons of God. What better proof could be adduced than this, that they themselves had received the Spirit and experienced His power?

Hoti is frequently = "that," and there is here probably an instance of the figure of speech called brachylogy, or condensation, in which case the ellipsis may be supplied from 3:11, above, "and that ye are sons is evident, for God sent forth," etc.

God sent forth—*exapostellō,* cp. Luke 24:49, where the Lord Jesus spoke of the Holy Spirit, "I send forth the promise of My Father upon you," another incidental testimony to the apostolic doctrine of the Deity of the Lord Jesus, inasmuch as He speaks of Himself as doing that which He elsewhere declares that His Father will do (John 14:16, 26), and which, in the nature of the case, only God could do. Who save God could speak of Himself as sending forth the Spirit of God?

the Spirit of His Son—i.e., the Holy Spirit, cp. Romans 8, 9, where He is called both "Spirit of God" and "Spirit of Christ," still another incidental testimony to the Deity of the Son; cp. also 1 Peter 1:11; Acts 16:7, "the Spirit of Jesus," and Philippians 1:19, "the Spirit of Jesus Christ." Cp. Isaiah 48:16, which seems to require an interpretation in accordance with this verse combined with v. 4, thus, "the Lord Jehovah hath sent Me [Messiah] and His Spirit." This is probably one of those utterances into which they who wrote them desired to look, 1 Peter 1:11, and which could be understood only in the light of the subsequent New Testament revelation. But in Hebrew and in Greek, as in English, the words are ambiguous, i.e., they may be read of the sending of Messiah by God and His Spirit, or, and more probably, as suggested above. Certainly in the New Testament the Lord Jesus is not said to have been sent by the Spirit; that He was "led by the Spirit," alike in His life and in His death, see Matthew 4:1; Hebrews 9:14, etc.

The words "Spirit of His Son" must not be taken to mean the character, purpose, or general sentiment of sonship (cp. "the spirit of Elijah," Luke 1:17), but must be understood in the sense demanded by the parallel passage in Romans 8:16, where the Spirit is said to bear witness, which is the function of a person, an intelligent and active agent.

The Holy Spirit is spoken of under various titles in the New Testament. A list of these follows. It is to be remembered that "Spirit" and "Ghost" are alternative renderings of the same Greek word, *pneuma;* the advantage of the word "Spirit" is that it can always be used, whereas "Ghost" cannot be used alone, but only with "Holy" prefixed to it. Occurrences with and without the article are distinguished below, but the reader must bear in mind that the article is sometimes necessary in English where it is absent in Greek, and sometimes must be omitted in English though it appears in Greek. Thus, e.g., in Matthew 3:16 the article is absent, but in English it must be supplied; "he saw Spirit of God descending on Him" would not be English at all. Conversely, "spirit of the grace" is not English, though it is a literal translation of the Greek words.

Spirit, Matthew 22:43;
Eternal Spirit, Hebrews 9:14;
the Spirit, Matthew 4:1;
Holy Spirit, Matthew 1:18;
the Holy Spirit, Matthew 28:19;
the Spirit, the Holy, Matthew 12:32;
the Spirit of promise, the Holy, Ephesians 1:13;
Spirit of God, Romans 8:9;
Spirit of (the) living God, 2 Corinthians 3:3;
the Spirit of God, 1 Corinthians 2:11;
the Spirit of our God, 1 Corinthians 6:11;
the Spirit of God, the Holy, Ephesians 4:30;
the Spirit of Glory and of God, 1 Peter 4:14;
the Spirit of Him that raised up Jesus from the dead (i.e., of God), Romans 8:11;
the Spirit of your Father, Matthew 10:20;
the Spirit of His Son, here;
Spirit of (the) Lord, Acts 8:39;
the Spirit of (the) Lord, Acts 5:9;
(the) Lord, (the) Spirit, 2 Corinthians 3:18;
the Spirit of Jesus, Acts 16:7;

Spirit of Christ, Romans 8:9;
the Spirit of Jesus Christ, Philippians 1:19;
Spirit of adoption, Romans 8:15;
the Spirit of truth, John 14:17;
the Spirit of life, Romans 8:2;
the Spirit of grace, Hebrews 10:29.

into our hearts,—for analysis of the New Testament use of this word see comment on *1 Thessalonians* 2:4.

crying,—i.e., the Spirit cries; the tense is present continuous; cp. Romans 8:15, "the Spirit of adoption whereby we cry." The Spirit makes His abode in the heart of the believer, or, as in 1 Corinthians 6:19, in his body; and so intimate is the relationship between the divine Spirit and the human spirit in the regenerate, that what is said in one place of the former is said in another place of the latter. It is the action of the Spirit of the Son on the spirits of the sons that enables them to cry, Abba! Father! Cp. Romans 8:26, 27.

Abba,—properly an Aramaic word, but one which appears in most languages in a form somewhat similar, cp. English "papa," e.g. It occurs again in Mark 14:36; Romans 8:15. In the Gemara (a rabbinical commentary on the Mishna, or traditional teaching of the Jews) it is stated that slaves were forbidden to address by this title the head of the family to which they belonged.||

Father.—*patēr,* the Greek equivalent of "Abba." Christ taught His disciples to address God as their Father, Matthew 6:9, e.g., and gives them His Spirit to enable them so to do.
   "Father" is not to be read in any of these three places as a translation of "Abba," supplied for the sake of readers ignorant of Aramaic. "Abba" seems rather to approximate to a personal name, while "Father" is, lit., "the Father" *(ho patēr),* and hence may be rendered "Abba, our Father." The words are to be taken together as the expression of the love and intelligent confidence of the child. "Abba" is the word framed by the feeble lips of the infant; it expresses simple unreasoning trust, the outcome of feeling rather than of knowledge. "Father" is the word of maturity, the considered expression of a relationship intelligently realized.
   To call God, Father! means more than merely to address Him by that name. It means that he who so invokes Him trusts and obeys Him also. It is the word of communion, the confidence and obedience of the son meeting its response in the complacent love of the Father, John 14:23. The Lord Jesus called Him, "Abba, Father," and lived the ideal filial life. He trusted God, Psalm 22:9, saying, "Thy will be done," and "the cup which the Father hath given Me, shall I not drink it?" Matthew 26:42; John 18:11. He obeyed God, learning in suffering what obedience is, Hebrews 5:8, and saying, "Lo, I am come to do Thy will," and "I do always the things that are pleasing to Him," Hebrews 10:9; John 8:29. He lived in unclouded communion with God, saying "I and the Father are One,"

and "I am in the Father, and the Father in Me," John 10:30; 14:11. Into this life of communion with the Father and the Son the sons of God are introduced by the Holy Spirit in order that the prayer of the Lord may be fulfilled, "that they may be one even as We are One," John 17:11, 22. How different this, the effect of the true gospel, and that state of bondage into which the false gospel of the Judaizing ritualists would inevitably bring them! See comment on *1 Thessalonians* 1:1.

4:7 So that—*hōste* = "with the effect that," it is translated "insomuch" at 2:13, above; here it marks the climax of the argument and introduces a direct and personal application thereof to those to whom it was addressed. The argument itself is twofold: first, the general proposition, their minority was at an end; second, the experimental fact, they had received the Spirit.

thou—the singular still further marks the climax and the narrowing down of the argument to its personal application, thus: v. 5, "we" "we Jews and Gentiles alike"; v. 6, "ye," "you Galatian believers"; v. 7, "thou," any and every one of you individually. This use of the singular pronoun in addressing a church is not without parallel in Paul's writings; see Romans 11:17; 1 Corinthians 4:7, and 6:1, below. "Thou, being a believer on Christ, having received and responded to the Holy Spirit, trusting God as Father, and obeying Him."

art no longer—i.e., though you once were.

a bondservant,—i.e., under bondage to law, being a Jew, v. 3, above, or to idols, being a Gentile, v. 8, below.
    When God through the gospel frees men from bondage to law or to idols, as the case may be, He appropriates to Himself those whom He so delivers; henceforth they are His bondservants, Romans 6:22, that is, they are Christ's, 1 Corinthians 7:22, or, as otherwise expressed, they become "servants of righteousness." True freedom is not liberty to do wrong, it is liberty to do right. Therefore it is that only as a man becomes the bondservant of the Lord Jesus Christ does he find himself free in the best sense of the word.

but a son;—i.e., not merely a child of God, though that certainly, but a child come to the full consciousness of his relationship with his Father through the operation of the Spirit; see at 3:26, above.

and if a son, then an heir—see note at 3:29, above, and cp. Romans 8:17, "if children then heirs."

through God.—cp. 1:1; the categorical statement that sonship involves heirship, that all sons are heirs, is confirmed by these added words, for men become sons and heirs of God not through efforts of their own but solely through the acts of the Triune God: the Father Who sent the Son, v. 4, the Son Who died to free us from bondage, v. 5, the Spirit Who quickened us into life, v. 6. Neither natural birth nor meritorious works avail here.

It is plain from these words that the apostle not only enjoyed the assurance of his own salvation, but that he assumed his readers to be in the enjoyment of a similar assurance of their relationship with God. To know God is to acknowledge His Fatherhood; to be known of God is to be acknowledged as His sons. All this is set out here and elsewhere in Scripture, not as a hope, a possibility of the future, but as a present fact, an actual and gracious experience for the comfort and encouragement of all who trust in Christ. "Hereby know we [*ginōskō*, have come to know] that we abide in Him [God], and He in us, because He hath given us of His Spirit," 1 John 4:13.

4:8 Howbeit—now the apostle turns to the Gentile element in the Galatian churches, reminding them of their state before the gospel reached them, and set them free from a bondage different from, but not less real than, that in which the Jews had been held, and appealing to them not to return thereto. "Howbeit," lit., "but," sets the two conditions, their former pagan bondage and their present Christian freedom, in strong contrast.

at that time,—i.e., before their conversion under the preaching of the gospel by Paul and his fellow missionaries, cp. Romans 6:21.

not knowing—*oida*, see at 2:9, above.

God,—the same description of the heathen appears in 1 Thessalonians 4:5; 2 Thessalonians 1:8, where see notes. In 1 Corinthians 1:21 and 1 John 4:8 the word translated "know" is *ginōskō*. The difference in the ideas expressed by the different words may be shown in a paraphrase, thus: "He that does not exhibit love in his dealings with his fellows makes it plain that he has not come to know God, whatever he may profess, for God in His very nature is love," 1 John 4:8. "The world by means of its wisdom did not get to know God, whatever else they may have got to know," 1 Corinthians 1:21. In these passages failure to realize an aim is the idea. Here, and in the verses in the Epistles to Thessalonians, the mere fact is stated, they were not acquainted with God.

Before the Fall man lived in the knowledge of God his Creator, Romans 1:21, but that knowledge was gradually lost to him altogether since he deliberately resigned and refused it, v. 28. Even so, the handiwork of God everywhere testifies to His being and power, cp. Psalm 19:1, so that man, albeit alienated from the life of God through the ignorance that had come to be ingrained in him, Ephesians 4:18, is without excuse that he does not get to know, *ginōskō*, God, Romans 1:19, 20.

In John 17:25 the world of which the Lord speaks is primarily that part of it with which He was then in immediate contact, and which was tested by His presence in it, namely, the Jewish nation. To them the oracles of God had been committed, Romans 3:2, and to them God had manifested Himself in Christ; even so they also, with all these advantages and opportunities, had not come to know, *ginōskō*, God.

ye were in bondage to them which by nature are no gods:—i.e., idols, concerning which see extended note, comment on *1 Thessalonians* 1:9. "Nature," *phusis,* is the emphatic word here, and in this statement the apostle includes demons, 1 Corinthians 10:20, and deified men, as well as idols; for these are gods, not in themselves, but as they have been made such by men, and hence are gods in name only. The negative used here, *mē*, does not merely deny the fact that these aforetime objects of their worship were gods, it denies the possibility that they could be gods; see 2 Chronicles 13:9.

4:9 but now—i.e., since their conversion through the gospel; in contrast with "at that time," above.

that ye have come to know God,—*ginōskō,* as above. This knowledge had been attained not by their own intellectual activities, neither as a result of progress toward moral excellence, but through the operation of the Spirit consequent on their acceptance of Christ; see John 17:3, where there is a brachylogy (a figure of speech in which the thought is greatly condensed) which, with part of v. 2, included to make the connection clear, may be paraphrased thus: "to them He gives eternal life, and this is the gift of eternal life [i. e., for this end was it given] in order that they should know Thee the only true God and Thy sent One, Jesus Christ." Eternal life is the new divine nature of which the believer is made partaker in the new birth, 2 Peter 1:4, and to which alone the faculty by which God is known belongs. This knowledge of God is not an attainment marked by finality, it is rather the beginning of such an understanding of the infinite One as may be possible to His finite creatures in virtue of their spiritual endowment in Christ. The prophets called upon Israel to know, to "follow on to know the Lord," Hosea 6:3; the apostle, in like manner, exhorts the Christian to "grow in the . . . knowledge of our Lord and Savior Jesus Christ," 2 Peter 3:18. The words of the Lord Himself make it plain, of course, that the knowledge of Christ is the knowledge of God, cp. John 14:8-10.

or rather to be known of God,—here *ginōskō* includes the idea of approval, and hence bears the meaning "to be acknowledged." In this sense God is said to know those who put their trust in Him, Nahum 1:7, and those who love Him, 1 Corinthians 8:3, and those who belong to Him, 2 Timothy 2:19; with this last cp. John 10:14, 27. These words are added apparently to emphasize the fact that the salvation they had experienced was due to God, not to themselves in any way. For an interesting parallel to the double statement of the apostle here, see John 1:43, where the Lord finds Philip, and v. 45 where Philip says "we have found Him."

how—i.e., "how comes it about that," cp. 2:14.

turn ye back—see note at 1 Thessalonians 1:9; the Thessalonians had turned to God; it seemed as though the Galatians were about to turn away from Him, cp. 1:6, above. Here, as there, the tense is present continuous = "how are ye turning?" Cp. 2 Corinthians 3:16.

again—*palin*, see at the end of the verse.

to the weak—*asthenes*, i.e., powerless to produce results; an epithet elsewhere applied to the law and in the same sense, Romans 8:3; Hebrews 7:18. Neither the Divinely appointed moral code and symbolic ritual of the Jew, nor the idolatry of the Gentile (the product of human reason and imagination at its best, Is. 44:9-20, the inspiration of demons at its worst, 1 Cor. 10:20) could deliver man from condemnation, justify him, or make him live; see 3:21, above. To the accomplishment of such ends as these no religious system has any power at all, and yet these are the profoundest needs of mankind. With this weakness contrast, "the exceeding greatness of His [God's] power to usward who believe," Ephesians 1:19, "the power of Christ," 2 Corinthians 12:9, "the power of the Holy Spirit," Romans 15:13.

and beggarly—*ptōchos*, (translated "poor" at 2:10, above, i.e., powerless) to enrich. Without spiritual wealth, without an inheritance, present or prospective, without any gift of life or of the Spirit, these religions of childhood, v. 1, and of bondage, were "poverty-stricken" indeed and could give nothing, for they had nothing to give. With this poverty contrast the riches of God "in glory," Romans 9:23, "in grace," Ephesians 1:7, "in wisdom and knowledge," Romans 11:33, all which, with much more beside, are "the unsearchable riches of Christ," Ephesians 3:8.

rudiments,—as at v. 3, where see note. This is the word which served to sum up the religion of the Jews, and which serves now to sum up the religion of the Gentiles. Different as these were in their origin and in their characteristics, they had this in common, an incurable inefficiency and incompetence for meeting the needs of men and for bridging the gulf that yawned between men and God.

whereunto ye desire—*thelō*, for which see comment on *1 Thessalonians* 2:18; 4:3; 5:18 and cp. John 5:40, "ye will not come to Me," or rather, for the word is the same, "ye do not desire to come to Me," and 7:17, "if any man willeth [desireth] to do His Will"; so also in Matthew 19:17, 21; 2 Timothy 3:12, e.g.

to be in bondage—in the best texts the tense is momentary = "to enter into bondage"; cp. Acts 15:10, "a yoke . . . which neither our fathers nor we were able to bear."

over again?—*palin* (which is translated "again" earlier in the verse, and is of frequent occurrence), *anōthen* (which does not occur elsewhere in Paul's Epistles). Luke uses *anōthen* of the starting point of his careful investigations into the earthly history of the Lord Jesus, 1:3, and, in a similar sense, of the Jews' knowledge of Paul's life story, Acts 26:5. Matthew 27:51, and Mark 15:38, use it of the rending of the veil of the temple "from the top," and John of the weaving of the seamless coat, 19:23; James uses it of heaven, the dwelling place of God, 1:17; 3:15, 17; so does John, 3:31 (where "He that cometh from above" and "He that cometh from Heaven" are alternative descriptions of Christ), 19:11 (where not imperial Rome but heaven—by metonymy for God who dwells there—is intended).

The usage in other parts of John's Gospel would perhaps be decisive in favor of the margin "from above" in 3:3, 7, but that the words of Nicodemus, v. 4, show that he understood them as meaning "born anew." Here also not "again" but "anew" is the apostle's thought, for though the bondage would be the same in essence and in effect, it would be new in that it would be no longer bondage to idols but to the law—the old bondage, in fact, but to a new master.||

4:10 Ye observe—*paratēreō*, a strengthened form of the verb *tēreō*, "to keep" (see comment on *2 Thessalonians* 5:23) is used, = "to observe carefully," cp. Psalm 130:3, where LXX has the same word; the middle voice suggests that this punctilious respect for days, etc., was with a view to their own profit and not from any disinterested motive. What the apostle now says is equally applicable to Jews and Gentiles, but the days, etc., are Jewish festivals; the apostle does not suggest that the Galatians were in danger of returning to idolatry, he is furnishing proof of the suggestion conveyed in his question, "how turn ye back again to the weak and beggarly rudiments?"

days,—i.e., the weekly sabbaths; see Romans 14:5; Colossians 2:16.

and months,—i.e., the new moons; see 1 Chronicles 23:31.

and seasons,—i.e., the three annual feasts of the Jews, see 2 Chronicles 8:13 where, in LXX, "times" is *kairos,* the word used here; see comment on *1 Thessalonians* 5:1 and Leviticus 23:4.

and years.—i.e., Sabbatic years, and years of jubilee; see Leviticus 25:1–8.

While it is probable that these were the occasions in the mind of the apostle when he wrote, still they must not be taken in a too literal sense, as though, e.g., the Galatians had actually been observing a year of jubilee. If they observed the least of them they acknowledged the principle, it was as though they observed all. Heretofore the apostle had mentioned circumcision only as indicative of the declension of these believers, but of course they could not draw the line at that; once they put themselves under the law, they became debtors to do all the law enjoined, see 5:3, below. Moreover, the religious observance of days is inconsistent with the spirit of the gospel; to keep a day is a tacit admission that that day is, in some sense, holier than other days, whereas, to the Christian, every day is holy.

This subject is dealt with from another point of view in Romans 14. There the apostle gives counsel as to the treatment of brethren who had a conscience in such matters, and to whom he speaks as "weak in faith." These, he declares, are the objects of the redeeming love of Christ, v. 15, the work of God, v. 20,

His servants, v. 4, and their brethren, v. 10. Moreover, weak though they may be, the conscience of such is "consciousness of God" (1 Peter 2:19, marg.), v. 6. Plainly, therefore, they are not to be denied the privileges of Christian fellowship, 15:7, even though they are, on account of this weakness of faith, unable to share the full burden of Christian responsibility, 14:1. Nor are such to be held in contempt or otherwise grieved, v. 15, or judged, v. 13; rather are they to be encouraged and considered, that all may be edified, v. 19. The strength of Christ is manifest in this that He bears with the weaknesses of the strong among His people; their strength is to be manifested in bearing with the weak among themselves, 15:1-3.

In Colossians 2:16 the matter is approached from yet another standpoint. The apostle warns the believers against permitting anyone to judge them in respect of these very things, meaning thereby, primarily, "let no one judge you for refusing to observe them," see v. 17; but that complete liberty which is secured to all in the gospel is best asserted absolutely, "let no one judge you either way." Liberty is either liberty for all or is not liberty at all.

4:11 1 am afraid of you,—apparently = "I am apprehensive about you": the words testify, *a*, to his sense of their danger, and *b*, to his deep interest in them.

lest by any means—as at 2:2.

I have bestowed labor upon you—*kopiaō;* see comment on *1 Thessalonians* 5:12. Cp. Romans 16:6. The measure of his apprehension about them is seen in this that he does not say "lest I should have," but "lest I have"; his labor was a fact, the result of it was contingent on their loyalty to what they had learned at the outset.

in vain.—as in 3:4.

4:12 *I* beseech you, brethren,—*deomai,* a word which is also used of prayer to God. After reasoning comes expostulation, after expostulation appeal. Much of the section thus introduced is occupied with reminiscences of the writer's first visit to the Galatians, and as there is no history of the circumstances to which the apostle refers, it is somewhat difficult to follow the connection of the thought. It is clear, however, that the relations between them had been of an unusually cordial character, and on this fact his appeal is based. He would have them think of him as one of themselves, so he calls them "brethren."

be as I *am*, for I *am* as ye are.—"*be*" is, lit., "become," and this suggests the rendering "become as I am, for I became as ye were," i.e., "I was once zealous for the law, [1:14], but I laid its supposed advantages, and my lifelong prejudice in its favor, [cp. Phil. 3:7], in order to take my place beside you Gentiles: now I appeal to you who have put yourselves under the law, or who contemplate doing so, to take your place beside me—be ye free as I am free," cp. 1 Corinthians 9:21.

Ye did me no wrong:—anticipating a possible suggestion that the vigor of the apostle's language was due to some personal grievance. The point tense shows that he has in mind the occasion of his first visit to them. The emphasis is on "no," lit., "in nothing did ye do me an injustice." Cp. 2 Corinthians 12, 13 where the apostle is ironical.

4:13 but ye know that—on the contrary, so far from doing him any injury that he might resent, he reminds them that the circumstances under which they first met were such as rather to put him under obligation to them, because of the kindness with which they treated him when his sickness might very well have repelled them.

because of an infirmity—another form of the word translated "weak" in v. 9, above.

of the flesh—i.e., some bodily ailment, of what nature is not stated, hence it is vain to speculate about it; see Intro. Note.

I preached the gospel unto you the first time:—lit., "I evangelized you the former time," see margin; i.e., on the former of two previous visits; see Intro. Note. His visit to the Galatian cities had not been premeditated, it was an indirect consequence of his illness.

4:14 and that which was a temptation to you in my flesh—this language suggests that the "infirmity," whatever it was, was of a kind to arouse feelings of repugnance in those with whom the sufferer came in contact. For "temptation" see extended note, comment on *1 Thessalonians* 3:5; here, as in most places of its occurrence, *peirasmos* = "trial."

ye despised not,—*excutheneō,* as in 1 Thessalonians 5:20; they had not treated him as the Jews, Acts 4:11, and as Herod and his soldiery, Luke 23:11, treated the Lord, and as the self-righteous treat other men, 18:9.

nor rejected;—*ekptuō,* lit., "to spit out"; so margin. The sentence is elliptical: "although my disease repelled you, you did not on that account refuse to hear my message."||

but—*alla* = "on the contrary."

ye received me—*dechomai,* translated "accepted" in 1 Thessalonians 2:13, where see note.

as an angel of God,—i.e., as a messenger from another world; see comment on *2 Thessalonians* 1:7.

even **as Christ Jesus.**—there is an ellipsis to be supplied here, "as ye would receive Christ Jesus," the messenger of God and Lord of all the angels. When the apostle first visited the Galatians they knew nothing of God or His angels or of Christ Jesus; but they had received him as they would have received Them had they known of Them. This is an instance of the rhetorical figure "climax," the effect of the words is heightened by the advance from "angel" to "Christ."

4:15 Where then is that gratulation of yourselves?—*makarismos,* which is translated "blessing" in Romans 4:6, 9. They had counted themselves happy when they heard the gospel from his lips. What had become of that spirit which animated them not so long ago? Cp. 1:6, above.||

for I bear your witness, that, if possible, ye would have plucked out your eyes and given them to me.—sufficient proof, indeed, of their sense of gratitude to the apostle and of their consequent love for him. The words have been understood as suggesting that the "infirmity" of which he speaks was an affection of the eyes, and some have found support for this theory in the blindness that ensued on the vision at the time of his conversion, and also in the incident recorded in Acts 23:1-5. All this is precarious and highly speculative at the best. Nor does it matter either way. The same is to be said of the identification of this "infirmity" with the "thorn in the flesh" of 2 Corinthians 12:7. Had "ye" been the emphasized word, as it is not, the sentence might have been understood to suggest an affection of the eyes, but the emphasis is on "eyes"; they would have parted with their most precious possession, see Deuteronomy 32:10, had there been any possibility of his profiting by the gift. As to the blindness on the way to Damascus, that was supernaturally inflicted and was complete; so with the cure, that also was the direct act of God, and so cannot have been other than complete.

4:16 So then am I become your enemy,—at the close of Acts 21:36 the words "down with our enemy" appear in some ancient authorities, and while it is not probable that they formed part of the original history, as written by Luke, yet they do probably represent a very early tradition. It is possible that "enemy" is a quotation from some report that had reached Paul of what his detractors had said; he seems to be intended by the word in the following passage from the *Clementine Homilies* (*circa* A.D. 160–188), the writer of which was a bitter opponent of the teaching of the apostle: "Some of the Gentiles . . . have accepted the lawless and foolish teaching of an enemy."

because I tell you the truth?—*alēthenō* = "to deal faithfully, or truly, with anyone," as in Ephesians 4:15. The idea of integrity of conduct as well as of truthfulness of speech is included in the word, see Genesis 42:16, LXX, "whether ye deal truly or no." Some reason there must be for their changed attitude toward him, so he partly asks, partly exclaims incredulously, "Can this be the consequence of my plain dealing with you, that you look upon me no longer as a friend but actually as an enemy, as one hostile to you?"||

"Tell the truth" is in the present continuous sense; it is possible that the reference is to something he had said to them on his second visit, but more probably he speaks of the contents of this letter. Cp. the Lord's description of

Himself as "a Man that hath told you the truth," John 8:40, and the proverb "faithful are the wounds of a friend," Proverbs 27:6.

4:17 They zealously seek you—*zēloō* (which is probably derived from a word meaning "to boil") is sometimes used in a bad sense = to be jealous, as in Acts 7:9; 17:5; to envy, 1 Corinthians 13:4; to covet, James 4:2; sometimes in a good sense = to desire earnestly, 1 Corinthians 12:31; 14:1, 39. In 2 Corinthians 11:2 *zēloō* = "to take a warm interest in," a meaning which suits the word here and in v. 18.||

in no good way;—*kalōs,* see comment on *1 Thessalonians* 5:21, i.e., the motives and the methods of the Judaizers were neither worthy in themselves nor were they calculated, nor intended, to further the true interests of the Galatian converts. The contrast suggested is between one who dealt plainly with them for the sake of their welfare and those who paid them court with other ends in view. He had proved his love for them in a way not to be mistaken; what proof of love or of any real interest in them had these would-be teachers offered?

This is just the difference between proselytizing and evangelizing; in the one there is zeal for a creed, in the other for a person. The Judaizers paid court to the Galatians in order to attach them to a party; Paul took an interest in them in order that he might win them to, and preserve them for, Christ.

nay,—*alla* = "but," "on the contrary," i.e., not in a good but in an evil way; as soon as by flattery and pretended interest they had succeeded in inducing the Galatian believers to submit to the yoke of the law their real intention would become manifest. The apostle had readily discerned what that was, namely, to deprive them of the freedom which they had in Christ, and to establish a lordship over their faith.

they—this is the first direct reference to the Judaizers since 1:7.

desire to shut you out,—i.e., as Gentiles, from the scope of the promises of God and so from Christ, from salvation, and from Christian fellowship. *Ekkleiō,* as in Romans 3:27.||

that ye may seek them.—If the Judaizers could persuade the converts, who had been taught that faith in Christ alone was necessary for salvation, that circumcision and submission to the law were also essential, the effect would inevitably be just what the apostle here describes. They must turn to their new teachers for that assurance of salvation which, they would suppose, the gospel as preached by Paul could not supply.

4:18 But—or, "however," introducing a general reflection intended to obviate the deduction from what had just been said, that the apostle was unwilling that anyone but himself should show an interest in them.

it is good—*kalos,* "admirable."

to be zealously sought—i.e., to be the object of a warm interest on the part of others.

in a good matter—*kalos;* always provided that the interest taken is of a healthy character and for a worthy end, as it was not in this case, for the Judaizers paid court to them "in no good way," v. 17. Cp. the "godly jealousy" of the apostle for the believers at Corinth, 2 Corinthians 11:2.

at all times, and not only when I am present with you.—the apostle, having an understanding in the ways of God, that one sows and another reaps, that one plants and another waters, that one lays a foundation and another builds thereon, and having also the spiritual welfare of the converts truly at heart, was glad that others as well as he should labor among them. His opposition to the Judaizers was not a merely unworthy jealousy lest any other servant of Christ should gain a place in the esteem and affection of those to whom he had brought the knowledge of Christ. From such pettiness his mind was happily free; cp. his language in 1 Corinthians 3:5 and in Philippians 1:15–18. True ministry of the true gospel he could only encourage, but those who would lead the converts away therefrom must be vigilantly and unrelentingly opposed. That the apostle's own interest in them had not ceased with his labors among them the present letter was sufficient evidence.

"With,"—*pros,* as at 1:18, above.

4:19 My little children,—*teknion* (a diminutive of *teknon,* for which see comment on *1 Thessalonians* 5:5, and at 3:26, above) is found here only in the letters of the apostle Paul. In the New Testament it occurs only in the plural, and in each place is a term of affection used by a teacher to his disciples under circumstances calling for tender appeal:

The Lord Jesus knew that He spoke to the Twelve for the last time before His death, John 13:33.

John was very old and yearned over the believers in view of the dangers that threatened their faith, 1 John 2:1, 12, 28; 3:7, 18; 4:4; 5:21.

Paul, as his whole letter shows, was deeply moved by the unscrupulous attack made upon the faith of the Galatian believers.||

Paul also uses *teknon* of his own spiritual children, whom he addresses with the tender solicitude of a parent, as in 1 Corinthians 4:14,15; 2 Timothy 1:2; Philemon 10; see comment on *1 Thessalonians* 2:11.

of whom I am—in travail—*ōdinō,* as in v. 27 and Revelation 12:2.|| Cp. the corresponding noun, *odin,* in 1 Thessalonians 5:3 and the somewhat similar metaphor in Colossians 2:1.

again—as once before he had labored for their souls when he preached the gospel to them at the first. Then his travail was for their deliverance from bondage to idols, v. 8, now it was for their deliverance from the formal and external religion of the Jews, v. 9. There is a suggestion of reproach in his words, as though he would ask them whether they had ever heard of a mother enduring the birth pangs twice for her children. There is no thought here of a second regeneration necessitated by their defection; for one reason because the apostle does not charge them with having actually turned away from the true gospel, but only with being in danger of doing so; see note at 3:26, above. He is thinking not so much of their need as of his own labor among them, and of the possibility of its proving abortive, and of his apprehensions on their account, now unhappily renewed; see 1 Thessalonians 3:5.

until Christ be formed in you,—*morphoō*.|| When the apostle brought the gospel to the Galatian cities, his aim was not merely to induce men to change their religion, to forsake polytheism, the worship of many gods, for monotheism, the worship of one God; it was that they might receive life in Christ. So now his anxiety on their account was not merely that they should be intellectually persuaded of, and confirmed in, the true nature of the gospel and its conditions, but that the new life therein imparted might grow in them. Doctrine is not something alien from life. What a man believes affects his character and his conduct. Doctrine that exalts Christ makes for holiness; doctrine that detracts from the excellence of His person, or from the completeness and sufficiency of His sacrifice, hinders, or prevents, the work of the Holy Spirit in the believer, which work is carried on by the presentation of Christ, in His essential deity, in His true manhood, in His perfect salvation; see John 16:13–15. The fatal defect of the doctrine of the Judaizers was that, by making something besides acceptance of Christ necessary to the obtaining of the promises, they presented a defective Savior. That Christ is supreme, Romans 9:5; sufficient, Colossians 1:19; "all and in all," 3:11, nothing less than this is the apostle's claim. But if on this point the Galatians were misled, how could they experience the power of truth they denied? To submit to circumcision, to seek justification by law, was to be severed from Christ and to lose all that the gospel offered, see 5:2–4, below. To trust Christ, and to trust Him alone, was to be justified from all things indeed, see Romans 3:28; 8:31–34; but more, it was to be "a new creation," 2 Corinthians 5:17, to live in Christ, and to have Christ living in the heart; see 2:20, above. Growth, moreover, is the evidence of life, and this the apostle desired for his converts that they might "all attain . . . unto a full-grown man, unto the measure of the stature of the fullness of Christ," that they might "grow up in all things into . . . Christ," Ephesians 4:13–15. How this is to be accomplished may be learned from his prayer that Christ might dwell in their hearts through faith, 3:17, and from the exhortation of Philippians 2:5, "Have this mind in you which was also in Christ Jesus." For as the exercise of faith occupies the heart with Christ the mind of Christ develops in the believer, and as a direct result of these inward processes his conduct is increasingly conformed to the example of Christ.

"That Christ may be formed in you" is, then, the desire of the apostle for the moral conformity of the believer to Christ here and now. The thought is similar to, or identical with, that of Philippians 3:10, "becoming conformed to His death." But conformity to Christ, though it begins in the moral sphere, does not end there. In due time, that which is now inward and spiritual will extend also to that which is outward and physical, for "the body of our humiliation" will, at the coming of the Lord, be "conformed to the body of His glory," Philippians 3:21.

The apostle's mind here, however, is not so much on the future, and the final outcome in them of faith in Christ, as it is that he longs for some present and satisfying evidence to confirm his confidence that God had indeed begun a good work in them; if he were only assured of that the ultimate issue would not be in doubt; see Philippians 1:6. But the ordinance of God is that the believer must enter into willing cooperation with Him for his own perfecting into the image of His Son; see Romans 8:28, 29, marg. The formation of Christ in the believer is at once the purpose of God and the ambition, inwrought by the Spirit, of all who are taught of Him.

With *morphoō* may be compared *metamorphoō*, which occurs in Matthew 17:2; Mark 9:2, of the change in the appearance of the Lord described by Luke in the words "the fashion of His countenance was altered," 9:29. The word *morphoō*, it is important to note, does not refer to what is outward and transient, but to what is inward and real. Hence on the Mount of Transfiguration that glory which was His own, essentially and eternally, shone out for a moment through the veil that concealed it during the days of His flesh. *Metamorphoō* occurs also in Romans 12:2 and in 2 Corinthians 3:18. The former of these passages reads, "And be not fashioned [*suschēmatizo* = to be made to resemble, as in 1 Pet. 1:14] according to this age: but be ye transformed by the renewing of your mind." Here an outward change in the character and conduct of the believer, to correspond with his inward spiritual condition, is intended. The second passage reads, "We all . . . are [being] transformed into the same image."||*

4:20 yea, I could wish—cp. Acts 25:22; Romans 9:3; though the word translated "could wish" is different in each place, the tense is the same. He was willing to come to them, but was unable to do so, therefore the ellipsis to be supplied is not "but I do not," it is "if that were possible."

The American Revisers suggest the substitution of a — for the comma after "yea," the better to represent the emotion of the apostle as he contemplated the danger in which his converts stood. He is not arguing with them, he is appealing to them.

to be present with you—"with" is *pros* as in v. 18, above; here he reverts to what he had said there.

_____

*The noun *morphē*, which corresponds to the verb *morphoō*, occurs in Mark 16:12; Philippians 2:6, 7, of the Lord Jesus in each case. It is impossible to deal incidentally with passages of such vital importance to sound doctrine concerning the person of Christ.||

now,—this is the emphatic word: "now, at this critical juncture in your spiritual history when the future of the work of the gospel in Galatia hangs in the balance." How much better it would be were he able to speak with them, how much more effective the voice than the pen!

and to change—*allassō*, = "to alter": said of the effect of the gospel upon the ordinances of the law, Acts 6:14; and of the effect of the return of Christ on the body of the believer, 1 Corinthians 15:51, 52, and of the ultimate renewal of the material creation, Hebrews 1:12. In Romans 1:23 *allassō*, = "to exchange," is used of the departure of the human race from God.||

my voice;—i.e., he desired to be able to speak to them with confidence in their fidelity to the true gospel, instead of with the mingled apprehension, expostulation, severity and appeal of this letter. This he could do only if they were to turn away altogether from their new teachers. He longed to be able to say to the Galatian believers as he was able to say to those at Corinth, "I rejoice that in everything I am of good courage concerning you," 2 Corinthians 7:16, cp. 1:23—2:4.

for I am perplexed about you.—*aporeomai*, lit., "to be without a way in which to go," and so = to be puzzled, to be at a loss what to think or what to do, as Jacob was about his brother Esau, Genesis 32:7; as Herod was about the Baptist, Mark 6:20; as the disciples were about the words of the Lord, John 13:22, and about the absence of His body from the tomb, Luke 24:4; as Festus was about the trial of Paul, Acts 25:20. That this perplexity about the best way to succor the Galatians was not an exceptional experience; see 2 Corinthians 4:8.||

Apostle though he was, Paul was not exempt from the trials that attend the servants of Christ, and this was equally true of external experiences, persecutions and the like, and of experiences of the mind and heart, perplexities included; see 2 Corinthians 11:28. He who lives by faith, 2:20, must walk by faith, 2 Corinthians 5:7, and he who walks and serves by faith knows, indeed, that the end is sure, but knows not the intermediate steps. Information concerning the future of any particular believer, or of any particular church, was not vouchsafed to the apostle. There was always room for fear of the worst to stimulate him to fresh labors, see 1 Thessalonians 3:5, 10, always room for hope of the best to give him confidence that those labors would not be in vain; see 1 Thessalonians 5:23, 24, and cp. Philippians 1:6, 7.

4:21 Tell me, ye that desire to be under the law,—i.e., the law of Moses; see at 2:16, above. The apostle now adopts a new line of argument. Earlier in the Epistle he had reasoned with them concerning justification and the reception of the Holy Spirit, 3:1-14, the nature of a covenant and the relation of the law to the promises, 15-29; now he appeals to an episode in the family history of Abraham, discerning in it an esoteric, that is to say, an inward, or mystic, significance. The Judaizers appealed to the Old Testament, so would he. They boasted in their descent from Abraham; he would show them how the superiority of the promise to the law, of faith to natural descent, was latent in the very foundation of Abraham's line. They claimed to have in their keeping the key to the Scriptures; he would show them once more that the true key was to be found in the gospel.

do ye not hear the law?—the story to which the apostle is about to refer is related in Genesis 16—18:15 and 21:1-21. "The Law" here, then, is not the moral and ceremonial code contained in the other books of the Pentateuch, but is either, *a,* the Pentateuch itself, as in Romans 3:21, or, *b,* the Old Testament as a whole, as in v. 19 (the quotations there grouped under this title are taken from Ps., Prov., and Is.); it does not seem to make any material difference whether the word is understood here in its wider or in its more limited sense. With *a,* cp. "the Book of the law," 3:10, and with *b,* "the Scripture," 3:8, above.

The question also may be taken in one of two ways, either, *a,* as = "is not the law continually read in your hearing?" cp. Acts 15:21; 2 Corinthians 3:14; or, *b,* as = "do ye not pay attention to the law when it is read to you?" cp. Matthew 13:13, 43, Luke 16:29. The meaning of the apostle may, perhaps, be expressed in a paraphrase: "You who are attracted by the teaching of the Judaizers and desire to come under the Mosaic Law, do you need to listen to their reasoning and to their deductions? Are you not accustomed yourselves to hear the Scriptures read? Then let me give you an illustration, drawn from a story with which you are familiar, of what that bondage which you desire so much will do for you."

4:22 For it is written,—see note at 3:10; this form of words ordinarily introduces a quotation from Old Testament; here it introduces a brief summary of an Old Testament history.

that Abraham had two sons,—Ishmael and Isaac.

one by the handmaid,—Hagar, an Egyptian, servant to Sarah and mother of Ishmael. *Paidiskē* is used only of a maidservant in the New Testament, and so in Genesis 16, but in Ruth 4:12 it occurs of the young widow of Chilion; thus it corresponds with the English word "handmaid," being used in the same general way.

and one by the freewoman.—Sarah, Abraham's half-sister and his wife, Genesis 20:12, and mother of Isaac. The article is attached to each of these words because they refer to persons whose history was well-known to Jews and Christians in Galatia.

4:23 Howbeit—*alla,* "but"; notwithstanding that they were children of one father, there was a further difference between them beyond that consequent on the different status of their respective mothers.

the *son* by the handmaid is born—*gennaō.*

after the flesh;—i.e., in the course of nature. Abraham and Hagar were united in accordance with natural counsels and with result after the order of nature. Sarah was aware, indeed, of the promise of God to Abraham that he should have a son, but her own name had not yet been mentioned in connection therewith, and assuming that the promise was impossible of fulfillment through herself, she planned to bring it about through another, Genesis 16:1, 2. To Sarah's device the apostle refers. From it sprang evils innumerable, first for Abraham and Sarah, then for Isaac, then for the people Israel, and then for the world at large. God's Word is settled forever in heaven, and cannot fail of its fulfillment; but God is not to be hindered or hurried of any. Whoever attempts the one or the other dooms himself to disaster. Scheming and faith are mutually exclusive. He that trusts God will not scheme; he that schemes makes manifest that he is not trusting God.

but the son by the freewoman *is born* through promise.—i.e., by the interposition of God in accordance with His promise, viz., that given subsequently to Sarah's scheme with Hagar, Genesis 17:15–19; 18:10–14; see also Romans 9:9. The first effect of the Word of God was to produce in Abraham, Romans 4:18–21, and subsequently in Sarah also, Hebrews 11:11, that faith which made them willing to accept the will of God; then in response to their faith God, contrary to the course of nature, imparted to them the power whereby the promise itself was fulfilled. In Romans 4 Abraham's faith is in view, in Hebrews 11 Sarah's; here the promise that produced that faith and the power that made the promise good.

Faith is the response of the soul to a word from God. God speaks, man accepts, submits, acts, as the word from God demands; that is faith, and to faith, in turn, God responds with the power necessary to make the word good, as it is written, "no word from God shall be void of power," Genesis 18:14, LXX, as quoted in Luke 1:37.

4:24 Which things—*hostis,* i.e., "which class of things"; cp. Colossians 2:23, "these ordinances and such as these"; Philippians 3:7, "things that seemed to promise advantage, whatever those things might be"; 2 Thessalonians 1:9, ("who") "persons of both classes mentioned." So here, what is said of this narrative may also be said of other narratives of the same character.

contain an allegory:—*allēgoreō,* to speak allegorically, i.e., not according to the plain sense of the words, but applying the facts of the narrative to illustrate principles. The presence of an allegorical meaning does not deprive the narrative of its literal meaning. Indeed, while it is at least conceivable that any given narrative may be capable of more than one allegorical meaning, it is plain that but one literal meaning can attach to it.

Scripture history differs from profane history in this, that while God is ever the disposer of the affairs of men, see Daniel 4:17, the latter cannot take account of His hand since the only sources of the information of profane history are human; it records events as seen from below. But the writers of Scripture history are directly concerned with the interpositions of God; guided by the Spirit of Inspiration they not only record events, they also record the part that God Himself took in those events, and this could only become known to them by revelation; Scripture history records events as seen from above. There are thus two possible conceptions of the origin of the Bible. Either men wrote of God and His ways what they were able to discover for themselves, which is the naturalistic view, or God revealed Himself and His ways to men and inspired the records they made, which is the Bible's own account of itself.

The Scripture histories are thus seen to be representative in character, embodying spiritual principles; which principles are always in operation, indeed, though they are not always recognized. Here the apostle shows how a particular principle worked in a particular history. He does not deduce the principle from the facts related, however, but declares the principle on quite other grounds. It was given to him "through revelation of Jesus Christ," 1:11, 12, above; he uses the history to illustrate it. Much caution is necessary in any attempt to apply the apostle's method of treatment of the story of Sarah and Hagar to other narratives of Scripture. Imagination and ingenuity are poor substitutes for apostolic guidance.

for these *women* **are**—i.e., they represent, as in Matthew 13:38, 39; Luke 22:19; John 10:7, 11, and 1 Corinthians 11:25, "This cup is the new covenant in My blood."

two covenants;—*diathēkē*, as in 3:17, above.

one—i.e., one of the two covenants. The other is not specified in the context, it is dealt with in v. 26.

from—*apo*, not as originating from Sinai, for which *ek* would have been appropriate, but as having been promulgated and received from Sinai.

mount Sinai, bearing children—in accordance with the allegory the apostle speaks of the covenant as bearing children.

unto bondage,—*douleia*, for which see at 5:1, below—naturally, Hagar being a bondservant, the property of her master, her children would be born into the same condition; spiritually, the apostle had reasoned, this was just the case of the Jews, and Hagar's son aptly illustrates it. The allegory does not, however, yield a harmonious sense in each detail, i.e., Hagar was a bondservant, so were her children; those under the law were bondservants, but here the analogy ceases, in no sense was the law a slave.

which is Hagar.—i.e., which is represented by Hagar in this allegorical use of the story.

4:25 Now this Hagar is—i.e., represents.

mount Sinai in Arabia,—whence the law was originally given with every circumstance of terror, suggesting not sonship but slavery; see Hebrews 12:18–21. There is no discoverable authority for the statement sometimes made that Sinai is, or was, known to the Arabians as Hagar; hence all interpretations of the passage based upon that supposition (the evidence for which Lightfoot declares to be "both deficient in amount and suspicious in character") must be dismissed.

Another reading (see Intro. Note) very well supported by the ancient authorities, and accepted by Lightfoot, is given in the margin: "For mount Sinai is a mountain in Arabia." This may very well be what the apostle wrote; the interpretation will be the same in either case.*

and answereth to—*sunstoicheō*, or, *sustoicheō*, = "to stand in the same file with"; the simple form of the word, *stoicheō*, occurs in 5:25; 6:16, below; see also note on "rudiments" at v. 3, above.

the Jerusalem that now is:—it is the old covenant, v. 24, allegorically Hagar and Sinai, that stands in the same file with the earthly Jerusalem. The apostle may have mentioned Arabia because its geographical position approximates to that of Egypt and because Hagar's descendants dwell there. His purpose seems to be to suggest the remoteness of Sinai from the Holy City of the Jews in a physical sense, and thus in turn to suggest the remoteness, in a moral sense, of the law from the promise.

for she is in bondage—to the Romans, literally and actually, when this letter was written. It is possible, however, that the political bondage is merely an accidental circumstance not in the apostle's mind, and that he is thinking of the spiritual bondage only, cp. 3:23—4:9. The meaning is the same in either case.

with her children.—i.e., the inhabitants of the city, in the literal sense; in the spiritual sense, all such as seek to be justified by the law wherever they may dwell, or to whatever nationality they may belong.

4:26 But the Jerusalem that is above—the apostle does not express all the terms of the antithesis; the complete parallel, with its double symbolism, may be thus set out: Hagar the bondwoman with her son Ishmael, born in the course of nature, points to the actual Jerusalem in Palestine with its inhabitants, in bondage, whether political or spiritual; and they in turn point to the Jewish people, whether in the land or of the Dispersion, in bondage to law, and with them all such Gentiles as put themselves under the law. Sarah the freewoman, with Isaac, born in fulfillment of a promise, point to the heavenly, the ideal Jerusalem with its inhabitants, under no control of this world; and

---

*It would be outside the scope of these Notes to reproduce the very intricate evidence that is adduced in favor of one or other of these readings, or of other readings not so well supported as either of these. Those of our readers who are interested will know where to look for technical discussions thereof.

these, in turn, point to those Jews and Gentiles who have trusted Christ and who are free from the law in Him. The different items in the allegory may be tabulated:

a. Hagar the bondwoman.	*a.* Sarah the freewoman.
b. Ishmael.	*b.* Isaac.
c. Sinai.	*c.* Zion.
d. Jerusalem, earthly.	*d.* Jerusalem, heavenly.
e. The Jewish people.	*e.* Believers in Christ.

In each column the different items are in file with, or "answer to," one another; see note at v. 25, above.

is free,—i.e., is not subject to ordinances, or bound by laws imposed from without. The law (i.e., the controlling power) of the living Spirit in Christ Jesus makes the believer free from the law (i.e., the controlling power) of sin and death, Romans 8:2.

which is our mother.—i.e., of Christians; still, of course, in the allegorical, or spiritual, sense. Cp. "metropolis," lit., "mother city," the capital of a country, the seat of its government, the center of its activities, and the place where the national characteristics are most fully expressed.

The idea of a heavenly counterpart of the earthly Jerusalem is not prominent in the Old Testament. The language of Psalm 46:4–7 is certainly inapplicable to the earthly city, inasmuch as no river with tributary streams flows in it, for it is built on a hill; see Psalm 48:1, 2; 87:1–3. These verses do, however, form a basis for the language of some passages in the New Testament, such, e.g., as those in the epistle to the Hebrews which declare that Abraham "looked for the city which hath the foundations, whose Builder and Maker is God," and that God "hath prepared for" the men of faith "a city," 11:10, 16. The same writer further declares that believers in Christ "are come unto mount Zion, and unto the city of the Living God, the Heavenly Jerusalem," 12:22. But while, spiritually and potentially, believers have already come to that city, yet, and indeed, on this account, they have here no permanent dwelling place, they "seek after the city which is to come," 13:14. In Revelation this city is "the New Jerusalem, which cometh down out of Heaven from . . . God," 3:12. And in due course John sees the city descending, 21:2, and is invited to a closer view of it under the guidance of the angel, 9, 10. The language is still figurative, the city exhibits the hosts of the redeemed in the renewed conditions of corporate life when the purposes of God have been accomplished and all things have been made new, v. 5. To this figure of an ideal city the language of the apostle Paul conforms, "Our citizenship is in Heaven; from whence also we wait for a Savior," Philippians 3:20. That city of God is dominated by "the powers of the age to come," the same powers that work in the believer now for his establishment in holiness and love.

A city is what its inhabitants make it. Men express their mental and moral characteristics in the surroundings they make for themselves. Jerusalem, however, was the Holy City, Matthew 4:5, for God dwelt there in the midst of His people, Psalm 46:5. Because of its commanding situation, because of its temple, its palaces and defenses. Psalm 48:2, 12, 13, because of the majesty of God that He put upon it, Ezekiel 16:14, the metropolis of Judah was known as "The Perfection of Beauty," and, "The Joy of the Whole Land," Lamentations 2:15. Such was the ideal, what God purposed Jerusalem should be. How different the real, what His people made it! Because of their rebellion it was given over to the enemy once and again. The Lord Jesus wept over it, for once more His own people had failed to recognize, in the presence of their rightful King among them, an opportunity for repentance, Luke 13:34; 19:41; therefore, conscious of their inveterate antagonism to Himself and to God, He prophesied its desolation, 21:20; 23. Centuries earlier Isaiah had called it "Sodom," 1:10, cp. 3:9, because of the ways of its people, and John describes it as "the great city, which spiritu-pally is called Sodom and Egypt, where also [the] Lord was crucified," Revelation 11:8. God had made Jerusalem His dwelling place for the display of His character; His corrupt people had given it their own.

4:27 For—i.e., the statement that the "Jerusalem that is above" is the mother, symbolically, of all such as are of faith, 3:9, finds its support in the language of Isaiah 54:1, see also vv. 2–6.

it is written,—the words were originally spoken for the comfort of Israel and Jerusalem when they were under the yoke of a foreign oppressor.

Rejoice, thou barren that bearest not; break forth and cry, thou that travailest not: for more are the children of the desolate than of her which hath the husband.—the apostle's use of the prophet's words suggest that Isaiah himself had the case of Sarah and Hagar in mind when he wrote, and 51:2 seems confirmatory of this. Sarah was the barren who had neither travailed nor borne, the desolate from whom her husband had turned to another. Hagar is that other to whom Abraham had turned. In time their places were reversed again, Sarah rejoiced, Hagar was cast out. As applied by the apostle, the works of the law had for a while superseded the promise by grace, see 3:17, above, but this was now reversed; grace had been restored to its old place, and the law had been dismissed from the position to which it had been temporarily appointed. In the end it would be found that the progeny of grace, those saved through the gospel, would greatly exceed those who had acknowledged allegiance to the law.

Primarily, no doubt, Isaiah 54 has reference to the prosperity of Israel when the nation is ultimately restored to the favor of God. But as always, so here, far-reaching principles are at work. God is one, His law one, and the universe in which He works according to His law is one, though as yet our knowledge is partial. The prophecy, even in its material aspect, is addressed not to Israel after the flesh, but to an Israel spiritually regenerate, and it is to this spiritual Israel that Jehovah stands in the relation of husband as well as maker and

Redeemer. But while the ultimate fulfillment of this specific prophecy in a national sense is assured, now, in the conversion of the Gentiles, the same principle asserts itself; grace and faith are fruitful, law and works are barren.

The connection between Isaiah 53 and 54 is that between the sufferings and the glory; the abundant fruitfulness of the Cross is foreshadowed in 53:11, "My Righteous Servant shall justify many."

4:28 Now we, brethren,—i.e., "we Christians," whether Jews or Gentiles. "We" is separately expressed in the original to emphasize the contrast between those who were spiritually akin to Abraham and the Jews who, though his lineal descendants, had nothing further in common with him, cp. Romans 2:28, 29.

as Isaac was,—lit., "after the manner of, or like, Isaac." His birth was consequent upon the divine interposition, so is that new birth of which every believer is the subject.

are children—*teknon*, for which see comment on *1 Thessalonians* 5:5.

of promise.—i.e., "children [of Abraham] by virtue [not of natural descent but] of promise." Cp. Romans 9:8, "the children of the promise," where the same contrast is made. There, because the promise in view is specified in the preceding verse, the articles are used; here, because the promise is not specified, but the fact that there was a promise is stated, the articles are omitted.

Whatever privileges the Judaizers could claim as descendants of Abraham, whatever they might hold out to others on condition of submitting to circumcision, Paul also could claim the same; see 2 Corinthians 11:22; Philippians 3:5. The Galatians, being Gentiles, could, of course, claim none of them. But Paul knew that neither did his natural descent confer any advantage upon him in the matter of salvation, nor did theirs disqualify them. He, Jew though he was, must be justified by faith, not by any work of, or on, the flesh. They, Gentiles though they were, could be justified through faith, impossible as that seemed to the Judaizers; see Romans 3:30. Thus he and they alike were children of God in virtue of the promise to Abraham, which promise had received its pledge of fulfillment in the birth of Isaac; see 3:6, 7, above; vv. 27 and 28 are an expansion of the words "our mother"—v. 27 of "mother," v. 28 of "our."

4:29 But as then—i.e., in Abraham's household after the birth of Isaac, which took place when Ishmael was about fourteen years old, cp. Genesis 16:16 with 21:5. Not improbably, however, the apostle has in mind the subsequent history of the boys, and includes with them their descendants, Israel in the one case, the Arabs, Hagrites or Hagarines, 1 Chronicles 5:10; Psalm 83:6, in the other.

he that was born after the flesh persecuted—in the narrative in Genesis it is not said that Ishmael persecuted Isaac, but only that he "mocked," or ridiculed, the aged mother and her newly weaned child. The apostle seems to have understood this mocking to indicate a hostile spirit, or he may have accepted rabbinic tradition that Ishmael, under pretense of play, shot an arrow at Isaac with intent to kill him. Moreover, the history of the descendants of the brothers shows their inveterate antagonism. The continuous tense of the verb, "was persecuting," lends support to the idea that the apostle has the Ishmaelites and the Israelites in mind.

him *that was born* **after the Spirit,**—the capital initial suggests the personal agency of the Holy Spirit in the birth of Isaac; this, however, may not have been the intention of the writer; see at 3:3, above. It is better to read "spirit" and to understand the words to mean "by supernatural power," in agreement with "after the flesh" which means "by natural power"; and of course this supernatural power is the power of the Holy Spirit.

In v. 23 the antithesis is between "after the flesh" and "through promise"; here it is between "after the flesh" and "after the spirit"; for the giving of a promise was part of the ministry of the Spirit, and so, like the redemption of all such promises, lay outside the operation of natural forces altogether, cp, "the promise of the Spirit," 3:14, above.

even so it is now.—i.e., "now in this time," Mark 10:30, throughout the present dispensation. If they were perplexed by the persecution of those whom they knew to be the appointed custodians of the revelation of God (see Rom. 3:2), let them not suppose that a strange thing happened to them, or something unforeseen (see 1 Pet. 4:12, and comment on *1 Thess.* 3:3). So it was at the beginning, as this allegorical interpretation of the history of the brothers shows; so had their Lord suffered, and the apostle; so, until the end, must those who seek salvation through grace and faith suffer at the hands of those who seek it through law and works.

4:30 Howbeit what saith the Scripture?—cp. notes at 3:8, 22, above. This persecution expresses the judgment of men on the children of God, of the flesh on the spirit. However, that judgment is not final, hence the question, which is equivalent to asking—what is God's judgment? for the Scripture is the revelation of His mind. Hence the question that is latent in this question is, shall that which is natural triumph finally, or that which is spiritual, the law or the gospel, works or faith?

Cast out the handmaid and her son: for the son of the handmaid shall not inherit with the son of the freewoman.—see Genesis 21:10; in the words actually spoken by Sarah, "this bondwoman," "my son," the personal element is prominent; she was zealous for her own and her son's rights, but the principle that found illustration in her action was not, apparently, in her thoughts. Therefore the apostle paraphrases Sarah's words, "son of the handmaid," "son of the freewoman," the better to display the principle that, in the very nature of things, that which is spiritual is free and abiding, that which is natural is in bondage and must pass away, cp. John 8:35.

Sarah's words, moreover, were endorsed by God, v. 12, and so became authoritative. This, however, does not mean that God commended Sarah in her jealousy of Hagar, or in any animosity she may have felt toward Ishmael, but merely that He made clear to Abraham that his wife's judgment was right as against his own natural feelings. The whole story is a tangle of the results of self-will; needless to say God did not instigate Abraham and Sarah to pursue the course described, it was self-selected; God interposed to overrule the issue to the accomplishment of His own purpose. Any plan made in self-will is bound to miscarry and to result in unforeseen and incalculable evils, but no self-will on the part of His agents can thwart or hinder the counsel of God.

According to the Targum, or Jewish paraphrase, Sarah spoke in the prophetic spirit, foreseeing the opposition of Ishmael and his descendants to the people of God. Sympathy with Hagar is naturally aroused by the story of the hard treatment meted out to her by those who had used her to further their own ends. However, God cared for her and for her son in the wilderness, vv. 17, 18.

The apostle thus reaches the climax of his argument from the historical narrative of Genesis, vindicates the claims of the gospel, and asserts its ultimate triumph. The circumstances under which he wrote the words must be remembered if the depth of his conviction of the certain triumph of the gospel is to be gauged aright. Lightfoot thus describes them: "One half of Christendom clung to the Mosaic Law with a jealous affection little short of frenzy, . . . while the Judaic party seemed to be growing in influence, and was strong enough, even in the gentile churches of his own founding, to undermine his influence and endanger his life." The apostle's conviction, and the courage with which he declared it, were in proportion to the clearness with which he apprehended the revelation of the purpose of God, and to the vigor of his faith in Him. Faith encourages faith, and this emphatic assertion would go far to strengthen the waverers in Galatia, and to confirm the believers in their allegiance to the gospel.

The words "shall not inherit" (ou me) are strongly emphatic; hence they are to be understood not merely as a prediction of what would happen, but as an assurance of the purpose of God. The apostle does not claim that those who trust Christ alone for salvation have a standing before God on an equality with those who add faith to the law; he asserts that they alone have such a standing, denying it explicitly to all who approach God on any other ground than that of faith. To support this denial, already maintained in various arguments, is the purpose of this allegory, for Isaac was not merely permitted to dwell with Ishmael, Ishmael was expelled from the house in his favor.

4:31 Wherefore,—The apostle, having fully established the difference between law and grace, flesh and spirit, bondage and freedom, and their incompatibility one with another, now makes direct application of the inference to be drawn from the allegory, which is that the inheritance is given by promise to faith, and cannot be obtained by works done in obedience to law.

brethren,—addressing all the Galatian believers, whether Jew or Gentile by birth.

we are not children of a handmaid,—the article is absent; hence the idea is "not of any person in a state of bondage."

but of the freewoman.—here the article appears, for though there may be many slaves there is but one true wife, one freewoman. So there are many ways along which men seek acceptance with God, there is but one of His appointment, and by it alone men may draw near to Him.

The close of the chapter at this point is unhappy, for 5:1 is obviously the conclusion of the argument developed in the preceding paragraph.

GALATIANS

CHAPTER FIVE

Verses 1–26

5:1 With freedom did Christ set us free:—the form of the expression is perhaps due to the influence of Hebrew (see Luke 22:15), and in that case the intention would be to emphasize the completeness of the liberty which the apostle has been urging upon them to realize as their own in Christ. The words may, however, be equally well read as in marg., "for freedom," and in that case the meaning may be expressed thus: "not to bring us into another form of bondage did Christ liberate us from that in which we were born, but in order to make us free from all bondage." On the whole this latter interpretation is to be preferred. True, the apostle does not in this Epistle state in so many words that we owe our freedom to Christ, but that is the underlying assumption throughout. Indeed he had already spoken of the believer as having been redeemed by Christ, and to redeem is to effect deliverance by the payment of a price; see 3:13, above. The writer seems to go back in his mind to what he said there, and in these vv. to sum up all he had said since; certainly the expressions are similar, "Christ redeemed us," "Christ set us free."

The apostle's words may, however, be read another way. Just as the most ancient MSS. are without distinctive initial letters so they are without punctuation. Hence some would read the passage thus: "we are not children of a handmaid, but with the freedom of the freewoman Christ set us free."

stand fast—*steko,* for which see comment on *1 Thessalonians* 3:8, where all the New Testament occurrences of the word are noted.

therefore,—*oun,* = "accordingly," introducing the natural inference from what has gone before.

and be not entangled—*enechō,* which is used of the plotting of Herodias against John the Baptist, Mark 6:19, and of the efforts of the scribes and Pharisees to induce the Lord to say something on which they might base a charge against Him, Luke 11:53.||

again—see 4:8, 9, and notes there. They had had an experience of bondage in their old life as idolaters; that surely should suffice them.

in a yoke—*zugos,* which in its literal sense means anything that joins two things together in such a way that neither can move independently, as scales, Leviticus 19:36; Revelation 6:5, and the rigid wooden structure that couples oxen engaged in haulage, Numbers 19:2. Figuratively it stands for responsibility and the discharge of duties and obligations, Lamentations 3:27. But in the figurative sense *zagos* is nearly always used of bondage or servitude of some kind, whether social, Isaiah 58:6, or tribal, Genesis 27:40, or national, Jeremiah 30:8, which latter, in the case of Israel, was the result of rebellion against God, Lamentations 1:14. In only one passage in the Old Testament is the will of God called a yoke, Jeremiah 5:5.

In the New Testament *zagos*, save in Revelation 6:5, appears only in a figurative sense, as of domestic slavery, 1 Timothy 6:1. In Acts 15:10 Peter uses it very much as Paul does here. The only occasion on which it has a good sense is Matthew 11:29, 30, where the Lord Jesus speaks of His service as a "yoke" which is "easy" and "light," in contrast with the cumbersome requirements of the law as interpreted by the scribes and Pharisees. This figure, however, is not to be taken to mean that the Lord and the believer are to be united under one "yoke," but that He is to be acknowledged as Master, while the believer becomes the willing servant, bearing the yoke that He appoints.||

A compound of *zugeō*, the corresponding verb, with *heteros*, = "different in kind," e.g. (see note at 1:6, above), *heterozugeō*, is used by Paul in 2 Corinthians 6:14, where the meaning is not different from the meaning here, though the circumstances are different. There persons are in view, here doctrines, but the danger in both cases is the curtailment of Christian liberty.||

Suzugos (*sun* = "with," and *zugos*) occurs in Philippians 4:3, but whom the apostle thus addressed cannot now be ascertained. Some suppose Epaphroditus, mentioned in v. 18, some a local leader into whose hands the letter would naturally be put on the arrival of the messenger who carried it, some, again, that Syzygos is a proper name. It does not seem possible, however, to get beyond guesswork, and that is vain.||

of bondage.—*douleia*, which is used in Romans 8:21 of that condition of the Creation into which it was brought by the Fall of man, its appointed head, and in v. 15 of that fallen condition of man himself which makes him dread God rather than love Him, and, in Hebrews 2:15, that makes him fear death; see also 4:24, above.||

For other forms of the word see comment on *1 Thessalonians* 1:9; 3:1.

Viewed religiously all men are in bondage, the Jews to a law, divinely imposed at the beginning, indeed, but long since abrogated because of its proved inadequacy to the end contemplated, Romans 8:3, the Gentiles to their own ideas of what God must be, ideas widely expressed in the form of idols (see at 4:8, above), but not exclusively so, for many who refuse idols yet know nothing higher than their own conceptions; their standard is still the creation of their own minds, not the revelation of God in Christ. Now only truth can set men free, John 8:32, and Christ Himself is the complete embodiment and expression of truth absolute, 14:6; the Holy Spirit is the Spirit of truth because He is the Spirit of Christ, Romans 8:9, cp. also Acts 16:7. Hence the declaration of the Lord Jesus: "If therefore the Son shall make you free, ye shall be free indeed," John 8:36, and of the apostle, "where the Spirit of the Lord is, there is liberty,"

2 Corinthians 3:17. He then that receives the Son is, by the Spirit of the Son, delivered from the slavish spirit that thinks of God only as an austere taskmaster, swift to mark failure and to punish it, Luke 19:21, and learns instead that God is love, 1 John 4:8. He that believes on the Son is delivered from bondage to the fear of death by the promise of the Lord Jesus to come again to take him to the place prepared for him in the Father's house, John 14:1-3, and by the assurance of resurrection, 11:25, 26.

In the present passage the bondage immediately contemplated is to those rites and ceremonies prescribed in a law that could not give either freedom in the present or hope for the future, Hebrews 7:18, 19; but the principle is of the widest application.

Human freedom, *eleutheria,* that in which man was originally created, is not liberty to do wrong or to indulge oneself, it is liberty to obey God. For man is so constituted that only as he pleases God can he be happy in the higher, the spiritual, part of his nature, and efficient for the great ends for which he was created. The essence of the Fall lay in this, that man used his endowment of freedom against the giver of it. Instead of enhancing and extending his freedom by his disobedience, however, man's first exercise of his will apart from God brought him into bondage to a new master, sin, see Romans 6:17, 18; 7:14, working through a threefold agency, the world, the flesh, and the devil; see 1 John 2:16, 17; 3:8. Thus sin is not the true master of men, but a usurper, ruling with rigor, albeit the rule is disguised so that not even the wisest seems capable of recognizing it apart from the teaching of the Spirit of God.

Christian freedom is secured for men in the redemption of Christ, which is to reach its full fruition at His coming again, cp. Romans 8:21 with 7:24, 25. Meanwhile the believer is to claim, to assert and to enjoy, the freedom that is his in Christ, but in so doing he will encounter many opposing forces, and these the apostle Paul usually sums up in the word "flesh" (for which see note at 3:3, above). Christian freedom is not liberty to the Christian to please himself; it is liberty for the new life which is his in Christ to develop in the leading of His Spirit, Romans 8:14, and according to its own nature despite the antagonism of the flesh, for "the flesh lusteth against the Spirit," i.e., the Spirit of Christ, v. 17, below.

The highest expression of Christian liberty is seen in the Lord Jesus, who said, prophetically, "Lo, I am come . . . to do Thy will, O God," Psalm 40:7, 8, and, in the days of His flesh, "I am come, . . . not to do Mine own will, but the will of Him that sent Me," John 6:38, and concerning whom the apostle wrote, "Christ . . . pleased not Himself," Romans 15:3.

The agent of Christ in bringing the believer into this freedom as an experience is the Holy Spirit, 2 Corinthians 3:17, who works within, in contrast with the Law of Moses which attempted to restrain the flesh and to encourage righteousness from without, Romans 8:2-4. Nevertheless the Scriptures in which that Law, together with the history of its effects upon men, are recorded, are indispensable to the Christian, for, with the gospel and the history of its development (which now forms an integral part of the whole Book) they constitute the "perfect law of liberty" into which he looks, and in the teaching of which he continues, and by which he will ultimately be judged, James 1:25; 2:12.

To the unregenerate the Law is an instrument of bondage, for it commands him to abstain from the things to which he is naturally inclined, and to do those things for which he has no desire. To the regenerate the Scriptures are a law of liberty, for they declare the will of God in which His children delight. They forbid the things he knows to be wrong and inexpedient, and command those things which the new nature desires. But the man who rejoices in his freedom to serve God according to his own conscience shrinks from the temptation to bring another into bondage. Tolerance of others is the evidence of the value attached to freedom for oneself.

The security of Christian liberty lies in this, that the Christian, discharged from every law imposed from without, is yet "under law to Christ," 1 Corinthians 9:21, and is "Christ's bondservant," 7:22; "he cannot sin, because he is begotten of God," 1 John 3:9.* Nevertheless, "the flesh" is always present in the believer, always active to mislead or to overcome him. The Christian, therefore, is to be upon his guard and to learn to discriminate against those specious promises of liberty which would only bring him into the old bondage again, 2 Peter 2:19, and see v. 13, below.

The flesh, moreover, hates the exercise of Christian liberty by others, and seeks to curtail it by espionage, by prohibitions, and by the presence of a sensitive conscience, 2:4, 14, above, 1 Corinthians 10:29.

Governments, indeed, are appointed of God to restrain, or at least to regulate, the grosser manifestations of the flesh, and the Christian yields a ready obedience to such laws as they may make (provided they are not in direct conflict with the higher laws of God, Acts 5:29) in order to contribute what he may to make life on the earth orderly and tolerable according to the will of God, 1 Peter 2:13-17; see also Romans 13:1-7.||

The verb *eleutheroō*, "to set free," occurs twice in the words of the Lord Jesus, in each case in the future tense, a promise and an assurance made in view of His death and resurrection, John 8:32, 36; three times Paul uses it in the past tense, here and Romans 6:18, 22, for where the Lord looked forward the apostle looked back. "Being made free from sin," that alien power which entered into the human race at the Fall, 5:12, the Christian enters into the possession of his true inheritance, Ephesians 1:3, and is free to work out what God works in him, Philippians 2:12, 13. But freedom in the full, large sense, freedom from the trammels of the old and groaning creation, awaits the coming of the Lord; hence in Romans 8:21 the tense is future.||

---

*This "cannot" plainly does not mean that sin is a physical impossibility to the Christian; it is a moral impossibility to him as it was to Joseph in the house of Potiphar, Genesis 39:9.

5:2 Behold, I Paul say unto you, that,—in three other places in his Epistles the apostle thus emphasizes what he is about to say, 2 Corinthians 10:1; Ephesians 3:1; 1 Thessalonians 2:18. The new section begins here: the apostle becomes more personal again, and, as he sets before the Galatians in the plainest terms the inevitable end of the path that was attracting them, his language takes on warmth with the vigor of his expostulation.

He mentions his name in this emphatic way for one or other, or for all, of three reasons: It may be, *a,* that he thus reminds them of the unique apostolic authority which he had asserted at the opening of his letter, or, *b,* that he states with studied emphasis his directly contrary teaching in view of the charge of himself advocating circumcision that had been laid against him, v. 11, below, or, *c,* that he would have them think that for him who has occasion thus to speak to them they would at one time have given their eyes, 4:15, above.

if ye receive circumcision,—cp. 1 Corinthians 7:18, where Gentile converts are categorically forbidden to submit to this rite, and Acts 15, where the decision of the Council at Jerusalem that it was not to be imposed upon them is recorded; see note at 2:7, above. This does not mean that no circumcised person can be saved, for the tense of the verb is present continuous (see comment on *1 Thess.*), hence the meaning is "if you continue to receive." Those who had been circumcised, whether in infancy, as in his own case, Philippians 3:5, or voluntarily in later years, as in the case of Timothy, Acts 16:3, are not thereby shut out from Christ, they are warned of the danger of pursuing the practice in the case of new converts and of maintaining the teaching of which circumcision is the symbol.

It is plain that "receiveth" is not to be understood of the performance of the rite itself, for that could be done but once. There is here a metonymy: to "receive" circumcision is to acknowledge it to be of divine authority and of Christian obligation, and in like manner to acknowledge all that for which it stood in the mind of the Jews. The apostle's intention was to bring to a decision adverse to the Judaizers whose converts who had been baptized into the Name of the Lord Jesus, but who, being Gentiles, had never been circumcised.

Christ will profit you nothing.—in life or in death, in time or in eternity; for plainly if salvation, and justification, and life, and the promises, and the gift of the Spirit, are obtainable by the works of the law, then there was no need for the Son of God to come to die to secure them for us; see 2:21, above. How great was the gulf between the apostle and his opponents may be judged from a comparison of these and the following words with those with which Acts 15 opens, "And certain men came down from Judaea and taught the brethren, saying, Except ye be circumcised, . . . ye cannot be saved"; see 4:11, above, and cp. Romans 2:25.

5:3 Yea,—*de,* which usually suggests a contrast more or less marked: not only would they be without advantage from Christ if they consented to be circumcised, they would thereby pledge themselves to do all that the law pre-scribes, to fulfill the whole law in all parts without distinction whether of ceremo-nial and moral, or of any other kind. And as this is not possible for any man, the law would not profit them either.

I testify—*marturomai,* see comment on *1 Thessalonians* 2:11.

again—with reference to the statement of the preceding verse, which is here extended, as noted above, and made more emphatic in form; "say" becomes "testify," "you" becomes "every man."

to every man that receiveth circumcision, that he is a debtor—*opheilō,* a conspectus of the New Testament use of this word see comment on *2 Thessalo-nians* 1:1. Cp. the parable of the ten thousand talents, Matthew 18:23 ff.

to do the whole law.—the unity of the law is asserted categorically by James, who declares that to offend in one point is to transgress the law as a whole, and so to become guilty of all; see 2:10, 11. In that case it is clear that zeal in one direction will not compensate for failure in another. The law is not to be conceived of as a bundle of separate strands, whereof if one be broken the rest may still remain intact, but rather as a sheet of glass which, if it be broken in any part, is broken as a whole.

The Lord Jesus also implied the integrity of the law in His reference to the necessity for the fulfillment of its every jot and tittle; see Matthew 5:18.

5:4 Ye are severed from Christ,—*katargeō;* for an analysis of New Testa-ment use of this word see comment on *2 Thessalonians* 2:8. The aorist, "point" sense marks the moment of decision to accept that the teaching of the Judaizers; when they did that, then and there they were separated from Christ as a branch is separated from a tree; henceforth Christ would profit them nothing at all. Cp. John 15:6; Romans 11:17. The apostle's claim is nothing less than this, that Christ must be everything or nothing to a man; no limited trust or divided allegiance is acceptable to Him. The man who is justified by the grace of the Lord Jesus Christ is a Christian; the man who seeks to be justified by the works of the law is not.

ye who would be justified by the law;—for this was the end contemplated in submitting to circumcision. The verb is in the present continuous tense, lit., "are being justified," which frequently expresses the purpose in view in pursuing a given course; for illustrations of this usage from other New Testament passages see comment on *1 Thessalonians* 2:4.

The emphasis of v. 4 is different from that of v. 2. There the stress falls on "Christ," in order to set in contrast the Son of God, the Savior, on the one hand and the law on the other. Here the stress falls upon "severed," to suggest the contrast between what they aimed at in submitting to circumcision, namely, that faith in Christ was to be a kind of filling up and rounding off of the law, and the actual effect of so doing.

ye are fallen away from grace.—again the aorist or point tense is used, lit., "ye fell away," for the apostle's mind is still upon the initial act which committed them to the works of the law. They had surrendered any hope based on the grace of God when they submitted to circumcision themselves or consented to its imposition upon others. The apostle is not here dealing with conduct or character, but solely with the ground on which justification is sought. Such defection is not primarily moral; a man may continue in the most rigorous obedience to law and in the cultivation of even the distinctive Christian virtues, striving earnestly to please God in his own strength and in accordance with his own ideas, when he has already fallen away from grace. The Christian position is described in language of striking contrast with this in Romans 5:2, "we have had our access by faith into this grace wherein we stand."

Ekpiptō is used in the New Testament, literally, of flowers that wither in the course of nature, James 1:11; 1 Peter 1:24, of a ship not under control, Acts 27:17, 26, 29, 32, of shackles loosed from a prisoner's wrist, 12:7, and, figuratively, of the Word of God (the expression of His purpose) which cannot fall away from the end to which it is set, Romans 9:6, and of the believer who is warned lest he fall away from the course in which he has been confirmed by the Word of God, 2 Peter 3:17. The present passage is closely parallel with that in Peter, this being addressed to those at the outset of the Christian course, that to those who had long been running therein. There is this difference, however, that whereas Paul is here dealing specifically with defection in doctrine, Peter is concerned with the behavior of Christians, and warns them against defection in morals.||

Indeed it is possible that Peter had these words of Paul in his mind when he wrote. Immediately before he had referred to some letter of Paul's written to those whom Peter himself was addressing. Peter's second epistle was sent to those to whom he wrote the first, 2 Peter 3:1, which was a circular letter addressed to saints at Galatia among others. It is difficult to resist the conclusion that it is to this epistle that Peter refers. And if so how gracious of that apostle to commend specifically the very letter in which his own weakness and vacillation on a momentous occasion is plainly recorded! With him, apparently, the edification of the saints was the sole consideration of weight.

These expressions must be understood as explicit denials of salvation to those who, in the face of the apostle's statements of what was involved, persisted in acknowledging circumcision, and so committed themselves to the works of the law as necessary to justification. Only by grace, and that the grace of the Lord Jesus, Acts 15:11, can any man be saved. How then could they be saved to whom Christ was of no advantage, who had been severed from Christ, who had fallen away from grace? All such as turn to the law for blessing find in it only a curse, 3:10, above, condemnation and death, 2 Corinthians 3:7, 9, for the law of God "worketh wrath," Romans 4:15, but the grace of God brings salvation, Titus 2:11.

The Christian is not to:

a. receive the grace of God in vain, 2 Corinthians 6:1;

b. fall away from grace, here;

c. do despite unto the Spirit of grace, Hebrews 10:29;

d. fall short of the grace of God, Hebrews 12:15;

e. turn the grace of our God into lasciviousness, Jude 4.

On the contrary he is to:

a. continue in the grace of God, Acts 13:43;

b. stand in grace, Romans 5:2, cp. 1 Peter 5:12;

c. be strengthened in the grace that is in Christ Jesus, 2 Timothy 2:1;

d. draw near with boldness unto the throne of grace, Hebrews 4:16;

e. be established in heart by grace, Hebrews 13:9;

f. grow in the grace of Christ, 2 Peter 3:18.

5:5 For—introducing the ground upon which the uncompromising statements of v. 4 are made. This is presented in the form of a declaration of the true Christian position, which is plainly incompatible with that of the Judaizing legalists.

we—i.e., "we Christians," we who repudiate the law and trust wholly in Christ for justification and the fulfillment of the promises of God. The pronoun is emphatic, "we, whatever others may do."

through the Spirit—*pneuma* is here without the article; it does not on that account follow that the Holy Spirit is not intended and that the capital initial is wrong, for the article is sometimes absent where the person is certainly meant, as in Acts 19:2, and is sometimes present where that is not the case, as in John 6:63; see comment on *1 Thessalonians* 1:5; *2 Thessalonians* 2:13. If "in spirit" should be read here, then the meaning is that whereas the Jew sought justification in the flesh, i.e., by the observance of ordinances and obedience to moral precepts, the Christian is justified by an act of the spirit, i.e., through faith, as indeed the apostle states. If, however, as is equally possible, "through the Spirit" is to be read, then the meaning is, "through the agency of the Holy Spirit," i.e., the believer is quickened by Him, and is taught by Him to cherish this hope, and is maintained by Him to continue therein. The Holy Spirit is received by an act of faith, and by the continued exercise of this receptive faculty, faith, the blessings He brings are appropriated. Thus the whole spiritual life of the Christian is a life of faith, life through the Holy Spirit; see note at 3:2, 3, above.

Whichever view of the passage is taken, it is important to remember that the sphere of the operations of the Spirit of God is the human spirit, Romans 8:16; 2 Corinthians 1:22. Every impulse along the line of obedience to the will of God in the spirit of a man is the result of His operations. And since the person who acts and the sphere of His activities are known under the same name, it is not always possible to say beyond question which the apostle intended. Moreover, it is conceivable that he was not always concerned to make a sharp distinction between the Spirit Who works and the spirit on, or in, which He works, just as it is not always possible to distinguish between the giver and His gifts, for where the gift is the giver is also, without Him the gift would be barren. It is a disadvantage inherent in human language that one word has to do duty for the Holy Spirit of God and for the spirit of man, for the giver and for His gifts.

by faith—*ek,* as at 2:16, above, see note there.

wait for—*apekdechomai,* "to look forward to," with the idea of expectancy always prominent, Romans 8:25; see comment on *1 Thessalonians* 1:10. In each of the other places of its occurrence in the New Testament the object of the expectation is either the coming of the Lord, 1 Corinthians 1:7; Philippians 3:20; Hebrews 9:28, or some immediate consequence thereof, as the change that is to be wrought in the bodies of the living saints, Romans 8:23, and the display of the sonship of the redeemed to all creation, v. 19. This use of the word elsewhere creates a strong presumption that here also *apekdechomai* directs attention to the consummation of the purposes of God to be ushered in at the return of the Lord Jesus.||

the hope—*elpis,* for which see comments on *1 Thessalonians* 1:3; *2 Thessalonians* 2:16. An ellipsis is to be supplied, "wait for the realization of the hope"; see note on "receive," 3:14, above.

of righteousness.—*dikaiosunē,* the character or quality of being right or just, formerly spelled "rightwiseness," which makes the meaning unmistakable. *Dikaiosunē* is found in the sayings of the Lord Jesus:

a, of whatever is right or just in itself, whatever conforms to the revealed will of God, Matthew 5:6, 10, 20, John 16:8, 10;

b, whatever has been appointed by God to be acknowledged and obeyed by man, Matthew 3:15; 21:32;

c, the sum total of the requirements of God, Matthew 6:33;

d, religious duties, Matthew 6:1 (distinguished as almsgiving, man's duty to his neighbor, vv. 2–4, prayer, his duty to God, vv. 5–15, fasting, the duty of self-control, vv. 16–18).

In the preaching of the apostles recorded in Acts the word has the same general meaning. So also in James 1:20; 3:18, in both Epistles of Peter and in the Epistles of John and the Revelation. In 2 Peter 1:1 "the righteousness of our God and Savior Jesus Christ" is the righteous dealing of God with sin and with sinners on the ground of the death of Christ. "Word of righteousness," Hebrews 5:13, is probably the gospel, and the Scriptures as containing the gospel, wherein is declared the righteousness of God in all its aspects; it is = "the oracles of God," v. 12.

This meaning of *dikaiosunē,* right action, is frequent also in Paul's writings, as in all five of its occurrences in Romans 6; Ephesians 6:14, etc., but for the more part he uses it of that gracious gift of God to men whereby all who believe on the Lord Jesus Christ are brought into right relationship with God. This righteousness is unattainable by obedience to any law, or by any merit of a man's own, or any other condition than that of faith in Christ; see 2:16; 3:11, above. The man who trusts in Christ becomes "the righteousness of God in Him," 2 Corinthians 5:21, i.e., becomes in Christ all that God requires a man to be, all that he could never be in himself. Because Abraham accepted the Word of God, making it his own by that act of the mind and spirit which is called faith, and, as the sequel showed, submitting himself to its control, therefore God accepted him as one who fulfilled the whole of His requirements, Romans 4:3. With the possible exception of Hebrews 11:7, this use of the word in the New Testament is not found outside the writings of the apostle Paul.

Righteousness is not said to be imputed to the believer save in the sense that faith is imputed ("reckoned" is the better word) for righteousness. It is clear that in Romans 4:6, 11 "righteousness reckoned" must be understood in the light of the context, "faith reckoned for righteousness," vv. 3, 5, 9, 22. "For" in these places is *eis,* which does not mean "instead of," but "with a view to." The faith thus exercised brings the soul into vital union with God in Christ, and inevitably produces righteousness of life, that is, conformity to the will of God; see also at 3:6, above.

The phrase "hope of righteousness," refers to the believer's complete conformity to all the requirements of the will of God at the coming of Christ. God, who knows the end from the beginning, needs not to wait the final issue of man's life before pronouncing His verdict, but accounts him righteous when he trusts in Christ. As to his past the believing man is without merit; as to his future he is without potentiality for good; but by the act of faith in Christ he accepts the condemnation of his past, and looks to Christ in his wisdom, power, and love for his future. No charge against him can lie since Christ died on his behalf, Romans 8:33, 34; and all things, i.e., all things accordant with the will of God, become possible to him, Mark 9:23; 2 Corinthians 1; 2:9, since Christ is alive from the dead, Hebrews 7:25. Thus, on the one hand, the believer stands justified before God, and on the other, looks with confidence to the perfecting of the good work begun in him, Philippians 1:6, when he will be completely conformed to the image of Christ. The thought conveyed by the words "hope of righteousness" is thus similar to that of such passages as Romans 8:29; 1 John 3:2.

Other phrases similarly formed with the word "hope" are found in Paul's Epistles and speeches, but not elsewhere, in the New Testament:

a, "the hope of the promise," i.e., of the fulfillment of the promise, Acts 26:6;

b, "the hope and resurrection of the dead," i.e., "the hope, that is to say, the resurrection of the dead," which was included in the hope of the promise,* Acts 23:6;

Kai, here translated "and," is sometimes used in an epexegetical or explanatory sense; see comment on *1 Thessalonians* 4:1; 5:23. The meaning of the apostle's words in Acts 23:6 is clear from 24:15.

c, "the hope of Israel," i.e., the expectation of the coming of the Messiah to restore the national glories, Acts 28:20;

d, the "hope of the glory of God," Romans 5:2, i.e., of "the appearing of the glory of our great God and Savior Jesus Christ," Titus 2:13; see also Colossians 1:27, where, as here, the reference is to the public manifestation of the Parousia with which it ends rather than to the rapture with which it begins; see comments on *1 Thessalonians* 2:14; *2 Thessalonians* 2:8. That Christ is in the midst of His people now is the ground of their hope that they will be around Him in that day;

e, "the hope of salvation," i.e., the hope of the rapture, or catching away, of believers that is to take place at the opening of the Parousia, 1 Thessalonians 5:8;

f, "the hope of His [God's] calling," i.e., the prospect before those who respond to the call of God in His Gospel, Ephesians 1:18;

g, the "hope of your [the believer's] calling," the same calling as *f*, but looked at from the point of view of those who are called, Ephesians 4:4;

h, "the hope of the gospel," a comprehensive term including the fulfillment of all the promises of God, Colossians 1:23;

i, "the hope of eternal life," which in the region of the spirit is the present possession of the believer, see John 5:24, but which is to have its full manifestation in the assumption of immortality by the mortal body at the Parousia of the Lord, 1 Corinthians 15:53; thus eternal life is at once a possession and a hope, Titus 1:2; 3:7.

Phrases similarly formed with the word "righteousness" are also found:

a, "the way of righteousness," Matthew 21:32, for which see *b* under "righteousness" above, and 2 Peter 2:21, where the gospel, wherein men are taught how to please God, is intended;

b, "enemy of all righteousness," Acts 13:10, one who naturally and instinctively sets himself to defeat what is right;

c, "word of righteousness," Hebrews 5:13, cp. Psalm 119:123, and see on "righteousness" above;

d, "king of righteousness," Hebrews 7:2, the translation of the Hebrew name of the King-priest (cp. "priest upon his throne," Zech. 6:13), Genesis 14:18;

e, "heir of the righteousness which is according to faith," Hebrews 11:7, i.e., one who obtains that righteousness which is possible only to those who are in vital union with God, the source of righteousness;

f, "the fruit of righteousness," Hebrews 12:11, i.e., righteousness in word and act; the effect of affliction is to teach and to train men in the right ways of the Lord, cp. Psalm 119:67, 71; in James 3:18 there seems to be an ellipsis, "the right seed that produces righteous fruit," i.e., righteousness, in oneself or in others, is not attained by strife and clamor, but by the quiet persistent doing of what is right without regard to advantage, cp. Isaiah 32:17; the figure is not infrequent in the Old Testament, cp. Proverbs 11:18, etc., and see below;

g, "a preacher of righteousness," 2 Peter 2:5, one who declared the righteous demands of God upon men, His right ways and their responsibility to walk therein.

The epistles of Paul supply the following:

h, "the gift of righteousness," Romans 5:17, righteousness as a gift, not as something earned; the gracious acceptance of men by God, not on the ground of their merit, but solely because Christ died for them, cp. *e,* above;

i, "instruments [better as margin, weapons, see comment on *1 Thessalonians* 5:8] of righteousness," Romans 6:13, the powers of the believer's mind and body yielded to God for the execution of His will and for the carrying on of His warfare against evil; with this may be associated:

j, "the armor of righteousness," 2 Corinthians 6:7, and;

k, "the breastplate of righteousness," Ephesians 6:14, in which right conduct, righteousness of thought, word, and deed is to be understood;

l, "servants [*doulos*] of righteousness," Romans 6:18, i.e., servants who obey the righteous will of God;

m, "ministers [*diakonos,* for which with its New Testament synonyms, see comments on *1 Thessalonians* 3:1] of righteousness," 2 Corinthians 11:15, see under *l;*

n, "a law of righteousness," Romans 9:31, i.e., such a law as would produce righteousness in life, and so effect a right relationship between men and God;

o, "the ministration [*diakonia, cp. diakonos*] of righteousness," 2 Corinthians 3:9, the equivalent of "the ministration of the spirit," v. 8, i.e., the gospel in which it is manifested that grace reigns through righteousness, Romans 5:21;

p, "the fruits (lit., fruit) of righteousness," Philippians 1:11, see on James 3:18, under *f,* above; in 2 Corinthians 9:10 "fruit" is, lit., "offspring," *genēma,* as in Luke 22:18, but the meaning is not different; to increase the fruits of righteousness means that to him that gives shall be given, to him that is liberal in spirit God will supply the means of expressing that liberality;

q, "the crown of righteousness," 2 Timothy 4:8, the rightly adjusted reward of faithful service; see comment on *1 Thessalonians* 2:19.

5:6 For in Christ Jesus neither circumcision . . . nor uncircumcision—see at 2:7, above. Since the death of Christ nationality does not confer any religious privilege upon men; before God all men stand on a common level of weakness, ungodliness, and enmity against Him; see Romans 5:6–10.

availeth anything,—*ischuō,* "to be effective," "to be capable of producing results"; in Hebrews 9:17 it appears to have the meaning "to be valid" ("of force"), a meaning which is common in Greek documents contemporary with the New Testament, but which would be inadequate in this passage; Acts 19:20, where it is said of the gospel, affords a better illustration of its meaning here.

A strengthened form of this word, *exischuō,* occurs in Ephesians 3:18, in the apostle's prayer that the believers may be "strong"; here also the capacity for producing the spiritual results described is directly connected with faith.||

Another, *katischuō*, occurs in Matthew 16:18, of the powerlessness of the "gates of Hades" to prevail against the Church, and in Luke 23:23 of the power of a determined mob to prevail over a weak ruler.||

but faith working—*energeō*, for which see at 3:5, above.

through love.—*agapē*, for which see comment on *1 Thessalonians* 1:3; 3:12.

These words have been understood in two ways:

a. That faith is formed by love, is the outcome of the exercise of love, thus making of faith a "work"; but against this interpretation is the fact that the verb is not in the passive voice, in which case the meaning would be "wrought, or produced by, love"; it is in the middle voice, and so means "exerting itself in, or producing, love." In the New Testament faith is consistently set in contrast with works as the means of justification. The two are not complementary the one to the other in this connection; they are mutually exclusive the one of the other. It is never love that justifies, but always and only faith. Faith produces works; works do not produce faith.

b. That faith expresses itself in love. The general teaching of Scripture is that faith is a living and active power, inasmuch as it brings a man into vital union with the source of all life, and so of all spiritual activity. But God is not only the source of spiritual life and power, God is love, and in the heart of the man who trusts in God His love is shed abroad by the Holy Spirit, Romans 5:5. This love of God so experienced begets love to God, 1 Corinthians 8:3, and love to men, 1 Thessalonians 4:9. Thus it is that faith expresses itself in love. It may be added, moreover, that the apostle is not here describing how a man may attain to be in Christ, but rather how the faith that brings him into union with Christ manifests itself in his life.

The recurrence here of Paul's triad, faith, hope, love, is to be noted, see comment on *1 Thessalonians* 1:3, where a reference to Romans 5:1, 5 should be added.

With these words should be compared:

"Circumcision is nothing, and uncircumcision is nothing; but the keeping of the commandments of God [is everything]" 1 Corinthians 7:19.

"Neither is circumcision anything, nor uncircumcision, but [it is necessary that a man become the subject of] a new creation," 6:15, margin, below.

Here also there is an ellipsis to be supplied—"Neither circumcision availeth anything, nor uncircumcision; but faith working through love accomplishes all things"; with this may be compared the words of the Lord in Matthew 17:20 and Mark 9:23. This categorical statement, as to the first part of it, is a concise summary of the argument of 3:1-9, and as to the second part, is a direct, explicit abrogation of the covenant with Abraham of which circumcision was the seal and symbol.

It is not the apostle's mind to deny that "circumcision," i.e., subjection to law, is a more advantageous condition than "uncircumcision," i.e., natural license restricted only by conscience already warped and blinded by sin; on the contrary, he has elsewhere declared that the advantage of the Jew over the Gentile is "much every way," Romans 3:1, 2. But faith in Christ frees the one from bondage to a law imposed from without, and the other from bondage to the impulses of a corrupted nature, by producing in both the essential characteristic of the nature of God, love, for God is love, 1 John 4:8.

There is complete agreement between Paul and James on the essential quality of faith; to both faith is something vital, effective, making a difference in the man who exercises it. With James faith produces obedience as with Paul it produces love. But whereas James distinguishes between true faith and spurious faith, James 2:14–26, Paul does not anywhere acknowledge a false or ineffective faith; see also at 3:6, above.

5:7 Ye were running well;—as at 2:2, above.

who did hinder you—*enkoptō* = "to cut into," and in general usage "to impede a person by cutting off, or breaking up, his way," hence "to hinder." Here the meaning is "who broke up the road you had begun to travel with so much promise?" So also Romans 15:22; 1 Thessalonians 2:18, there, however, of actual journeys; in Acts 24:4 of detaining a person unnecessarily, and in 1 Peter 3:7 of the effect of a low ideal of family life upon prayer.||

The figure of a race is found also in Romans 9:16; 1 Corinthians 9:24–26, and Hebrews 12:1; cp. Acts 20:24; 2 Timothy 4:7.

that ye should not obey—lit., "be persuaded by," *peithō*, which in the active voice = "to persuade," "to win over," as in Matthew 27:20, and in the passive voice = "to be persuaded," "to be won over," as in Acts 5:36, 40; 21:14. It suggests, not obedience in submission to authority, but obedience resulting from persuasion, of which Acts 27:11 is a good example; see Romans 2:8; 14:14, and 1:10, above, with note there.

A strengthened form, *anapeithō*, occurs in Acts 18:13; it is always used in an evil sense, "to induce" (of course the Jews thought that Paul was doing an evil thing in persuading the people to accept the gospel); see Jeremiah 36:8, LXX; so also the papyri.||

Peithō and *pisteuō*, "to trust," are closely related etymologically, the difference in meaning is that the former implies the obedience that is produced by the latter, cp. Hebrews 3:18, 19, where the disobedience of the Israelites is said to be the evidence of their unbelief. Faith is of the heart, invisible to men; obedience is of the conduct and may be observed. When a man obeys God he gives the only possible evidence that in his heart he believes God. Of course it is persuasion of the truth that results in faith (we believe because we are persuaded that the thing is true, a thing does not become true because it is believed), but *peithō* in the New Testament suggests an actual and outward result of the inward persuasion and consequent faith.

the truth?—the article though printed in the Greek text of R.V. is not found in the oldest MSS.; if it is to be retained then the meaning is, "the gospel, the true doctrine of the Scriptures in the light of the coming and death of the Son of God." If, as is almost certainly the case, it is to be rejected, then the meaning is "that which in the nature of the case is true, in view alike of its vital power as you have experienced it, and of the reasons already adduced from Scripture"; see comment on *2 Thessalonians* 2:10, 13; cp. 2:5, 14, above. In either case a contrast is suggested with the false gospel of the Judaizers (that salvation is dependent upon works, wholly or in part) which does not accord with the Scriptures on which it was professedly based, when those Scriptures are rightly read, 3:6–22, above, and which in their own experience was void of any vitality or power, 3:1–5, above.

The language of metaphor is soon dropped for that of reality; "to run well" is to obey.

5:8 This persuasion—i.e., "this influence that has won you over, or that seems likely to do so"; *peismonē*, which from its similarity in sound and meaning with *peithō*, v. 7, suggests a play upon the words, a paronomasia; see comment on *2 Thessalonians* 3:11.||

came not of him that calleth you.—present continuous tense, ct. 1:10, above. The reference is to God; see comment on *1 Thessalonians* 2:12; 5:24; *2 Thessalonians* 2:14. Apparently the ellipsis would be better supplied by the present tense, "cometh," as A.V.; the sentence may be paraphrased, "you would not be persuaded by the truth, and the persuasion to which you are yielding is not the persuasion of God, Who is calling you to a life of unreserved faith in His Son."

5:9 A little leaven leaveneth the whole lump.—this somewhat abrupt allusion to a commonly known effect in material things may be made in anticipation of a plea that the Judaizing party was small in number, or that whether a person observed the law in one particular (circumcision) was a matter of no great moment. On the contrary, the apostle urges, evil spreads surely and rapidly, and must be opposed in its beginnings if it is to be opposed successfully. It is a mistake to despise "the day of small things," whether of good or of evil, Zechariah 4:10; "great oaks from little acorns grow," and just as one plague-infected person may bring devastation upon a city, so may one teacher of doctrine subversive of the gospel corrupt a whole community of believers.

The question whether the apostle here refers to persons, as in 1 Corinthians 5:6, or to doctrines, as in Matthew 16:6, cp. v. 12, is perhaps best answered "to both." Both have just been mentioned in the context, the hinderer, v. 7, and the persuasion, v. 8. Doctrines in the Scriptures are not dissociated from the persons who maintain them.

Leaven is not used in a metaphorical sense in the Old Testament, and in the New Testament is only once found it its literal sense, Matthew 16:12. Elsewhere it is always a symbol of the pervasive power of evil; there seems to be no valid reason for excepting Matthew 13:33. This phrase was probably a current saying, for it occurs again in 1 Corinthians 5:6, there of moral evil as here of doctrinal.

5:10 I have confidence—*peithō,* as in v. 7, but here in the tense of completeness and finality, "I am persuaded." The paronomasia already noticed is continued. "I" is emphatic, "whoever he may be who is hindering your fidelity to and progress in the gospel, I, Paul, who first brought that gospel to you, have not lost the confidence concerning your call from God of which I was then persuaded."

There is a twofold difference between this passage and Romans 8:38. Here, as noticed above, "I" is emphatic, there the emphasis is on the verb. Here he is giving expression not to the result of experience or of argument, but to a desire of the consummation of which he is hopeful; it is "I feel sure." In Romans 8:38 he is declaring the result in his own mind of the reasons he had adduced, combined with his experience of the power of the Lord to save. These had carried him irresistibly to the conclusion that whatever the future might contain for him and for his readers, nothing could hinder the consummation of the purposes of God for them; it is "I am sure."

to you-ward in the Lord,—see comment on *2 Thessalonians* 3:3. "To you-ward" differs nothing from "toward you" in actual meaning, though the departure from the usual form may, perhaps, suggest that these words form the subordinate and unemphatic part of the sentence. Paul's confidence is not in them, it is in the Lord for all things, their spiritual welfare included.

that ye will be none otherwise minded:—*phroneō* = "to think," "to form a judgment"; but in the New Testament never merely "to hold an opinion," always it is contemplated that action will be taken upon the judgment formed, cp. Philippians 4:10, e.g., Paul was not merely in their minds to think about, their thought for him had been translated into acts. The ellipsis to be supplied here is to the effect that he is sure that in their final judgment and consequent conduct they will not differ from what they had been taught at the beginning, what they had accepted as the counsel of God for their salvation, and what is now confirmed to them in this Epistle, and that therefore they will resist and shun the Judaizers and their teaching.

but he that troubleth you—as at 1:7, above.

shall bear—*bastazō,* to support as a burden, whether physically, John 19:17, or spiritually, Luke 14:27, and so, to lift up, John 10:31, and to carry away, Acts 3:2. Here it is used of the burden of the sentence of God to be delivered in due time. For an analogy in temporal affairs cp. 2 Kings 18:14, LXX; occurs also in 6:2, below.

his judgment,—the apostle had given his own judgment upon the aim and teachings of the Judaizers, a judgment based upon varied and good grounds fully set forth, not upon prejudice or any mere personal feeling or pique that his teaching and influence had been set aside. There was, however, a court of appeal, even to God whose decisions, *krima*, are according to truth, Romans 2:2, and from which there is no appeal and no escape.

Krima is usually the decision which results from an investigation, just as *krisis* (see comment on *2 Thess.* 1:5) is the process of investigation; sometimes the two are interchanged, as in 1 Peter 4:17, *krima*, where the process of judgment rather than the resulting decision seems to be intended. Hence *krima* is used of the estimate one man forms of another, Matthew 7:2, and of the decision of human tribunals, Luke 23:40, of the decisions of God, in general, Romans 11:33, and in particular concerning the devil, 1 Timothy 3:6, and man, Mark 12:40 and here.

This judgment is usually unfavorable to the person judged, but Revelation 20:4 may be an exception, for if those who sat upon the thrones are those described in the remainder of the verse then the judgment is a decision in their favor; it may be, however, that the words are to be understood by 1 Corinthians 6:2.

In John 9:39 the Lord declares that He is in the world "for judgment," *eis krima*, i.e., to bring men to decision, to be the touchstone of the destiny of men. In Revelation 18:20 "judged (*krinō*, see comment on *2 Thess.* 2:12, *e*) your judgment" is probably to be understood as "executed the judgment that you had passed upon her," though it may mean "executed upon her the judgment that she had passed upon you."

In most cases the decision includes the sentence pronounced in consequence of the decision, but where it is necessary to distinguish between them, as in Romans 5:16, *krima* is the decision, *katakrima* is the sentence, "the decision was formed on one trespass of one man, and in accordance therewith sentence was passed upon all men." *Katakrima* occurs again in Romans 5:18 and 8:1.||

Another compound of *krima* is *prokrima*, "prejudice," i.e., a sentence passed before trial, or investigation, 1 Timothy 5:21; a not uncommon evil among Christians, the magnitude of which may be inferred from the language in which it is here forbidden. Prejudice is at once folly and shame to a man, Proverbs 18:13.||

whosoever he be.—for of course there is no respect of persons with God, see at 2:6, above. "Who did hinder you?" the apostle asked, v. 7, but not to elicit information, for "whosoever he may be" it matters not, though it be Peter himself on the one hand, or the most ignorant and malicious of the Jews on the other; he is "a troubler" of God's people, and must "give account of himself to God," Romans 14:12. Cp. the words of the Lord Jesus, "Whoso shall cause one of these little ones which believe on Me to stumble, it is profitable for him that a great millstone should be hanged about his neck, and that he should be sunk in the depth of the sea . . . woe to that man," Matthew 18:6, 7.

5:11 But I, brethren, if I still preach—*kērussō*, as at 2:2, above.

circumcision,—the apostle turns suddenly to meet a charge of inconsistency, perhaps of insincerity, made against him by the Judaizing party, one to which indeed he had already somewhat indirectly referred, 1:8, 9, above. His action in regard to Timothy may have afforded ground for this charge. But the case of Timothy differed from that of Titus 2:3, above, in an important particular. Titus was a Gentile born of Gentile parents; Timothy's mother was a Hebrew, his father a Gentile, he was therefore the offspring of a union plainly prohibited by the Mosaic Law. It may have seemed expedient to the apostle on this account to circumcise Timothy in order to conciliate some who through ignorance, or through weakness in the faith, were sensitive on the point. However that may have been, the apostle soon learned that any attempt to conciliate the Judaizers was foredoomed to failure, and would probably involve the churches in disaster. The time arrived when it became necessary to oppose them at all points, and to attack their hybrid system of salvation by works and faith with every legitimate weapon available. The pressure in favor of circumcision was renewed when Titus came to Antioch, but now the apostle did not yield. So long as he hoped to further the interests of the gospel by conciliating the Judaizers he endeavored to conciliate them, perhaps even hoped to win them; now he saw clearly that these interests could be preserved and furthered only by bold and insistent attack upon those who opposed them.

why am I still persecuted?—the answer to the charge seems conclusive; is it conceivable that they would deliberately persecute one who actively maintained their own doctrines?

The former "still" refers either, *a,* to the period before his conversion, the latter to the period since, or, *b,* the former refers to the period after his conversion during which the apostle had himself sanctioned circumcision in the case at least of Jews, the latter to the subsequent period during which he had so strenuously opposed circumcision and all that of which it is significant. On the whole *b* seems to be the better sense.

It may be that by this second "still" the apostle intends a delicate reminder that when they accepted his gospel they too were persecuted, see 3:4, above, and suggests that their change of doctrine had brought about an alleviation of their troubles. Could it be that the prospect of relief from persecution had weighed with them when they were tempted to "receive circumcision"? It was possible that such considerations weakened the will to obey the truth at whatever cost.

It is also possible that the first "still" is quoted directly from some utterance of his antagonists, the second is his "counter thereto"; perhaps a subtle way of suggesting that they had always persecuted him throughout his ministry of the gospel. It may well be that he knew that in fact the opposition of the Judaizers arose out of their reluctance to preach the gospel to the Gentiles at all, or at least that they wished to make of them Jewish proselytes first, and Christians after. But Paul did not share their mind that Christianity was in any sense "a sect of the Jews."

then—"in that case," i.e., if he still preached circumcision; for it was the Cross, and the doctrines of which it is the symbol, so repugnant to the Jew, and indeed to men generally, that had provoked the persecution to which Paul and others had been subjected.

hath the stumbling block—*skandalon,* originally the name of that part of a trap to which the bait is attached, and hence the trap or snare itself, as in Romans 11:9, quoted from Psalm 69:22, which see, and in Revelation 2:14, for Balaam's device was rather a trap for Israel than a stumbling block to them, and in Matthew 16:23, for in Peter's words the Lord perceived a snare laid for Him by Satan.

In the New Testament *skandalon* is always used metaphorically, and ordinarily of anything that arouses prejudice, or becomes a hindrance to others, or causes them to fall by the way. Sometimes the hindrance is in itself good, and those stumbled by it are the wicked. Thus Christ Himself, because He came in circumstances entirely different from those in which He was expected by the Jews; because His teaching and His experiences were entirely different from their preconceptions of what they would be; and because He abrogated the works of the law in favor of the obedience of faith as the ground of justification and the way of access to God, became a stumbling block to them, as indeed the prophets had foreseen would be the case, Romans 9:33; 1 Peter 2:8, where Isaiah 8:14 is cited. And if He was a stumbling block to them in the manner of His life, and in the matter of His teaching, much more was He a stumbling block to them in the manner of His death, but above all were their most virulent prejudices aroused by the apostolic declaration of the significance and purpose of that death, to which the writer refers here and in 1 Corinthians 1:23.

In His teaching the Lord frequently bade the disciples to beware lest in their words, or by their conduct, they should become stumbling blocks to other people, and especially to the less mature among those who believed on Him; to offenders in this matter His warning is couched in language of quite exceptional severity, Matthew 18:7; Luke 17:1, cp. Leviticus 19:14, which may, indeed, have been in His mind. It is to be noted, moreover, that men become stumbling blocks not merely by their words and by their actions, but also by that less easily controlled and more subtly effective thing called personal influence. As to the future the Lord declared, when He explained the parable of the tares in the field, that "all things that cause stumbling" shall be gathered out of His kingdom when He comes to establish it on the earth, Matthew 13:41.

The apostle John asserts that the man who loves his brother does not present any stumbling block to others, i.e., since love works no ill to any, Romans 13:10, and never fails in seeking the welfare of any, 1 Corinthians 13:8; where love rules the heart personal influence tells not for evil but for good, 1 John 2:10. Hence it follows that the cultivation of love (for which see comment on *1 Thess.*

3:12) is the best security against the woes pronounced by the Lord Jesus upon those who stumble others. The apostle Paul also warns the believer against putting "an occasion of falling" in his brother's way, with reference to the use of Christian liberty in such a way as to prove a hindrance to another, Romans 14:13, and with reference to the teaching of things contrary to sound doctrine, 16:17.||

A synonym of *skandalon, proskomma,* = "an obstacle against which one may dash his foot," is also used. The two words appear together in Romans 9:32, 33; 1 Peter 2:8, of the Lord Jesus Christ. The gospel of a crucified Messiah was in direct conflict with the religious conceptions of the Jews; it was diametrically opposed to all their thoughts concerning God and His Messiah. They conceived of God as One who only commands His creatures, whereas in the gospel He entreats them, 2 Corinthians 5:20; they conceived of Him as the receiver of the homage expressed in sacrifice, whereas in the gospel it is declared that He Himself made the supreme sacrifice in behalf of His creatures, John 3:16. And the Christ who was condemned justifies; He Who did not save Himself from a death of shame saves others; He who died gives life. The very glories of the gospel were to the Jews blasphemy against God and dishonor to men. Both words appear again in Romans 14:13 of the believer, who is to be ever on his guard lest by any selfishness in the use of his liberty he should become a hindrance to the spiritual progress of another, for that is an evil thing to do, v. 20. The matter is summed up in 1 Corinthians 8:9, and urged particularly in 2 Corinthians 6:3 (where *proskopē,* another form of the word is used). From these passages it is plain that the spiritual well-being of others is to be the paramount consideration with the Christian; to this end he is to subordinate his own preferences, desires, privileges, and legitimate interests, in which, indeed, Christ Himself is his constant pattern, Matthew 17:27, where the verb *skandalizo* appears.||

In some Old Testament passages warnings are given against things that affect adversely the spiritual welfare of men, that, in the language of 1 Peter 2:11, "war against the soul." Recognition of, or acquiescence in, or association with the idolatries of the Canaanites would cause their gods to become a stumbling block, *proskomma,* to the Israelites, Exodus 23:33, cp. Hosea 4:17. "Ephraim partaking with idols hath laid stumbling blocks *(skandalon)* in his own path." See also Proverbs 16:18, "a haughty spirit (becomes) a stumbling block," *proskopē,* i.e., to oneself. In each case the reference is to LXX.

of the cross—*stauros,* a stake, a pole, to which criminals were nailed and left until death ensued. To this form of capital punishment peculiar ignominy attached, it was reserved for slaves and for malefactors of the lowest type; see at 3:13, above.

Besides its literal meaning, *stauros* is also in the New Testament used in metonymy as under:

a, of things from which, though not in themselves evil, men recoil, and which they naturally endeavor to shun, but which are appointed by God for the discipline of the spirit, and as such are to be accepted by the believer. This meaning is found only in the words of the Lord Jesus who Himself submitted to such things daily, and who knew that He would "lay down His life" of His own deliberate choice, the preordained instrument of His death providing the figure under which He urges upon all who name His Name the life of self-renunciation in which He set them an example, Luke 9:23;

b, the instrument of the death of Christ is put for the death itself, 6:14, below;

c, and for the purpose of that death as at once confirming the universal condemnation of men (inasmuch as Christ Himself came under it when "He bare our sins in His Body upon the Tree," 1 Pet. 2:24), and providing a way of escape therefrom (inasmuch as in bearing our sins He put them away, Heb. 9:28), Ephesians 2:16.

been done away.—*katargeō*, see at v. 4, above (and for analysis of the New Testament occurrences see comment on *2 Thess.* 2:8).

The real ground of the persecution of Paul and those associated with him was, of course, that the abrogation of circumcision effectually broke down the religious monopoly which the Jews claimed for themselves under the old covenant. But if the death of Christ did not render circumcision nugatory, and if Paul still insisted on circumcision, then he also maintained that monopoly. Why then persecute him, as undoubtedly they were still doing? It was absurd; they could not have it both ways; either he still preached circumcision and was no longer persecuted, or if he was persecuted it was because he opposed circumcision, and in so doing denied to the Jews a monopoly of the favor of God.

The conclusion is plainly inconsistent with the facts; he was still persecuted, and for preaching "the Word of the Cross," 1 Corinthians 1:18; his gospel had not changed; there was no more ground in fact for this calumny of the Judaizers than there was basis in Scripture for their teaching.

5:12 I would that—*ophelon*, an exclamation which here and in 1 Corinthians 4:8; Revelation 3:15 would have been more effectively rendered without "I," as in 2 Corinthians 11:1.‖

they which unsettle you—*anastatoō*, "to upset," as Paul and his companions were said to "turn the civilised world upside down," Acts 17:6; in Acts 21:38 it is rendered "stirred up to sedition."‖

The continuous tense is used, "those who are attempting to unsettle you."

would even cut themselves off.—*apokoptō*, to amputate, as a hand or foot, Mark 9:43, 45, or an ear, John 18:10, 26; to divide, to sever, as a rope, Acts 27:32. The Judaizers attempted to excommunicate the Galatian believers, 4:17, the apostle desired that they would excommunicate themselves, and so relieve the troubled churches of their presence altogether.‖

5:13 For—referring back to the statement of v. 1. Verses 2-12 form a parenthesis of mingled warning and encouragement and indignant expostulation. Here the more directly practical section of the Epistle begins; the apostle is about to show that the doctrines upon which he so strenuously insists are vitally related to the character and conduct that become confessors of Christ, and thus, incidentally, to dispose of the common objection that the doctrines of grace encourage license in behavior, see Romans 3:7, 8; 6:1.

ye, brethren, were called—as at v. 8, above. "Ye" is emphatic, apparently in order to bring home to them that this was not a merely academic discussion, that the truth for which the writer contended was of vital consequence, affecting each of them personally. Let them beware, then, lest the very purpose of God in their calling should be missed, and they themselves lose the blessing of the freedom that Christ had purchased for them, and that God intended them to enjoy.

for—*epi*, here = "with a view to" as in 1 Thessalonians 4:7, where see note.

freedom;—*eleutheria;* slavery, established and regulated by law, was an integral element in the social fabric of the apostle's day. Provision was made, among other things, for the liberation of the slave, and this was effected by a legal fiction according to which he was purchased by a deity, Apollo or another; the purchase money was in fact provided by the slave who, as he had no legal standing, no civil rights, could not purchase himself. To meet this difficulty the sum appointed was paid into the temple treasury, whither master and slave proceeded. There, when the money was paid over, a document was drawn up and duly attested, to the effect that so-and-so had been purchased by the deity at such a price; in some of these documents the same words that are used by the apostle here, "for freedom," i.e., "with the object of setting him free," were inserted. Henceforth the erstwhile slave is his own master, and may do "the things that he will," nor may any man bring him into bondage again inasmuch as, in theory at least, he is now the property of the god who purchased him.*

In the New Testament men are declared to be in bondage, the Jews to law, 4:3, above, Romans 7:1, the Gentiles to idols, 4:8, above, 1 Corinthians 12:2, and all to sin, Romans 6:6, 17; therein, too, the way to freedom is declared in language which is largely that of the manumission from social slavery just described. The seed from which this conception of salvation as deliverance from bondage afterwards developed is found, however, in the words of the Lord Jesus, cp. Matthew 20:28, "the Son of Man came . . . to give His life a ransom for many," and Luke 21:38, "your redemption draweth nigh," and John 8:36, "If . . . the Son shall make you free [lit., free you], ye shall be free indeed." Thus men are set at liberty by Christ who purchased them at a price, 1 Corinthians 6:20; 7:23, which is His own blood, Acts 20:28; 1 Peter 1:18, 19, for He actually did

*Deissman, "Light from the Ancient East."

at His own cost what the god did fictionally with money provided by the slave. Thus those who were in bondage to law, idols and sin, become the bond servants of Christ, of God and of righteousness, Romans 6:18, 22; 1 Corinthians 7:22. And he who thus becomes "the Lord's free man" must beware lest he should submit to any other bondage, or lest he should be robbed of his liberty, 2:4; 5:1, above, Romans 6:12, 14; 1 Corinthians 7:23. Henceforth being "under law to Christ," 1 Corinthians 9:21, sealed and indwelt by the Holy Spirit, Ephesians 1:13, 14, and bearing "the fruit of the Spirit," he makes it his aim "to be well-pleasing unto Him" who set him free, 2 Corinthians 5:9. Thus it is that when a man is set free from the law through the death of Christ "the ordinance, or requirement, of the law" is nevertheless fulfilled in him inasmuch as he "walks" no longer "after the flesh, but after the Spirit," Romans 8:4.

only use not your freedom for—*eis*, "unto," i.e., with this end in view. Privilege is always attended by the danger of abuse, and liberty is not an exception to this rule; as, therefore, the apostle had encouraged them to respond boldly to God's call to liberty, so now he warns them against the misuse of it. The Christian must not allow himself to be persuaded to renounce his liberty indeed, but for the sake of others he may be called to forego the display of it.

an occasion—*aphormē*, which, among other meanings, was used in writings contemporary with the New Testament of a base of operations in war; it occurs as follows:

a, the law provided sin with a base of operations for its attack upon the soul, Romans 7:8, 11;

b, the irreproachable conduct of the apostle provided his friends with a base of operations against his detractors, 2 Corinthians 5:12;

c, the apostle by refusing temporal support at Corinth deprived these same detractors of their base of operations against him, 2 Corinthians 11:12;

d, unguarded behavior on the part of young widows (and the same is true of all believers) would provide Satan with a base of operations against the faith, 1 Timothy 5:14.||

to the flesh,—the seat and organ of sin in man; see at 3:3, above.

Paul's teaching on the subject of Christian freedom here may have been one of those "things hard to be understood, which the ignorant and unsteadfast wrest . . . unto their own destruction," 2 Peter 3:16, and this is the more likely if, as seems to be the case, Peter also addressed the Galatian churches, see at v. 4, above. For in his denunciation of the "false teachers" he declares that they "promise liberty" to those who are "just escaping the defilements of the world" in order to entangle them again therein, that they may be overcome thereby, 2 Peter 2:19, 20. But notwithstanding their use of Paul's words, plainly this liberty is not the liberty of Christ and His Spirit of which Paul spoke, but that license in which the flesh finds a base for its operations against the spirit, and which in fact brings a man into bondage to corruption, those filthy and death-doomed things which God hates, Jeremiah 44:4.

Peter's teaching in this passage, that if a man indulges in any of the world's defilements he is made its slave, is closely parallel with Romans 6:16, where Paul declares that if a man yields to sin he becomes sin's servant, and with Titus 3:3, "serving divers lusts and pleasures." This principle, however, was first asserted by the Lord Jesus, "Every one that committeth [present continuous tense, = he who is committing] sin is the servant of sin," John 8:34.

but—*alla,* "but on the contrary."

through—*dia,* "by the way of," "by means of."

love—that love fulfills the law the Lord Jesus also showed in His "Golden Rule," Matthew 7:12, "All things therefore whatsoever ye would that men should do unto you, even so do ye also unto them: for this is the law and the prophets." This is love's law, to put oneself in another's place and to act toward that other as though he were oneself. Thus will the Christian not merely work no ill to his neighbor, Romans 13:10, he will, as need arises and as opportunity offers, spend himself in his neighbor's service, for would not he have his neighbor do the like for him? This is what James calls "the perfect law, the law of liberty," "the royal law," 1:25; 2:8. By it is the Christian bound, and in it finds that "a life of self-renouncing love is a life of liberty."

be servants—*douleuō,* for which see comment on *1 Thessalonians* 1:9; the tense is continuous, "let it be your habit to serve." The paradox, or apparent contradiction, is noteworthy, "for freedom . . . be servants"; the Christian is free in order that he may serve.

The Lord Jesus is the true servant, the type to which the servants conform; hence the apostle writes that in His self-humiliation the Son of God took "the form, *morphē,* of a servant," Philippians 2:7; but *morphē* means not merely the outward appearance, what meets the eye of an observer, it conveys the idea that what is seen is the expression of the essential nature that underlies the appearance. Thus the Lord Jesus not only seemed to be a servant, He had become a servant in verity. In Him, moreover, love is seen to be the motive of true service. Because He loved the Father, John 14:31, therefore He became obedient even unto death, Philippians 2:8; because He loved His disciples there-fore He washed their feet, John 13:1; because He loved the church therefore He gave Himself up for it, Ephesians 5:25; cp. the apostle's own course described in 1 Corinthians 9:19. Where love is the motive, service is without constraint; where love is not, service is an irksome burden.

one to another.—among men the natural ambition is to attain to a position in which it will be possible to lord it over others, see Mark 10:42–45, and hence come jealousy and strife. Over against this natural ambition Christ sets His own example as that to which all who name His name are to be conformed. Where

His precept is obeyed and His example followed no one will take advantage of another, for each will live to serve after the pattern of Christ, and none to lord it over the rest after the corrupting example of the world. Any attempt to dominate the brethren is evidence of the absence of love, which is due, in turn, to alienation from the spirit of Christ. Against the danger of self-indulgence, which attends so closely upon liberty, the best safeguard is to hold liberty as a trust from the Lord in the interests of the brethren, not as an end in itself, but as a means to an end, the welfare of others.

The Galatians had been tempted to exchange an old bondage for a new; Christ offered them a bondage better than either, a bondage in which the highest freedom is preserved, for to live in love is to be at once bond and free. If, as is possible, charges of antinomianism had been brought against the apostle on account of the doctrine of grace which he preached, see Romans 6:1, here was his answer: grace produces love, and he who abides in love abides in God, for God is love, 1 John 4:16. He who becomes a bond servant of God, then, must not, and will not, use his freedom as a cloak for anything base, 1 Peter 2:16.

5:14 For—a reason for such a command is now provided; they desire to be under the law; here then is the sum and substance of the law, and the acceptance of the gospel would not hinder them, but, on the contrary, would enable them to do what the law aimed at, indeed, but could not accomplish, that is, to live according to the will of God.

the whole law—the Greek phrase differs somewhat from that rendered in the same way in v. 3, above. There the law is viewed as made up of separate commandments, each of which is essential to the whole, and consequently must be obeyed; here the separate commandments are viewed as combined to make a complete law summed up and expressed in one comprehensive word.

is fulfilled—*plēroō,* as in Romans 13:8; the tense is that which expresses completeness, effected in the past and continued into the present. The words may mean either, *a,* that the full intention of the law is expressed in one precept, or, *b,* that the whole law is fulfilled where this one precept is observed. In Romans 13:8–10, where the apostle deals with the same subject at greater length, the separate commandments of the law are enumerated and "summed up" in the same precept. This consideration favors the former interpretation, but at the close of the paragraph in Romans 13 he asserts that "love . . . is the fulfillment of the law," thus favoring the latter meaning. It is probable then that the two ideas are combined here, that the distinction is not made in the earlier and briefer treatment here that is made in the later and longer one in Romans. Indeed it follows that if all the commandments of the law are summed up in one precept, then to keep that precept is to keep the whole law.

in one word, even in this;—*logos,* here = a precept or commandment, cp. "decalogue," from *deka,* ten, and *logos,* a word, "the ten words," i.e., the Ten Commandments, Deuteronomy 10:4, cp. "in this word," Romans 13:9.

Thou shalt love thy neighbor as thyself.—cited from Leviticus 19:18. "Neighbor" is *plēsios,* "the near one"; but in the law the Jew only was intended, for "neighbor" is parallel with, and hence is an equivalent of, "the children of thy people"; cp. also vv. 16, 17, "thy people," "thy brother." The question of the scope of the word had apparently been raised among the lawyers of Israel, for one of them, when the Lord Jesus quoted this passage, asked Him, "And who is my neighbor?" Luke 10:25 ff. The effect of the parable of the good Samaritan, given in reply, was to answer "not fellow-nationals but fellowmen"; the claim of one man upon another rests not upon consanguinity (in the narrower, non-Scriptural sense, see Acts 17:26) but upon need.

The teaching of the present passage also appears to be based directly on that of the Lord Jesus, Matthew 22:34–40, who, however, made a distinction between love to God and love to one's neighbor, and declared that all that God had revealed in the law and in the prophets "depends" upon these two. The thought conveyed by the language of the apostle is not really different.

The Lord represents the various commandments as radiating out from these two, the apostle represents the commandments as converging upon them. That the apostle does not refer either here or in Romans 13 to "the great and first commandment" is perhaps due to the fact that his immediate purpose was to urge upon believers their responsibilities toward all men, whereas the Lord was answering a question about the right interpretation of the law.

Both the Lord Jesus and the apostle, on the occasions mentioned, appealed to the essentials of the law as proclaimed in the law itself, and this because of the condition of those addressed in each case. The lawyer asked concerning the law, and out of the law the Lord answered him; the Galatians desired to submit to the law, and out of the law the apostle directed them to the true way of submission to the law. There was a higher standard, however, for those who had made, or promised to make, progress. "The new commandment" was not merely "that ye love one another"; the newness lay in the different standard; "as thyself," said the law, "as I have loved you," said the Lord, John 13:34; 15:12. So also Paul, "walk in love, even as Christ also loved you," Ephesians 5:2; cp. 1 John 3:16.

5:15 But—having asserted that true liberty expresses itself in mutual love, the apostle adds a necessary warning against the false liberty which is self-assertive and which issues inevitably in mutual destruction. Love takes account of infirmity, makes no demands, imposes no conditions, looks for no compensations, delights to serve. Law, on the contrary, knowing neither mercy nor compassion, unable to relent, or to relax the least of its provisions, must condemn all that fall short of the absolute perfection it demands. And thus, finding fault itself, law produces a fault-finding, censorious spirit. Hence the apostle warns them of yet another result of adhesion to law.

if ye bite—*daknō,* which, like the English word, besides its literal, has a wide range of metaphorical meaning.||

and devour one another,—*katesthiō,* lit., "to eat up," in the New Testament used of the effect of fire, Revelation 11:5; of the unscrupulous rapacity of the scribes, Mark 12:40; Luke 20:47; and of that exploiting of one another which is the antithesis of love, 2 Corinthians 11:20, and here.||

take heed—*blepō,* to look, to see, whether with the physical eye, Matthew 6:4, or in mental vision, Romans 7:23, or of inanimate things, Acts 27:12. It also means "to attach importance to," Matthew 22:16, and "to be on one's guard against," Mark 12:38, and here.

that ye be not consumed one of another.—*analiskō,* as in Luke 9:54; 2 Thessalonians 2:8, marg.; in those places literally, here metaphorically. If they lived in mutual love they would be "knit together" and would make "increase of the body unto the building up of itself," Ephesians 4:16, but if they were possessed by the opposite spirit they could only work havoc among themselves with the certain result that their corporate testimony would be laid in ruins.||

The ideal picture of a church is of brethren dwelling together in unity because they are indwelt by the Holy Spirit of God, Psalm 133:1; here the apostle presents a contrast, savage beasts making of each other a prey. Thus he warns them that party strife never ends in victory for either side, but always in mutual destruction. There is here an instance of the figure of speech called climax, "bite . . . devour . . . consume"; for another instance of the same figure, "steal . . . kill . . . destroy," see John 10:10. "Bite" and "devour" are in the continuous tense, they describe a process; "be consumed" is in the momentary, or point, tense, it describes the result of the process.

5:16 But I say,—as at 4:1, above. In the preceding passage they were urged to use their freedom aright and to exercise their love in mutual service. Still the Christian life is not merely the response to law imposed from without, however excellent that law may be, it is the result of a new spirit quickened within. Nevertheless, just as law must be obeyed, so must the spirit of the believer yield to the guidance, and receive the power, communicated to it by the Holy Spirit of God.

Walk—*peripateō* for which see comment on *1 Thessalonians 2:11.*

by the Spirit,—see at v. 5, above.

and ye shall . . . fulfill—*teleō,* which may mean, *a,* simply to end anything, as a journey, lit., Matthew 10:23, or metaphorically, 2 Timothy 4:7, or a discourse, Matthew 11:1; 13:53; 19:1; 26:1, or an experience of trial, Luke 12:50, or a period of time, Revelation 20:3, 5, 7. It may also mean, *b,* to "complete," as an appointed work is completed, John 19:30; Revelation 11:7; but of course these meanings overlap at times, so that it is not always possible to exclude one in favor of the other. The following list covers the remaining passages in the New Testament:

c, to exhaust, of the wrath of God, Revelation 15:1, 8;

d, to obey a law, whether of purpose, Luke 2:39, James 2:8, or unconsciously, Romans 2:27;

e, to give effect to, here;

f, to pay a tax, Matthew 17:24; Romans 13:6;

g, of the accomplishment of a purpose, Revelation 10:7;

h, said of the coming to pass of the prophetic word, Luke 18:31; 22:37; John 19:28; Acts 13:29; Revelation 17:17.||

not—*ou mē,* which in 1 Thessalonians 4:15; 5:3, and many other places is translated "in no wise." The sentence may be read either, *a,* as an assurance to the believer that if he walks by the Spirit, i.e., if he submits to the leading of the Holy Spirit of God, refusing to order his life according to the promptings of the flesh and the conventions of the age, then he shall not be overmastered by the desires of the flesh, but on the contrary shall have the victory over, and be enabled to live superior to, them; or, *b,* as a command followed by a prohibition, the first positive, "submit to the leading of the Holy Spirit"; the second negative, "refuse to order your life according to the promptings of the flesh and the conventions of this age." It is not possible to decide between these interpretations on purely grammatical grounds. The negative is strongly emphatic; if a prohibition is intended (*b,* above) no exception is permitted, if an assurance is intended (*a,* above) then there is no possibility of any miscarriage or failure of the divine power.

the lust—*epithumia,* for which see comment on *1 Thessalonians 2:17; 4:5;* this leads easily and inevitably to the biting and devouring just mentioned.

of the flesh.—*sarx,* see note *i* at 3:3, above.

5:17 For—introducing the ground on which the assurance *(a)* or prohibition *(b)* of v. 16 is based. The Spirit and the flesh are mutually antagonistic in nature, and where the expressed condition is fulfilled the victory of the Spirit is assured to the believer.

the flesh lusteth—*epithumeō,* which is used of the Lord Jesus, Luke 22:15 ("desire"), and of the angels, 1 Peter 1:12, and of the desires of good men for good things, Hebrews 6:11, and of the desires of men for things without moral quality, Luke 15:16, as well as of desires evil in themselves, Acts 20:33.

against the Spirit, and the Spirit against the flesh;—the Holy Spirit is intended, as in the preceding verse. As he had exhorted them to walk by the Spirit, so he warns them to expect opposition in endeavoring so to do. The verb is not repeated after "Spirit," but must of course be supplied; it is as suitably used of the Spirit as of the Lord Jesus, see above, but since in modern English the word "lust" is used exclusively in a bad sense it is therefore unsuitable as a rendering of *epithumeō* where the word is used in a good sense.

for—introducing the explanation of the opposition between the flesh and the Holy Spirit.

these are contrary the one to the other;—*antikeimai,* for which see comment on *2 Thessalonians* 2:4. The flesh, what man became in his nature in consequence of the Fall, with his propensity for evil, and the Holy Spirit, who is God, are, in the nature of the case, mutually antagonistic and impossible of reconciliation.

that—*hina,* which may be understood in one of two ways; if the preceding words are to be read as a parenthesis then the connection is "the Spirit resisteth the flesh in order that ye may not do the things that ye [otherwise] would"; but if these words are not parenthetic then the connection is "these are contrary the one to the other, so that ye may not do the things that ye would." In the first case the thought is that the object of the striving of the Spirit in the believer is that he may be saved from yielding to the evil tendencies of his own nature; in the other case it is that the conflict in the believer which hinders his doing the things that he would, whether good or evil, is explained by the contrariety of the two forces at work within him. The former of these interpretations is to be preferred.

ye may not do the things that ye would.—more literally and expressively "in order that the things you desire these you may not do," i.e., the things toward which fallen man naturally turns, and which are enumerated in v. 19 as "the works of the flesh." This is the characteristic of Christian liberty as an experience; since the believer is indwelt by the Holy Spirit it is no longer inevitable that he must yield to the evil motions of the flesh, he shall, if the condition of vv. 16 and 18 is fulfilled, enjoy happy liberty from all such bondage. And not only so, as he yields himself to the guidance and strengthening of the Spirit he is enabled to refuse "to do those things which are not fitting," Romans 1:28, and to bear that "fruit" of which the apostle is shortly to speak.

5:18 But if ye are led—*agō,* which includes the idea that he who is led not merely follows but does so willingly and intelligently; see comment on *1 Thessalonians* 4:14. This figure is complementary to that of v. 16; the believer walks in the counsel and by the power of the Spirit, the Spirit guides the believer in his way.

by the Spirit,—i.e., if a man submits himself to the will of God as it is revealed in the gospel, or as otherwise expressed, if a man is a Christian, a believer on the Lord Jesus Christ. The same words are used in Romans 8:14.

ye are not under the law.—neither as a way of life, nor as a means of justification, nor as a rule of conduct; cp. "ye also were made dead to the law by the body of Christ; . . . we have been discharged from the law," Romans 7:4, 6, and "not being myself under the law," 1 Corinthians 9:20.

The connection is not immediately evident, but apparently the apostle reverts to the idea of law as the provoker of transgression, see note at 3:19, above. There is a double antagonism, *a,* the Spirit versus the flesh, and, *b,* the Spirit versus the law. The law dealing with what is outward, with the conduct of men, did not avail to regulate it, because conduct is under the control of the heart, and the heart in turn is controlled by sin, cp. "I am carnal, sold under sin," Romans 7:14. But the heart of the regenerate man is just the sphere in which the Spirit carries on His work, see note at v. 5, above; there He gains His victories, which victories are manifested as His "fruit," see v. 22, below. So also the flesh, depraved human nature with its ineradicable sinward tendencies, is incapable of adequate response to law, which demands nothing less than obedience absolute and perfect; whereas by the act of the Spirit there is a new man brought into being "which after God is created in righteousness and holiness of truth," Ephesians 4:24, and hence is capable of responding to those impulses toward holiness and righteousness which are imparted to it by the Spirit. Romans 6:14 is closely parallel. The believer is assured that the lordship of sin over him is no longer of necessity, inasmuch as he is no longer under law, which demands obedience, but which cannot supply the power without which obedience is not possible. On the contrary, he is under grace, where inherent weakness is met by sufficient and instantly available strength, Ephesians 3:16.

5:19 Now the works of the flesh—cp. "lust of the flesh" in v. 16. The one term describes the inner motions of the soul, the natural tendency of men in their fallen estate toward things evil and toward things forbidden. The other describes the display of the effects of these motions in thought, in word, and in deed.

"Works" in the New Testament are not merely the results of the exercise of power under the direction of intelligence, as in John 5:36; 1 Corinthians 15:58; the outward and tangible expressions of character are also so described. What a person does testifies to what he is. From His works God is known, and the Son of God, John 10:37, 38. So also the character of Satan is manifested in his works, 8:41, as is that of his servants, i.e., preachers of a false gospel, 2 Corinthians 11:15. So also in the case of Cain, 1 John 3:12, and of the scribes and Pharisees, Matthew 23:3, and the ungodly Jews generally, Luke 11:48; indeed all manifestations of evil are summed up as "works of darkness," Romans 13:12, an expression closely akin to that of the text; cp. "the works of the world" in John 7:7, and contrast "works worthy of repentance" in Acts 26:20.

are manifest,—unlike lust, which is hidden.

which are these:—*hostis,* as at 4:24, above, and so = "these things and such things as these," the list does not exhaust the capacity of the flesh for evil; cp. 1 Timothy 1:10.

The catalogue of evil things which follows may perhaps be divided thus: 1–3, sensual sins, 4, 5, religious sins, 6–13, social sins, 14, 15, personal sins. But it may well be that the list lacks order and symmetry to suggest the chaos and confusion that characterize sin alike in its inner workings and in its manifestations.

fornication, uncleanness, lasciviousness,—the apostle puts at the head of the list the sins which set at defiance the primal laws of God which govern the continuation of the human race, and which are essential to its well-being, physical and moral, see Genesis 2:23, 24; Mark 10:6-9, and cp. 1 Corinthians 6:15-20. See also comment on *1 Thessalonians* 2:3; 4:3. There is a distinct climax in the order of the words: first a specific sin, then a general condition of impurity of mind, and finally an insolent disregard of decency. These three words are found together again in 2 Corinthians 12:21.

5:20 idolatry,—for which see comment on *1 Thessalonians* 1:9.

sorcery,—*pharmakia,* as in Revelation 9:21; 18:23, from which the English word "pharmacy" is derived, though the former belongs to superstition, the latter to science. Among pagan peoples the use of the simplest drugs is usually accompanied by an appeal to occult powers intended to impress the patient, and the uninitiated generally, with the mysterious resources of the physician. Cp. the magic of Egypt, Exodus 7:11, and of Babylon, Isaiah 47:9, 12, the "curious arts" of Ephesus, Acts 19:19, the "medicine" of present-day Africa, and the spiritism of civilized countries. These two, idolatry and sorcery, are vices in the religious sphere; the first open and evident, practiced by all, the second secret and obscure, practiced by the few. All five of these "works of the flesh" were associated with the pagan religious cults and with contemporary temple service; those who practice them are to suffer "the second death," Revelation 21:8.||

enmities,—*echthra,* which is the opposite of love, whether to God, Romans 8:7; Ephesians 2:15, 16; James 4:4, or to man, Luke 23:12. Its association with the following words, and the use of the plural, indicate that here the apostle has the mutual animosities of men in mind.||

jealousies,—*zēlos,* from which the English word "zeal" is derived. It is used in the New Testament in a good as well as in a bad sense; in John 2:17, e.g., of the devotedness of the Lord Jesus; in Hebrews 10:27 of the judgments of God; in 2 Corinthians 11:2 Paul speaks of his own "godly jealousy" over the converts. Here the meaning is wholly bad; this jealousy arises not out of love but out of enmity, and is an advance upon strife if only because the personal element is more prominent in it.

wraths,—*thumos,* in Revelation used seven times of the wrath of God, but elsewhere, save in Romans 2:8, only in a bad sense. Jealousy smolders in the heart until it breaks out in wrath.

factions,—*eritheia,* party-making, and taking sides for or against party leaders; it is frequently associated with jealousy, see James 3:14, 16, "where jealousy and faction are, there is confusion and every vile deed." The order is significant;

jealousy is the root of which faction, like wrath, is the fruit. These four words appear in the same order in 2 Corinthians 12:20.

divisions,—*dichostasia,* lit., "standing apart" in which party-making and side-taking are bound to result. Not only is the believer to beware of causing divisions himself, he is to be on his guard against those who manifest this disposition, and to "turn away from them," Romans 16:17.

heresies,—*hairesis,* = "a choosing" (cp. the verb *haireomai,* for which see comment on *2 Thess.* 2:13). Instead of submission to the gathering and combining power of truth, personal preference, or promise of advantage, leads to division, and so to the formation of sects or "parties," as margin. "Sect," indeed, is the translation of the word throughout Acts, see 5:17, e.g. The difference between the words seems to be that a division is the initial stage of a sect, a sect is a division matured and established. Sectarianism is thus the ultimate issue of the spirit of enmity. The advance to a climax in these seven "works of the flesh" manifested among men in their mutual relationships is readily discernible.

5:21 envyings,—*phthonos,* which is always in the New Testament (save in the difficult passage, James 4:5) used in a bad sense. Envy differs from jealousy in that the former desires merely to deprive another of what he has, whereas the latter desires as well to have the same, or a similar, thing for itself. On this account envy is said to be "as the rottenness of the bones," Proverbs 14:30; Trench, *Synonyms,* § xxvi., calls it "the meaner sin" of the two.

drunkenness,—*methē,* excessive indulgence in strong drink; lit., "drunken-nesses," as in Romans 13:13, but in Luke 21:34 "drunkenness."||

revelings,—*kōmos,* the consequence and concomitant of drunkenness; it is mentioned again in Romans 13:13; 1 Peter 4:3; in each place it is in the plural.||

and such like:—lit., "and things similar to these"; cp. notes on "which are these," above, and cp. "such things," below.

of which I forewarn you, even as I did forewarn you,—*prolegō,* as at 1 Thessalonians 3:4 (where see note) and 2 Corinthians 13:2. In each case the margin is probably to be preferred; the idea is not so much that he had prophesied a certain result if such things were permitted, but that he had told them, and now repeated his warning, of the inevitable consequence of permitting such things.||

that they which practice such things—*prassō,* in v. 17 the verb is *poieō,* which corresponds to the English "do," and has as wide a range of meaning. Speaking generally, in the Epistles of Paul *poieō* denotes an action complete in itself, whereas *prassō* denotes rather the habit that comes of the repetition of an act; both words appear in Romans 1:32, where the difference is readily discernible. Again, *poieō* emphasizes the accomplishment of something, as in

Romans 4:21, "perform," *prassō* the process whereby something is accomplished, as in 2:25, "doer." In v. 17, above, *poieō* is used because separate actions are contemplated, but *prassō* appears here because not an isolated act but a course of conduct is intended.

John, in his epistles, does not use *prassō* at all, but expresses the same idea by the continuous tenses of *poieō*, the present tense, as in the words "we do . . . the things that are pleasing in His sight," 1 John 3:22, or the present participle, as in "the doers of righteousness," v. 7, "the doers of sin," v. 8, for example. The teaching of v. 10 is similar to that of the present passage, which runs, literally, "all the not doers of righteousness are not of God," i.e., all those who do not practice righteousness are not born of God, whatever they may profess.

In the parallel passages, 1 Corinthians 6:9, 10; Ephesians 5:5, the apostle does not speak merely of persons doing or practicing certain things, he presses home the danger even more closely by speaking of persons to whom such things have become so habitual that a man can be characterized by the name of the vice he practices, so yielding himself to it that he has become its slave, Romans 6:16. Here drunkenness and idolatry, e.g., are specified, there the drunkard and the idolater, men who have not merely fallen into the sin of excess, or of worship of false gods, as into a snare, but men to whom these things have become habitual. The man who is overtaken in a trespass is to be restored by spiritual men, 6:1, below, but the man who makes the same sin the habit of his life not only sins against light, he refuses the power of Christ to free him from his bondage. And since by his fruits alone can the reality of a man's profession be judged, Matthew 7:16, the evidence of the new birth in such a case is absent. The list of Romans 1:29-31 is of like character with this, indeed many items are common to both, and concerning those who "practice such things" it is added that they "are worthy of death." But more, the man who does, *poieō*, such things is warned against judging those who practice them, *prassō;* he is not to reckon that he himself will escape the judgment of God, 2:2, 3. Nevertheless there is always a call to repentance, and an opportunity to repent, even for those who have practiced evil, 2 Corinthians 12:21; hence "except they repent" is to be understood in the present and the parallel passages. On the other hand, the practice of evil is evidence of hatred of the light, John 3:20, and those who have manifested that character shall come forth from the grave to "the resurrection of judgment," 5:29. See also Revelation 21:8, where the "part" of such persons is said to be "in the lake that burneth with fire and brimstone, which is the second death," and 22:15, where they, or such as they, are said to be without the city.

shall not—*ou*, the negative in its simple form, "shall not as a matter of fact."

inherit—*klēronomeō*, which is used in the New Testament as under:

a, birthright, that into the possession of which one enters in virtue of sonship, not because of a price paid or of a task accomplished, is said to be inherited, 4:30, above, Hebrews 1:4; 12:17;

b, that which is received as a gift, in contrast with that which is received as the reward of law-keeping (see 3:14–22, above, and notes) is said to be inherited, Hebrews 1:14; 6:12 ("through," i.e., "through experiences that called for the exercise of faith and patience," but not "on the ground of the exercise of faith and patience");

c, that which is received on condition of obedience to certain precepts, 1 Peter 3:9, and of faithfulness to God in the face of opposition, Revelation 21:7, is also said to be inherited;

d, the reward of that condition of soul which forbears retaliation and self-vindication, which expresses itself in gentleness of behavior, seeking not its own, 1 Corinthians 13:5 (and to which, therefore, "its own," Luke 16:12, is secure), Matthew 5:5.

The phrase "inherit the earth," or "land," occurs several times in the Old Testament, indeed the whole of this saying of the Lord Jesus is found in Psalm 37:11, 22. It seems to refer, in the first place, to the undisputed and undisturbed possession of the Promised Land by renewed Israel under the glorious rule of Messiah, in contrast with the uncertain tenure and harassed condition of Israel in the psalmist's day and in the days of the Lord's humiliation;

e, of the reward (in the coming age, Mark 10:30) of the acknowledgment of the paramountcy of the claims of Christ, Matthew 19:29.

In the three accounts given of this incident, see Mark 10:17–31, Luke 18:18–30, the words of the question put to the Lord are, in Matthew, "that I may have," in Mark and Luke, "that I may inherit." In the report of the Lord's words to Peter in reply to his subsequent question, Matthew has "inherit eternal life," while Mark and Luke have "receive eternal life." It seems to follow that the meaning of the word "inherit" is here ruled by the words "receive" and "have," with which it is interchanged in each of the three Gospels, i.e., the less common word "inherit" is to be regarded as equivalent to the more common words "receive" and "have." Cp. Luke 10:25;

f, of the reward of those who have shown kindness to the "brethren" of the Lord in their distress, Matthew 25:34, where "to inherit the kingdom" is alternated with "to enter into eternal life," see v. 46;

g, the incompatibility of the present physical constitution of man with the new order to be ushered in at the coming of the Lord is declared in the words "flesh and blood [the living] cannot inherit the Kingdom of God; neither doth corruption [the dead] inherit incorruption," 1 Corinthians 15:50;

h, so also of the morally corrupt, neither shall they inherit the kingdom of God, here, and 1 Corinthians 6:9, 10, cp. Ephesians 5.

In the present passage, and indeed throughout the epistle, the idea of the inheritance is always of something given in grace and received apart from works, see 3:18 and 4:7 above; in fact the meaning *a* is appropriated to spiritual uses. No man could qualify himself to inherit the kingdom of God, however assiduously he might practice the virtues to which these vices are opposed. On the other hand, the practice of the vices is presumptive evidence of the absence of that new birth which is the sole qualification for heirship. On this point the words of the Lord are explicit, "Not every one that saith unto Me, Lord, Lord, shall enter into the Kingdom of Heaven; but He that doeth the will of My Father, which is in Heaven," Matthew 7:21.||

For analyses of the New Testament usage of the words "inheritance" and "heir" see at 3:18, 29, above.

the kingdom of God.—see comment on *1 Thessalonians* 2:12. The parallel passage, Ephesians 5:5, has "the Kingdom of Christ and God." This expression cannot be confined to the millennial period, as though such as failed to inherit that would find their bliss in a later age. Neither does it seem possible in the descriptions given in these verses to recognize Christians, believers in, and disciples of, Christ ("the disciples were called Christians," Acts 11:26), men "in Christ." The apostle sets the two classes in contrast one with the other: "The unrighteous shall not inherit the Kingdom of God . . . And such were some of you; but ye were washed, but ye were sanctified, but ye were justified," 1 Corinthians 6:9-11.

Moreover, these very things call for "the wrath of God upon the sons of disobedience," hence the solemnity of the warning to those who name the name of the Lord to depart from unrighteousness, 2 Timothy 2:19, a warning which is also conveyed in the words "be not partakers with them," Ephesians 5:7. Rather the purpose in each of these passages seems to be to apply a moral test whereby the true may be distinguished from the false, the mere professor from the regenerate soul. Some men may, indeed, escape from the defilements of the world for a time through the knowledge of the Lord and Savior Jesus Christ, yet does it eventually happen to them according to the true proverb, the dog turns to his own vomit, the washed sow to her wallowing in the mire, 2 Peter 2:20-22. Such cannot have an inheritance of even a limited character in the Kingdom of God; their end is to endure the wrath of God, their portion is "the second death."

5:22 But the fruit—*karpos,* which occurs frequently in the New Testament in its natural sense of that which is produced by the inherent energy of a living organism, Matthew 13:8, and also, in a derived sense, of the result, in the spiritual and moral sphere, of the energy of the Holy Spirit operating in those who through faith are brought into living union with Christ, John 15:4, 5. "Fruit" is thus the outward expression of power working inwardly, and so in itself beyond observation, the character of the fruit giving evidence of the character of the power that produces it, Matthew 7:16. As lust manifests itself in works, the restless and disorderly activities of the flesh, or principle of evil, in man, so the Spirit manifests His presence in His "peaceable," Hebrews 12:11, and orderly fruit.

In this connection "fruit" presents an advance upon "works." "Works" gives prominence to the notion of activity; "fruit" directs attention to the power that works within.

The Christian graces here described, as to their origin, as "the fruit of the Spirit," in Philippians 1:11 are summed up as to their character, as "fruit [see margin] of righteousness."

"Fruit" is also used by the apostle Paul of the converts resulting from his ministry, Philippians 1:22; and of the manifestation of the character of Christ in the lives of believers in consequence of his ministry of the Word among them, Romans 1:13; and of the care of the believers for the poor, for this is the fruit, or outward expression, of love, attesting its reality, Romans 15:28; and of the care of laborers in the gospel, for this is the fruit, or outward expression, of thankfulness to God for spiritual blessings enjoyed, attesting its reality, Philippians 4:17.

In Ephesians 5:9 "the fruit of the light" is the manifestation, in goodness, righteousness, and truth, of the living union of the believer with God, Father, Son, and Spirit, inasmuch as the three virtues enumerated are three of the attributes of God. The believer is to display goodness because of his relationship with God his Father, for God is good, Mark 10:18, and it is the goodness of God which leads men to repentance, Romans 2:4; he is to display righteousness, because the Son of God, his Savior, is called "the Righteous One," Acts 7:52; and he is to display truth, because the Spirit, the indweller, is "the Spirit of [the] Truth," John 16:13. Cp. 1 John 1:5, "God [i.e., Father, Son, and Spirit, one God] is Light."

The singular form, "fruit," is used here perhaps to suggest the unity and harmony of the character of the Lord Jesus which is to be reproduced in the believer by the power of the Holy Spirit, in contrast with the discordant and often mutually antagonistic "works of the flesh." In Christ actually, and in the Christian potentially, the fruit of the Spirit is harmonious, the various elements being mutually consistent, and each encouraging and enhancing the rest in happy coordination and cooperation in that "new man, which after God hath been created in righteousness and holiness of truth," Ephesians 4:24.

"Good fruits" are also said to be the manifestation of "the wisdom that is from above," James 3:17, and of "righteousness," i.e., of that rectitude of spirit which belongs to the man in Christ, v. 18.

The verb "fruit-bearing," *karpophoreō,* is found in the New Testament in both the natural, Mark 4:28, and the spiritual sense, Matthew 13:23; Mark 4:20; Luke 8:15. The two states of men, the regenerate and the unregenerate, are contrasted in Romans 7:4, 5; in the former "the passions of sins," i.e., sinful impulses, see at v. 24, below, bore fruit unto death, that is these activities arose out of a state of alienation from God; in the latter the power of the indwelling Spirit, who unites the soul with the risen Lord, bears fruit unto God; so also Colossians 1:10. Colossians 1:6 corresponds with Philippians 1:22, mentioned above.||

The negative word "unfruitful," *akarpos,* is used in giving warning both by the Lord Jesus, in the parable of the sower, Matthew 13:22; Mark 4:19, and by Peter, 2 Peter 1:8. Jude uses it in his indictment of those who oppose the gospel the while they pretend to be its friends, v. 12. Paul speaks of "the unfruitful works of darkness," warning Christians against involving themselves therein,

Ephesians 5:11; again, he encourages them "to maintain good works for necessary uses," or perhaps, as margin, "to profess honest occupations," in order
that they may not be "unfruitful," Titus 3:14, referring not to the extraordinary
activities of the preacher, but to the ordinary life of all, to "the trivial round,
the common task," "providing for one's own," 1 Timothy 5:8, and "as we have
opportunity," "working that which is good toward all men, and especially toward
them that are of the household of the faith," 6:10, below; for thus, in the
language of the New Testament, is fruit borne unto God.

In 1 Corinthians 14:14, "If I pray in a tongue, my spirit prayeth, but my
understanding is unfruitful," the apostle's words imply that though the spirit and
tongue may be in exercise in prayer, yet is there no profit to the Church unless
the "understanding" is also engaged.||

of the Spirit—for "firstfruits of the Spirit," Romans 8:23, see comment on
2 Thessalonians 2:13.

is love,—*agape*, as in vv. 6, 13, above.

joy,—*chara;* see comment on *1 Thessalonians* 5:16.

peace,—*eirēnē;* see comment on *1 Thessalonians* 5:3, 23.

long-suffering,—*makrothumia;* see comment on *1 Thessalonians* 5:14.

kindness,—*chrēstotēs,* i.e., goodness, but not merely goodness as a quality,
rather it is goodness in action, goodness expressing itself in deeds; yet not
goodness expressing itself in indignation against sin, for it is contrasted with
severity in Romans 11:22, but in grace and tenderness and compassion.

It is said of God that He is rich in goodness, i.e., in beneficent acts, Romans
2:4, and this goodness found its supreme manifestation in the gift of His Son to
be the Savior of men, Ephesians 2:7; Titus 3:4. It is said of man that "there is
none that doeth good," Romans 3:12, which is the testimony, not indeed of man
himself, for it is a chief evidence of his sinful state that he is deceived about it,
but of God, who alone has complete knowledge of the human heart; see Jeremiah
17:9, 10. The Christian, on the other hand, having become the child of God, is
to show the kindness to others that has been shown by God to him, 2 Corinthians
6:6; Colossians 3:12, and here.||

goodness,—*agathōsunē;* see comment on *2 Thessalonians* 1:11. This word is
a synonym of the preceding (i.e., a different word with a similar meaning). They
are not readily distinguished, but that they occur together in this list shows that
the apostle did not intend the same idea in each. It may be that, whereas
chrēstotēs describes the more benign aspects of goodness, *agathōsunē* includes
its sterner qualities, i.e., doing good to others, but not necessarily by gentle
means. Trench, *Synonyms*, § lxiii., sees an illustration of the latter in the Lord
Jesus when He drove the buyers and sellers out of the temple, Matthew 21:12,
13, and when He denounced woes upon the scribes and Pharisees, 23:13, 39,

and of the former in His dealings with penitents such as are recorded in Luke 7:36–50. On the other hand, Lightfoot distinguishes them as between a kindly disposition toward others, *chrēstotēs,* and a kindly activity for the benefit of others, *agathōsunē.* The other New Testament occurrences are Romans 15:14; Ephesians 5:9; 2 Thessalonians 1:11.||

In 1 Corinthians 13:4 the verb *chrēsteuomai* occurs, "love . . . is kind," where the thought closely corresponds with Trench's illustration of the noun.||

faithfulness,—*pistis;* see comment on *1 Thessalonians* 3:2. In the majority of its frequent occurrences earlier in this Epistle *pistis* signifies the abandonment of oneself, insofar as hope of salvation through merit or works is concerned, and the casting of oneself therefore solely upon God in Christ, as in 2:16, e.g. But neither this meaning, nor the less common one of 1:23 (where it = "what is believed") seems to suit the context here. Faith, in the sense of confidence in God for salvation, would necessarily come at the head of such a list as this if it were to appear at all. *Pistis* is, however, sometimes = "faithfulness," as here rendered; see Romans 3:3 (of God), and Matthew 23:23; Titus 2:10 (of man). There is also a third idea which *pistis* may express, that of trustfulness, the habit of mind which does not doubt that God is working all things together for good with those who love Him, Romans 8:28, that seeks to realize the truth of the apostle's word concerning love that it "believeth all things," 1 Corinthians 13:7. Suspicion of God, whether of His love or of His wisdom (few doubt His power), is a work of the flesh, and so is suspicion of those around us; it darkens and embitters the soul, hinders efficiency in service, and makes fellowship impossible. The choice lies between the second and third of these meanings, and on the whole the last is perhaps more likely to be the intention of the apostle.

5:23 meekness,—*praotēs,* sometimes written *prautēs,* a word the meaning of which is not readily expressed in English, for the terms meekness, mildness, commonly used, suggest weakness and pusillanimity to a greater or less extent, whereas *praotēs* does nothing of the kind. Nevertheless, it is difficult to find a rendering less open to objection than meekness; "gentleness" has been suggested, but as *praotēs* describes a condition of mind and heart, and as "gentleness" is appropriate rather to actions, this word is no better than that used in both English versions. It must be clearly understood, therefore, that the meekness manifested by the Lord and commended to the believer is the fruit of power. The common assumption is that when a man is meek it is because he cannot help himself; but the Lord was "meek" because he had the infinite resources of God at His command. The believer is to cultivate meekness for the same reason. Described negatively, meekness is the opposite to self-assertiveness and self-interest; it is an equanimity of spirit that is neither elated nor cast down, simply because it is not occupied with self at all. This is well illustrated in the case of the Lord Jesus Christ, who was neither depressed by the rejection of His service nor elated by the plaudits of the multitudes that would have crowned Him, for He was "meek . . . in heart," Matthew 11:20–30.

In 2 Corinthians 10:1 the apostle appeals to the "meekness . . . of Christ," with obvious reference to Matthew 11:29, and to the quotation from Zechariah 9:9 in Matthew 21:5, "thy King cometh unto thee, meek . . . ." Christians are charged to show "all meekness toward all men," Titus 3:2, for meekness becomes "God's elect," Colossians 3:12, since they are "builded together for a habitation of God," Ephesians 2:22; 4:1, 2. To this virtue the "man of God" is urged; he is to "follow after meekness" for his own sake, 1 Timothy 6:11, with which the present passage may be associated; and in his service, and more especially in his dealings with the "ignorant and erring," he is to exhibit "a spirit of meekness," 1 Corinthians 4:21, and 6:1, below; even "they that oppose themselves" are to be corrected in meekness, 2 Timothy 2:25. So for the apostle Paul. James exhorts his "beloved brethren" to "receive with meekness the implanted word," 1:21, and declares that a life lived and good works done, not in an ostentatious way, but in that meekness which characterizes wisdom, is evidence of a "wise and understanding" heart, 3:13. Peter commends to women "the incorruptible apparel of a meek . . . spirit," 1 Peter 3:4; and to all "meekness" in setting forth the grounds of the Christian hope, 3:15.||

In Matthew 11:29; 21:5; 1 Peter 3:4, quoted above, and in Matthew 5:5, quoted from Psalm 37:11, *praos (praus)* the corresponding adjective is used.||

temperance:—*enkrateia,* = "self-control," as margin, which is to be preferred because temperance has been limited in modern times to self-control in a particular direction, whereas *enkrateia* is self-control in all things; it is the responsibility that attaches to a creature with a will, or power to choose his own course. God in His wisdom has endowed man richly in many directions, and each of his powers is necessarily capable of abuse as well as of use. The right use of this endowment demands the exercise of the will, and this is called self-control; see Acts 24:25 (where "righteousness" = the claims of God upon man, "self-control" = the responsibility of man to respond to those claims, "the judgment to come" = the inevitable day of account, when God shall call upon man to answer for his failure to respond to the divine claims). For man, trusting to his own wisdom and strength, has failed in this as in all other items of the list, which, therefore, are possible only as men become the subjects of the operations of the Holy Spirit through faith in Christ.

"Self-control" follows "knowledge" in Peter's catalogue, 2 Peter 1:6, as though to suggest that what the Christian learns he is responsible to put into practice, for the operation of the Spirit in the believer demands the cooperation of the believer himself; only in him who submits to be led by the Spirit can the fruit of the Spirit be borne.||

Enkratēs, Titus 1:8, and *enkrateuomai,* 1 Corinthians 7:9; 9:25, also occur; in the latter passage figuratively, of athletes who in preparing themselves for the games exercised a rigid self-restraint for the sake of the prize offered, denying the natural appetites lest by self-indulgence they should lose it. The meaning of these words does not vary from that given above.||

The number 3 is widely recognized as the arithmetical symbol of perfection, and the arrangement of the items of the fruit of the Spirit in three triplets may well have this significance, though on the other hand "against such" below, with its suggestion that the list is not exhaustive, must not be overlooked.

Inasmuch as man sustains a threefold relation to the universe, i.e., to God, to the world, and to himself, "instruction in righteousness" necessarily falls into three categories; cp. Titus 2:12, "we should live soberly [in ourselves], and righteously [in relation to others], and godly [in relation to God] in this present age." It may be that a similar division is intended here, and in that case the first three are Godward, the second three are manward, and the remaining three are internal graces of the Spirit.

"The love of God hath been shed abroad in our hearts through the Holy Spirit," begetting love in our hearts in return, see 1 John 4:19; therefore we "rejoice in hope of the glory of God," and we "have peace with God through our Lord Jesus Christ," Romans 5:1-5.

The selfishness of men, their pride, self-will and ambition, make it inevitable that they should impose a strain upon those with whom they are brought into contact, for these different manifestations of sin in anyone individual bring him into conflict with others in whom also the same evil forces are at work. Hence it is to long-suffering the first place is assigned in the triplet that prescribes the Christian's relation to his fellows. Kindness and goodness follow, for it is not enough that one should merely bear with others (and he must not forget that others have to bear with him), he is called to active beneficence, to do good to all men after the pattern of Christ.

The final triplet is composed of those personal virtues which are to be cultivated in the heart for their own sake; they describe what the believer should be in himself apart from any question of his relations with other people. And though these are mentioned last yet is it certain that on their vigor the manifestation of the Godward and manward graces that precede them in the list will largely depend.

against such—i.e., "such things," corresponding with "such like," v. 21, above; this list, like the other, is not complete, it is not intended to exhaust the graces of the Spirit.

there is no law.—the ostensible aim of the law is to restrain the evil tendencies natural to man in his fallen estate; yet in experience law finds itself not merely ineffective, it actually provokes those tendencies to greater activity. The intention of the gift of the Spirit is to constrain the believer to a life in which the natural tendencies shall have no place, and to produce in him their direct contraries. Law, therefore, has nothing to say against the fruit of the Spirit, hence the believer is not only not under law, v. 18, above, the law finds no scope in his life, inasmuch as, and insofar as, he is led by the Spirit. While Christianity is not a system of ethics, morality, i.e., instruction in conduct, being, doing, and suffering, occupies a considerable place in the teaching of the Lord Jesus and in the writings of His apostles. The section Matthew 5—7 is representative of the former, this "fruit of the Spirit" of the latter. While the morality of the New Testament retains much that was taught in the Old Testament, and necessarily includes much of the moral teaching of the Gentiles ("the law written in their hearts," Rom. 2:15), as a whole it is unique not only in its scope but in its character, and most of all in this, that whereas men have presented to their fellows defective ideals without pretending that those ideals had been realized, the New Testament presents a faultless ideal which had been actually embodied in a life lived before it was taught at all. It is the glory of the Lord Jesus Christ as a teacher that He not merely taught, He practiced what He taught, and before He taught it, leaving an example to those who name His name that they may follow His steps, John 13:15, cp. 1 Peter 2:21; 1 John 2:6. In the Sermon on the Mount He eulogized those who "do and teach"; and, in harmony with this word of the Lord, Luke speaks of "all that Jesus began both to do and to teach," Acts 1:1; see comment on *2 Thessalonians* 2:17. Hence it is to be concluded that all the precepts He laid down for the guidance of His disciples were just those that He Himself had observed during the silent years of His unrecorded life, always of course with this provision, that He "who knew no sin," found no occasion to pray "forgive us our debts." So also with the morality of the Epistles. It is the function of the Spirit to take what pertains to Christ, and to declare these things to the disciples, John 16:14. Those elements, then, in the apostolic testimony that prescribe the walk and conversation that become the Christian, are drawn from the example of the Lord Jesus as presented to the minds of the writers by the Holy Spirit. The fruit of the Spirit here described was exhibited in harmonious perfection in the walk and conversation of the Lord Jesus, and is here written for the guidance of His people. Allowing these things, and such things as these, to occupy their minds they are in fact occupied with Him in Whom these things had their embodiment. As the believer takes account of things true, honorable, just, pure, lovely, and of good report, the worthy things and the pleasing things, he is taking account of Christ, for the things that were to be seen in Paul were the things that Paul had seen in Christ; see Philippians 4:8, 9 and cp. 1 Corinthians 11:1. The ideal Christian life is an extension of the life of the Lord Jesus; the things that in the days of His flesh He manifested in His own way among men, He manifests now by the power of His Spirit in the lives of His people.

5:24 And they that are of Christ Jesus—i.e., that belong to Him; in contrast with those who are "under the law"; cp. "ye are Christ's," 1 Corinthians 3:23, "he is Christ's," 2 Corinthians 10:7. The phrase is the equivalent of the title Christian, applied to believers; they are Christ's property, the gift of His Father, John 17:6, and redeemed by His Blood, 1 Peter 1:18, 19; they are under law to Him, 1 Cor. 9:21; they call Him "Master (*despotēs* = "absolute ownership and uncontrolled power") and Lord," Jude 4.

have crucified—*stauroō*, point tense, referring to a definite act, lit., "they . . . crucified." This and 6:14 are the only New Testament instances of *stauroō* used in a figurative sense, but to these must be added *sustauroō*, "jointly crucified," in Romans 6:6, and 2:20, above, where see note. In each of these places the apostle speaks of something that is accomplished in the case of each believer when he receives Christ as his Savior. He does not, here or elsewhere, exhort them to crucify the old man, or the flesh, or themselves. He declares that the believer has already "crucified the flesh," that "the old man was crucified with Christ," that the believer "was crucified with Christ," that he "died with Christ," Romans 6:6. It is on the basis of this fact in the experience of the soul that the believer is now bidden to "reckon himself to be dead unto sin," v. 11, and "to put to death [forbid absolutely] the practices of the body [here looked upon as the organ of those appetites which war against the soul]," 8:13. The same exhortation is expressed in slightly different language in Colossians 3:5, "put to death your members which are upon the earth." The parallel between the two passages supplies the key to the meaning of the latter; in the first there are the body and its practices, in the second a catalogue of those practices; the "members that are upon the earth" are the members of the body in their unholy activity when they are yielded "unto sin as instruments of unrighteousness."

"Crucifixion" and "death" in these passages are used in a figurative way and are not to be taken literally, as though either the flesh or its passions and lusts had been so dealt with either by God or by the believer himself that they had ceased to exist. On the contrary, they are still with him and in him, ready to leap into activity again should the restraint of faith in the will and power of Christ to overcome them by the Holy Spirit be removed. Both in Romans 6 and in the present context the statements concerning the crucifixion and death of the man who has received Christ are accompanied by exhortations to make the corresponding realities good in his experience. "You were crucified with Christ—you died with Christ—reckon yourself to be dead unto sin," and "you crucified the flesh—walk by the Spirit and ye shall not fulfill the lusts of the flesh."

Hence there is no latent contradiction between the lusting of the flesh in v. 17 and the crucifixion of the same flesh in v. 24. The believer, when he "heard the word of the truth, the gospel of his salvation," Ephesians 1:13, there and then acquiesced in the sentence of death upon himself, or, as this most impressive figure puts it, crucified his flesh in his deliberate association of himself with Christ in His death on the cross. But inasmuch as the believer thus voluntarily entered into fellowship with God in Christ in his condemnation of sin (which is a comprehensive term for the flesh and its works), let him now so present himself to God that he may obtain the victory over the crucified flesh in all its passions and lusts. In response to faith in the Lord Jesus Christ the believer is given a certain standing before God as having died and risen with Christ; in response to obedience to the Word of God, God maintains the believer in a certain spiritual state corresponding to that standing, a state of victory over sin and of liberty and power to holiness and righteousness. But just as obedience is the only evidence of faith, so the state of the professed believer, as manifested in his walk and conversation before men, is the only competent evidence of his standing before God.

the flesh—for which see 3:3, above.

with the passions—*pathēma,* which, like its English equivalent, has two distinct meanings, *a,* suffering, *b,* emotion. It is used of the sufferings of Christ in 2 Corinthians 1:5, and of Christians in Romans 8:18. Here and in Romans 7:5 it is used of the workings, or emotions, of the flesh. Though *a* is the original meaning of "passion," this sense is seldom associated with it in modern English, but see Acts 1:3, "His Passion," i.e., His suffering of death, where the corresponding verb appears. The connection between these diverse meanings of the word is that the emotions, whether good or evil, were contemplated as the result of the exposure of the mind to external influences which it suffered.

and the lusts thereof.—as at v. 16, above. These words, "passions and lusts," do not in themselves necessarily carry an evil meaning; they are good or evil according as that with which they are associated is good or evil.

5:25 If we live—as we do; the fact is assumed, "since we live." For "live," *zaō,* see comment on *1 Thessalonians* 5:10.

by the Spirit,—there is no article in the Greek text, but the Holy Spirit, the originator and sustainer of the life of the man in Christ, seems to be intended, see at 5:5, above. Cp. "the Spirit of life" in Romans 8:2; He it is who frees men from that which produces sin and death.

by the Spirit let us also walk.—*stoicheō,* for which see comment on *1 Thessalonians* 2:12. The walk of v. 16 is the general manner of the life of the individual believer considered in itself; here it is his manner of life in relation with others. That is an exhortation to walk boldly and firmly as guided and enabled by the Holy Spirit; this is an exhortation to keep step with one another in the same strength and guidance. Submission of heart (for the comprehensive use of this word in the Scriptures see comment on *1 Thess.* 2:4) to the Holy Spirit alone secures peace to the individual and harmony to the church. He who walks by the Spirit in his private life is the man who, by the same Spirit, keeps step with his brethren. The obvious way to uniformity of step is that each should keep step with the leader of all, that is, with Christ. To be in step with Him is to be in step with all who walk with Him. Hence in order to attain to unity in the church each is to watch not his brother, but his Lord. Accordingly the new section begun here and extending to 6:10 (see Analyses) is devoted to instruction concerning church life.

This injunction and its condition arise directly out of the contrast developed in the preceding paragraph; it is indeed the practical conclusion to which the whole argument of the Epistle leads. Let not such as belong to Christ attempt to regulate their lives by rules and ordinances, imposed from without, and shown already to be at once inadequate and ineffective; let them rather submit themselves to the Holy Spirit of God, so that in His power they may become imitators of Christ.

As in Romans 12 so here, the apostle opens his "instruction in righteousness" with directions concerning behavior "in the house of God, which is the church of the living God," 1 Timothy 3:15, as though to suggest that the distinctively Christian virtues are to be cultivated in the congenial atmosphere of the brotherhood, 1 Peter 2:17, in order that they may grow strong enough to withstand the antagonism of the world. If a man fails to bear the fruit of the Spirit in the church there is little hope that he will do otherwise among "them that are without." If he cannot love the brethren, how will he show love in the world? Yet he is called to do both, 2 Peter 1:7.

5:26 Let us not be—*ginomai*, "become"; an act repeated becomes habit, habit reflects character; an empty word or action which is not promptly judged and condemned prepares the way for another of more pronounced type, and thus the vainglorious character is formed. Therefore the believer is to be on guard against the beginning of an evil.

The tact of the apostle is seen in his use of "become," for he thus suggests that these things were not actually characteristic of them, though he had ground for suspecting the danger. Moreover, he says "us," not "ye" in the same tactful spirit, but perhaps also because he knew that not even an apostle was immune from the motions of the flesh.

vainglorious,—*kenodoxos*, a compound formed from the two words *kenos*, "empty," and *doxa*, "glory," for which see at 1:5, above. There are true grounds for Christian glorying, see comment on *1 Thessalonians* 2:19; these, however, are not found in the man himself, nor in his religious attainments, nor in the observance of laws and ordinances, but in what he is by the grace of God, and what God in His grace is pleased to do through him. This "empty-glory" is commonly called conceit; it is stupid as well as carnal.||

"Vainglory" in Philippians 2:3, *kenodoxia*, is the corresponding noun.||

provoking one another,—*prokaleō*, "to call forth," as to a contest, and hence to arouse to activity what is evil in another.||

envying one another.—*phthoneō*; the corresponding noun appears in v. 21, above.||

These words are continuous participles, and describe character in its active manifestations; "do not become provokers, enviers." Vainglorying challenges competition, to which the stronger-natured respond in kind, while those who are weaker are moved to envy. The "us" suggests that the apostle has in mind not so much those who were deserting the true gospel, as those of whom he was hopeful that they would continue in it. Not orthodoxy merely but character counts, therefore let those who are "sound in [the] faith" be "sound in love" also, Titus 2:2. Of what profit is it to hold "a form of godliness" if the power thereof be not experienced in the inner man and be not evident in the walk and conversation?

GALATIANS

CHAPTER SIX

Verses 1–18

6:1 Brethren,—this word, describing their mutual relationship in the Lord, provides the ground for the exhortation that follows, and is introduced here, in the middle of a section, apparently with the purpose of reminding them that all their dealings one with the other, of whatever kind, must be ruled by this fundamental fact. Those who were not brethren could not be dealt with by them at all, 1 Corinthians 5:12; those who were, however grave the fault, must be dealt with as brethren, that is, in love, or not at all.

even if—again the apostle is tactful; he supposes a case in language which suggests no more than a possible contingency; he was "persuaded better things of them, even things that accompany salvation, though he thus spoke," Hebrews 6:9.

While it is true that those who practice such things as are enumerated in the preceding section until they have become characteristic ("second nature" as it is sometimes expressed), are thereby manifested as outside the ranks of the regenerate, it is also true that even those who have been born anew may fall a prey to one or other of these ever-present and ever-ready lusts of the flesh. The apostle now gives instruction regarding the treatment of such cases.

a man—i.e., any member of the church, of either sex. This is the general word, *anthrōpos*, "person"; there is a distinct word, *anēr*, "male," used when it is necessary to distinguish between the sexes.

be overtaken—*prolambanō*, "to anticipate anything," as Mary, by anointing the Lord Jesus, anticipated, was beforehand with, His burial, Mark 14:8, and as selfish believers forestalled, and consequently lost the opportunity of sharing with, those less favored than themselves in material things, 1 Corinthians 11:21.‖

in any trespass,—*paraptōma*, lit., "a fall beside"; it is used of breaches of the law of God, whether that given to Adam, Romans 5:15, or that given through Moses, Romans 5:20, or in a wider, more general sense, including that "written in the heart," Matthew 6:15; Romans 5:16, and of laws that regulate human intercourse, Matthew 6:14, 15. The same things are here in view as are above described as the works of the flesh; cp., "such things" with "any trespass"; the net is purposely cast very widely.

The corresponding verb, *parapiptō*, "to fall away," occurs in Hebrews 6:6.‖

These words present some difficulty; they have been understood to mean "even if man should be surprised in, detected in, a trespass," "taken in the act"; but this interpretation gives an unexampled meaning to the word, and does not harmonize with the context. It would, moreover, tend to encourage espionage and censoriousness rather than that self-judgment and care for others which the apostle urges upon them. It is more likely, considering the remoter context, see especially 5:21, that the thought is of the fault getting beforehand with the caution of the believer, finding him off his guard, and so taking advantage of him. This interpretation provides a vivid contrast with the deliberate and premeditated practice of evil dealt with immediately above, and harmonizes with the closing words of the verse.

The modern Greek version runs, "even if a man, through lack of circumspection, should fall into any sin," and this seems to express the mind of the apostle.

ye which are spiritual—*pneumatikos,* a word which always connotes the ideas of invisibility and of power. It does not occur in the LXX, nor in the Gospels, it is in fact an after-Pentecost word. In the New Testament it is used as under:

a, the angelic hosts, lower than God but higher in the scale of being than man in his natural state, are called "spiritual hosts," Ephesians 6:12;

b, things that have their origin with God, and which, therefore, are in harmony with His character, as His law is, are said to be "spiritual," Romans 7:14;

c, "spiritual" is prefixed to the material type in order to indicate that what the type sets forth, not the type itself, is intended, 1 Corinthians 10:3, 4;

d, the purposes of God revealed in the gospel by the Holy Spirit, 1 Corinthians 2:13*a,* and the words in which that revelation is expressed, are said to be "spiritual," 13*b,* "matching, or combining, spiritual things with spiritual words" (or, alternatively, "interpreting spiritual things to spiritual men," see *e,* below); "spiritual songs" are songs of which the burden is the things revealed by the Spirit, Ephesians 5:19; Colossians 3:16; "spiritual wisdom and understanding" is wisdom in, and understanding of, those things, Colossians 1:9;

e, men in Christ who walk so as to please God are said to be "spiritual," here and in 1 Corinthians 2:13*b* (but see *d,* above), 15; 3:1; 14:37;

f, the whole company of those who believe in Christ is called a "spiritual house," 1 Peter 2:5*a;*

g, the blessings that accrue to regenerate men at this present time are called "spiritualities," Romans 15:27; 1 Corinthians 9:11, "spiritual blessings," Ephesians 1:3, "spiritual gifts," Romans 1:11;

h, the activities Godward of regenerate men are "spiritual sacrifices," 1 Peter 2:5*b;* their appointed activities in the churches are also called "spiritual gifts," lit., "spiritualities," 1 Corinthians 12:1; 14:1;

i, the resurrection body of the dead in Christ is said to be "spiritual," i.e., such as is suited to the heavenly environment, 1 Corinthians 15:44;

j, all that is produced and maintained among men by the operations of the Spirit of God is termed "spiritual," 1 Corinthians 15:46.||

The adverb "spiritually," *pneumatikōs*, occurs in 1 Corinthians 2:14, where its meaning is as *j*, above, and in Revelation 11:8, where its meaning is as in *c*, above.||

The qualifications for such delicate work as the apostle has in mind here, and which he sums up in the comprehensive term "spiritual," are set forth in detail in 5:16–26, above. The spiritual man is one who walks by the Spirit both in the sense of v. 16 and in that of v. 25, and who himself manifests the fruit of the Spirit in his own ways. By no lesser standard than that provided by the Spirit of God must a man judge himself.

According to the Scriptures, the "spiritual" state of soul is normal for the believer, but to this state all believers do not attain, nor when it is attained is it always maintained. Thus the apostle, in 1 Corinthians 3:1–3, suggests a contrast between this spiritual state and that of the babe in Christ, i.e., of the man who because of immaturity and inexperience has not yet reached spirituality, and that of the man who by permitting jealousy, and the strife to which jealousy always leads, has lost it. The spiritual state is reached by diligence in the Word of God and in prayer; it is maintained by obedience and self-judgment. Such as are led by the Spirit are spiritual, but, of course, spirituality is not a fixed or absolute condition, it admits of growth; indeed growth in "the grace and knowledge of our Lord and Savior Jesus Christ," 2 Peter 3:18, is evidence of true spirituality.

Somewhat after the same fashion, when he had expounded the relation between the "strong" and the "weak" conscience in Romans 14, the apostle proceeded to urge upon those whose conscience was "strong" their obligations toward the "weak" brethren, 15:1.

restore such a one—*katartizō*, for which see comment on *1 Thessalonians 3:10*. It was applied, among other things, to the setting of a broken bone, an operation obviously calling for skill, delicate handling and much care, but not for more than is demanded by a case of spiritual dislocation among Christians. The end of ministry is to put, and to keep, in joint the members of the body. Such work is not to be lightly undertaken, nor is it to be undertaken at all by anyone lacking the qualification of spirituality. The tense is present continuous, for patience and perseverance are also essential. The word does not suggest punishment even remotely.

in a spirit of meekness;—as in 5:23, above. Cp. 1 Corinthians 4:21. Lightfoot's comment is to the point: "Gentleness is a characteristic of true spirituality. By their conduct toward wrongdoers their claim to the title 'spiritual' would be tested." It is necessary to discriminate, however. A spirit of meekness does not mean an easygoing toleration of evil. On the contrary, it is intolerance of evil that provides the occasion for the manifestation of the meek spirit. The Lord Jesus possessed the balanced temperament; intolerance of evil because it is evil, and meekness in dealing even with evil men, in Him were in perfect equipoise, and he is the pattern of His people. No doubt the apostle chooses this grace of Christ for emphasis here inasmuch as, in dealing with the erring, men are tempted to self-righteousness and to censoriousness, and to the assumption of an air of superiority which is hurtful as much to the would-be physician as to the patient. Cp. 2 Timothy 2:25.

looking—*skopeō*, "to pay attention to," as to:

a, one's motives that they be disinterested, for selfishness is darkness, generosity is light, Luke 11:35; Philippians 2:4;

b, the course of leaders in the churches, lest one should encourage division, Romans 16:17, or fail to strengthen the hands of those who labor for the welfare of the saints, Philippians 3:17;

c, the unseen things of the Spirit which are indeed the real, the eternal things, lest one should be brought under the power of things seen and material, which are indeed the unreal and the temporary things, and thus joy be lost, efficiency be impaired, and reward missed, 2 Corinthians 4:18.||

to thyself,—"ye which are spiritual" is plural, but in order to bring what he is about to say closely home to the individual, the apostle proceeds in the singular, "thyself . . . thou."

lest thou also be tempted.—i.e., in like circumstances, for you may find yourself situated as he is someday. Cp. 4:7, above, where the same change from plural to singular is made.

When a believer has realized his responsibility to an erring brother, he is in danger of thinking of himself as the other's judge, rather than as being one with the delinquent in natural tendencies and in liability to sin. If this thought is harbored spirituality departs, and with it all hope of succoring the fallen brother. Hence the apostle does not say "lest thou also fall," but "lest thou also be tempted," as though to suggest that the difference between the two men is not that both were tempted, that one resisted and one fell, but that one was tempted and fell, the other did not fall only because he had not been tempted. Therefore the man of true spirituality will say under such circumstances, "but for the grace of God I had been in his place," thus encouraging that spirit of meekness in himself without which he may make mischief but cannot do good. The use of the point tense suggests a sudden temptation, and is in harmony with "overtaken," above.

For "tempted," *peirazō*, see comment on *1 Thessalonians* 3:5.

The apostle, probably because he realized the danger, to which evangelists, pastors, and teachers are peculiarly exposed, of neglecting one's own spiritual welfare in zeal for the care of others, and well aware that if the former be not cultivated the latter will become mechanical and formal, repeatedly urged upon Timothy the importance of his own spiritual state and of maintaining it by rigorous application to himself of all that to which he exhorted others. He was:

to exercise himself (*gumnazō*, = "to strive with the body stripped," i.e., strenuously) unto godliness, 1 Timothy 4:7;

to give heed to himself (hold himself to strict account, *epechō*) and to his teaching, i.e., to see that his practice did not lag behind his precepts, so that he might save himself as well as his hearers (from the world, the flesh, and the devil), v. 16;

to keep himself pure, i.e., from indulgence in the things that defile the spirit, 5:22;

to be such a workman in the opening up of the Word of God as God will approve, 2 Timothy 2:15.

Titus also, like the apostle himself, was to be an example of the good works to which he exhorts others, 2:7.

6:2 Bear ye—as at 5:10, above. The tense is present continuous; not merely on occasion, or fitfully; this is to be a guiding principle, a habit of life. The believer is to remember that he is in the world not for what he can get out of it but for what good he can do in it, for what help he can render while he is here. So was it with Christ, so must it be with the Christian, Matthew 20:28.

one another's burdens,—*baros,* which is used of anything that presses upon one physically as labor does, Matthew 20:12, or that makes a demand upon one's resources, whether material, 1 Thessalonians 2:6 where see note, or spiritual, here; or of religious observances, Acts 15:28; Revelation 2:24; in one passage by a bold figure of speech the future state of the redeemed is described as "an eternal weight of glory," 2 Corinthians 4:17. In contemporary writings *baros* is used of faults, moral delinquencies.||

The corresponding verb, *bareō,* is used of approaching sleep, Matthew 26:43; Luke 9:32, and the stupefying effect of gluttony, Luke 21:34, of the present state of the regenerate soul confined in "the earthly house of this tabernacle," 2 Corinthians 5:4, of the effect upon Paul of the attack of the Ephesians, Acts 19:23, 2 Corinthians 1:8, and in 1 Timothy 5:16 of an unnecessary charge upon the material resources of the church.||

Cp. also *epibareō,* see comment on *1 Thessalonians* 2:9, and *katabareō,* 2 Corinthians 12:16.||

and so—or "thus," = "in this way."

fulfill—*anaplēroō,* which is compounded of *ana,* here = "up to," as a vessel is filled "up to" the brim, and *pleroo,* = "to fill," and in reference to the law "to keep"; hence *anaplēroō* = "to fill adequately, completely." It is used of the prophecy of Isaiah concerning the rejection of God by Israel, which came to pass fully in the rejection of His Son, Matthew 13:14; of the status of a person in the church, 1 Corinthians 14:16; of substituted service acknowledged to be adequate, 16:17, Philippians 2:30; and of the persistence of the Jews in pursuing their course of sin against God, 1 Thessalonians 2:16, where see note.||

the law of Christ.—this may either be the law given by Christ, as in John 13:14, 15; 15:12, and, more at length, in the Sermon on the Mount, Matthew

5—7, or it may be the law, or principle, by which Christ himself lived, Matthew 20:28, John 13:1. These, however, are not really alternative interpretations, for the law that Christ imposes upon His disciples is not a merely arbitrary dictate of authority, it is the law according to which He Himself lived in the days of His flesh.

Or it may be that the words were intended to suggest a contrast with the Law of Moses for which some of them were so zealous. They would impose a burden upon others; Christ would have them each take the other's burden on himself, as becomes those saved not by their own works but by His grace. Hence the emphasis, marked by the position of the words at the opening of the sentence, is, "one another's burdens do ye bear."

Romans 15:1-3 is parallel with, is indeed an expansion of, this passage. There also is the law of the spiritual and the erring brother, of the strong and the weak, and there, too, is the law of Christ who "pleased not Himself."

The burden here is the sense of weakness and of shame, the sense of the dishonor done to the name of the Lord Jesus, which is the portion of a believer who has been "overtaken in a trespass." It is not unnatural in such cases that the rest should hasten to repudiate the fallen brother and to dissociate themselves from him, lest the world should suppose they were careless about wrongdoing; yet it may be readily discerned that not concern for the name of the Lord but self-righteous pride prompts to this course. Here, in marked contrast to the way of men, is the law of Christ, who was at once jealous for the honor of His Father and meek and lowly in heart. Therefore, "let him that thinketh he standeth take heed lest he fall," 1 Corinthians 10:12, and with this sense of community of danger let him seek the restoration of his brother. Cp. the apostle's own example in 2 Corinthians 11:29.

6:3 For—the apostle is still dealing not with the defaulter but with those who are responsible for his restoration. "For" introduces the reason why the believer who approaches an erring brother should beware lest through an overconfident spirit he also fall, Romans 11:20. If a man fails in this it is because he has a wrong opinion of himself; such is the apostle's diagnosis of the case.

if a man—lit., "anyone."

thinketh himself—*dokeō*, as at 2:2, where see note.

to be something,—"anything," as in 2:6, above, where see note. See also Acts 5:36.

when he is nothing,—lit., "being nothing," i.e., whereas in himself he has neither wisdom nor power, but is entirely dependent upon the grace of the Lord Jesus alike for his deliverance from the dominion of sin and for his maintenance in the way of holiness. The words are not to be understood to mean "if he should be nothing," as though some among them might not answer to that description. It is a statement of fact concerning all believers, "that no flesh

should glory before God," 1 Corinthians 1:29; cp. the apostle's words concerning his own service, "I am nothing," 2 Corinthians 12:11, and "by the grace of God I am what I am . . . I labored . . . yet not I, but the grace of God which was with me," 1 Corinthians 15:10. Cp. also his words in Romans 12:3, "I say . . . to every man . . . not to think of himself more highly than he ought to think; but . . . to think soberly."

he deceiveth himself.—*phrenapataō*, a compound of *phrēn*, = *"mind,"* and *apataō*, = "to deceive" (see comment on *2 Thess.* 2:3); hence = "deceived in one's mind," suggesting that self-conceit is a sin against common sense. Cp. James 1:26, "deceiveth his heart."||

The corresponding noun occurs in Titus 1:10.||

6:4 But let each man prove—*dokimazō*, = "to test," "to try"; see comment on *2 Thessalonians* 2:3, 4, 6. The tense is continuous; not an isolated act but a habit is intended. Nothing is to be taken for granted in the Christian life; the Scriptures provide the readily accessible standard by which the believer is to test alike what he is, what he does, and what he allows. He is to "prove himself," 1 Corinthians 11:28, not indeed in hope of discovering any moral or spiritual worthiness in himself to justify him in partaking of the Supper of the Lord, but rather to reassure himself that he is "in the faith," 2 Corinthians 13:5, i.e., that he is partaking as a sinner owing his salvation solely to the death of Christ. He is to find in the needs of poor saints the opportunity of proving the sincerity of his love, 2 Corinthians 8:8, for if he "shutteth up his compassion from" such "how doth the love of God abide in him?" 1 John 3:17. He is to avoid the ways of darkness and to walk in the light, and thus is to prove, i.e., to learn by experience, what is well-pleasing to the Lord as distinguished from what is merely to his own liking, Ephesians 5:10; and as he increases in love he learns from God to judge all things by a spiritual standard in prospect of the day of account when the Lord comes, Philippians 1:10.

The present passage is another form of the same exhortation to that rigorous self-judgment which is repeatedly urged upon believers in view of the natural tendency to sit in judgment upon others. But whereas self-judgment is profitable to godliness, judgment of others is a usurpation of the functions of the Lord Jesus, John 5:22. Here, however, the person is not mentioned but his works, for a man, by applying the test of the Scriptures to what he has done, may readily discover what his own spiritual condition is. "Happy is he that judgeth (see comment on *2 Thess.* 2:12) not himself in that which he putteth to the test," Romans 14:22, margin.

The believer is thus charged to impose tests upon himself here and now with a view to the elimination of what is evil from, and the strengthening of what is good in, his life. At the same time God also is testing him, and, as he is found faithful in lesser things, trusts him with new responsibilities; cp. Matthew 25:21; Luke 19:17. The final testing comes with "the Day," i.e., "the Day of Christ," and that final test will be "the fire" (by which it may be that the eyes of the Lord are intended; see Rev. 2:18), 1 Corinthians 3:13.

his own work,—*ergon,* for which see comment on *1 Thessalonians* 1:3. The word must be taken here in the widest possible sense; it is almost the equivalent of "conduct"; see note at 5:19, above.

and then shall he have . . . glorying—*kauchēma,* "the ground or matter of glorying," as *kauchēsis,* 1 Thessalonians 2:19, is "the act of glorying." For illustrations of this distinction see Romans 3:27, "where then is the glorying?" *(kauchēsis)* with 4:2, "he hath whereof to glory" *(kauchēma),* and 2 Corinthians 8:24, where the apostle declares that he had been glorying *(kauchēsis)* in the liberality of the Corinthians, with 9:3, where he exhorts them not to deprive him of the ground whereon he had so gloried *(kauchēma).*

his—lit., "the," that glory which is distinctively his own; cp. 1 Corinthians 4:5. "then shall each man have his (lit., "the") praise from God," not, as A.V. suggests, that every man shall have some commendation from God, but that each shall certainly receive the commendation he has deserved. "Then" does not necessarily refer to the future, but in this passage it seems to point to the Judgment Seat of Christ, as it certainly does in 1 Corinthians 4:5.

in regard to himself alone, and not of his neighbor.—lit., "the other," *heteros,* for which see note at 1:6. The foolish habit of "measuring themselves by themselves and comparing themselves with themselves" is inveterate among men; and here implicitly, as in 2 Corinthians 10:12, explicitly, the apostle condemns it.

6:5 For each man shall bear—*bastozō,* as in v. 2 and 5:10, above.

his own burden.—*phortion,* which, with the exception of Acts 27:10, is used only in a metaphorical sense in the New Testament; of discipleship, whether of the scribes, Pharisees, and lawyers, Matthew 23:4; Luke 11:46, or of the Lord Jesus, Matthew 11:30.||

The corresponding verb, *phortizō,* is similarly used in Matthew 11:28; Luke 11:46.||

The difference between *baros,* v. 2, and *phortion* is that *phortion,* as its derivation from *pherō,* "to carry," shows, is something borne; be the load light or heavy, its weight is not the point. With *baros,* on the other hand, weight is the essential thing. Thus *phortion* is used in Matthew 11:30, "My burden is light," where *baros* would be unsuitable. The burden of the transgressor is of necessity a heavy one, hence *baros* appears in v. 2; but the burdens that all must bear are some lighter, some heavier, the point is that, heavy or light, each must bear his own; hence in v. 5 *phortion* is used.

The statements refer to different times. Verse 2 indicates an opportunity for present service to Christ in sharing the burdens of His people; v. 5 is a reminder that each man must, at the Judgment Seat of Christ, answer for himself how he has discharged the obligations of discipleship.

The only legitimate grounds for glorying are, first, in God, and in Christ, and in His Cross, and then in what a man has himself received by the grace of God, and in what he has been enabled to suffer and to do for the Lord, and that altogether apart from any reference to the experiences of other men; see further comment on *1 Thessalonians* 2:19. Moreover, if salvation is to be secured by individual merit, comparisons among men will inevitably be instituted, and self-glorification will result, as in the case of the Pharisee and the publican. But if salvation is by grace alone, then in the nature of the case glorying of any kind is excluded, see Romans 3:27; 4:2. Glorying one against another would be obviously incongruous in men who realize that they are under a common condemnation because of common failure, Romans 3:22, 23, and who share in a common salvation, Jude 3, to which individual merit contributes nothing, but which is due solely to the grace of God in Christ. And yet the danger threatens even these, for it is fatally easy for a man to become puffed up as the result of an almost unconscious comparison between his own virtues, real or fancied, and the failings of others. Moreover, for those who are called to deal with the erring this danger is aggravated by the subtlety of sin, and particularly by the subtlety of self-righteous pride. Hence the apostle's warning, and his concern that only spiritual men should undertake this responsibility, and these only as they remember their accountability to Christ. Self-approval is not a true criterion of merit, and in the spiritual man this testing can only induce such a sense of failure and dissatisfaction with one's best efforts as will forbid any comparison to the disadvantage of another.

6:6 But let him that is taught . . . him that teacheth—*katēcheō*, "to teach by word of mouth"; cp. English "catechize," to impart instruction by means of question and answer, and "catechumen," one who is so instructed. The word is used of Theophilus, Luke 1:4, and of Apollos, Acts 18:25, who received oral instruction in the Christian faith, see margin; and of the mass of Jewish believers at Jerusalem who had heard certain things said about the apostle Paul, Acts 21:21, 24; and of the Jews who had had the traditional, but then as yet unwritten, interpretation of the law imparted to them by the lips of the rabbis, Romans 2:18: and of the function of the teacher in the churches, which function Paul esteemed as among the highest of the endowments of the Spirit, 1 Corinthians 14:19.||

in the word—*logos*, i.e., the gospel.

communicate unto—*koinōneō*, to take part, actively or passively, with another, whether in things evil, 1 Timothy 5:22; 2 John 11, or good, as in all the remaining places of its occurrence in the New Testament. The thought conveyed by the word is not so much that of communicating to, as of communicating, i.e., sharing, with. Thus each man shares blood and flesh with all other men, for that is an essential element in their common humanity, Hebrews 2:14; the believer when he undergoes trial shares in the sufferings of Christ, inasmuch as he suffers for Christ's sake, and inasmuch as Christ suffers with each afflicted member (see Acts 9:4, 5, and 16) 1 Peter 4:13; the Gentiles share the blessings of the gospel with the Jews, Romans 15:27; the prosperous believer is to share his temporal supplies with his necessitous brethren, Romans 12:13; the church at Philippi shared its substance with the apostle that he might be the more free to preach the gospel to others, Philippians 4:15. In each case not giving but sharing is the idea prominent in the word.||

Cp. *koinōnia*, "fellowship," in 2:9, above.

in all good things,—*agathos*, good in the sense of useful, as distinguished from good in the sense of beautiful, admirable; see comment on *1 Thessalonians 5:15*, 21. Here, as in the passages mentioned above, by fellowship in "good things" temporal supplies are intended, cp. the same word as used in Luke 1:53, "the hungry he hath filled with good things," and 12:18, 19, of the rich fool's "goods," cp. 16:25.

The apostle here introduces a new subject, one not arising out of the preceding section, nor yet with any apparent relation to it, though both are immediately concerned with the responsibilities of church life. It may be that the messengers who had acquainted him with the major trouble among the Galatians had informed him also of these relatively minor, though still very important, matters. Fellowship with those by whom the Word is ministered is another of the responsibilities of discipleship for the discharge of which each believer must give account to God.

This obligation toward the teacher on the part of those who were taught would be new to the Gentile converts at least. Teaching functions were not attached to the pagan priesthoods. The offerer brought his offering and paid the fee prescribed by law or custom. Idolatry does not appeal to the intelligence but to the fears of the worshiper, who desires to ward off undefined evils by a sacrifice of such value as will demonstrate to the deity the esteem, or at least the dread, in which he is held. Ignorance, not knowledge, is the atmosphere in which superstition flourishes. The effect of the gospel, on the contrary, is to awaken, not the fears of men, but the conscience and the intellect. Growth in the knowledge of God and of His will, and of all that pertains to Him, is the divine requirement, and becomes the inevitable ambition and exercise of every renewed soul. See Colossians 1:10; 1 Peter 2:2; 2 Peter 3:18, etc. To this end God has designed the ministry of the Word among His people by those of them whom He calls and fits for that work. See Ephesians 4:7–16; Colossians 2:19. The Christian, on his part, is to recognize those whom God has thus called to, and fitted for, this particular service, by ministering to their needs in temporal things as they themselves have been prospered therein by Him from whom all supplies, spiritual and temporal, come, and to whom account of the use of all His gifts, of whatever kind, must ultimately be given.

6:7 Be not deceived;—*planaō,* "to lead astray." The same warning appears again in 1 Corinthians 6:9 concerning the inevitable consequence of evil practices, and in 15:33 of the effect upon character of association with teachers of doctrines subversive of the faith, and in James 1:16 of the result of yielding to evil enticements. In each of these cases the meaning is "do not deceive yourselves," and so here. Cp. Mark 12:24, 27, "ye do greatly deceive yourselves."

God is not mocked:—*muktērizō,* "to turn up one's nose at," i.e., to treat with contempt. Such a warning, couched in such unvarnished terms, might well provoke the protest that it is inconceivable that any man, professing to be a worshiper of God, could possibly treat Him with contempt. Yet it is true that men, even professing Christian men, will thoughtlessly do to God in act what they would shrink with horror from saying in word. Actions afford a better clue to the state of the heart than do words.||

The apostle does not deny that men attempt to mock God, for see Proverbs 1:30, "They despised all My reproof," where LXX uses the same word. He throws into strong contrast the essential difference between God and man. However it may be possible to deceive men by words and outward show, God, since He knows and judges by the thoughts of the heart, Jeremiah 17:10, cannot be imposed upon.

A strengthened form of the same word, *ekmuktērizō,* is used of those who "scoffed at" the Lord Jesus as He taught, Luke 16:14, and as He died, 23:35.||

for—because of the unerring operation of a universal law of God which is now stated under a figure drawn from the unvarying process of nature; cp. Job 4:8, etc.

whatsoever a man soweth,—*speirō,* which is used in the New Testament, and in LXX, as well in a metaphorical as in a literal sense. The apostle speaks of himself and his fellow-laborers as having sown "spiritual things" in their preaching and teaching, 1 Corinthians 9:11. The steward of God in things temporal is said to sow in prospect of a harvest proportionate to his sowing, when he gives to relieve the necessities of others, 2 Corinthians 9:6, 10; the honest and gracious words and ways of those who, being "sons of peace," Luke 10:6, desire and work for the peace of the saints, are the seed they sow from which comes "the fruit of righteousness," James 3:18.

that shall he also reap.—*therizō,* for which see the passages quoted under "soweth." "That" is emphatic; "that and nothing but that," for to the law of seed time and harvest there is no exception in either the physical or the spiritual realm. But what we reap is what we sow, not what we meant to sow, or thought we had sown, but that which we actually do sow.

6:8 For he that soweth unto—*eis,* in the interests of.

his own flesh—*sarx,* for which see at 3:3, above; here used of the natural needs, desires, proclivities, which are the common heritage of all the children of Adam. "Own" is inserted apparently in order to suggest that the selfishness of such sowing is its plain condemnation, for whatever has oneself for its object is, on that account alone, alien to Christ who "pleased not Himself," Romans 15:3.

shall of—*ek*, "out of."

the flesh—the selfsame soil in which he sowed.

reap corruption;—*phthora;* the result of the withdrawal of life (which alone maintains the physical organism in effective being) is the dissolution of the body; this process is called corruption, and is attended by conditions repugnant to the senses of the living. This idea of repulsiveness is extended to the moral sphere. Hence corruption is used in the New Testament, *a,* of death and decay in the physical sphere, Romans 8:21; 1 Corinthians 15:42, 50; 2 Peter 2:12; *b,* of moral decadence, 2 Peter 1:4; 2:19; *c,* of that which in its nature is necessarily shortlived, transient, Colossians 2:22, and here.||
 The corresponding verb is *phtheirō,* and the adjective *phthartos.*

but he that soweth unto—*eis,* as above.

the Spirit—notwithstanding the presence of the article with *pneuma* here it seems better to understand it of the new nature in the believer of which he is made a partaker in Christ, 2 Peter 1:4, through the new birth, 1 John 3:9. For the New Testament usage of "spirit" with and without the article see at 5:5, above.

shall of—*ek,* as above.

the Spirit—here also of the new nature.

reap eternal—*aiōnios,* for which see comment on *2 Thessalonians* 1:9.

life.—*zōē,* which is used in the New Testament of life as a principle, life in the absolute sense, life as God has it, that which the Father has in Himself, and which He gave to the incarnate Son to have in Himself, John 5:26, and which the Son manifested in the world, 1 John 1:2. From this life man has become alienated in consequence of the Fall, Ephesians 4:18, and of this life men become partakers through faith in the Lord Jesus Christ, John 3:15, who becomes its author to all such as trust in Him, Acts 3:15, and who is therefore said to be "the life" of the believer, Colossians 3:4, for the life that He gives He maintains, John 6:35, 63. Eternal life is the present actual possession of the believer because of his relationship with Christ, John 5:24; 1 John 3:14, and that it will one day extend its domain to the sphere of the body is assured by the resurrection of Christ, 2 Corinthians 5:4; 2 Timothy 1:10. This life is not merely a principle of power and mobility, however, for it has moral associations which are inseparable from it, as of holiness and righteousness. Death and sin, life and holiness, are frequently contrasted in the Scriptures.

Zōē is also used of that life which is the common possession of all animals and men by nature, Acts 17:25; 1 John 5:16, and of the present sojourn of man upon the earth with reference to its duration, Luke 16:25; 1 Corinthians 15:19; 1 Timothy 4:8; 1 Peter 3:10.

"This life," is a term = "the gospel," "the faith," "Christianity," Acts 5:20.

A synonym of *zōē* is *bios,* which is the usual word for lifetime, 1 Peter 4:3, but always with reference to this life only, Luke 8:14; it also, and frequently, signifies the means of livelihood, Mark 12:44. Another synonym is *psuchē,* for which see comments on *1 Thessalonians* 5:23. Speaking generally, *psuchē* is the individual life, the living being, whereas *zōē* is the life of that being, cp. Psalm 66:9, "God . . . which holdeth my soul *(psuchē)* in life *(zōē),*" and John 10:10, "I came that they might have life *(zōē),*" with v. 11, "the Good Shepherd layeth down His life *(psuchē)* for the sheep."

"Eternal life" is used alternatively with "life," cp. John 5:24; see further comments on *1 Thessalonians* 5:10. The expression is found in the Old Testament only in Daniel 12:2, LXX.

To sow to the flesh does not necessarily mean to do gross, immoral things, though these would be included in the larger sense of the word; there is nothing in the context, however, to show that it does so here. But if the believer considers only his material needs, the needs of the body, devoting his substance solely to the supply of these, then, since the material is temporal and the body in its present condition must pass away ("meats for the belly and the belly for meats; but God shall bring to nought both it and them," 1 Cor. 6:13), this man's harvest ends with this world. But if, taught by the Spirit in the Scriptures, he takes the larger, and the true, view of life, and uses his substance to encourage that ministry of the Word which God has made necessary to the maintenance and development of the life of his spirit, then, since the spirit is eternal, this man's harvest will extend into the region of "life which is life indeed," 1 Timothy 6:19, and will be reaped in eternity, as well as in time. The apostle dwells on this subject in 1 Corinthians 9:7–14, using the same figure, but with a different application, in v. 11. Cp. also 1 Timothy 5:17, and see comment on *1 Thessalonians* 2:6.

It is noteworthy that whereas the apostle charges the Galatians, 1 Corinthians 16:1, as well as the Macedonians and Corinthians, to share their substance with the poor at Jerusalem, there is no recorded commendation of the obedience of the former, though there is of both the latter, Romans 15:26. Did they who were so zealous for the law fail in sympathy with their needy brethren who shared that zeal (Acts 21:20)? In that case the words of v. 7 take on a new significance and are doubly appropriate. It is not law but grace that produces the love which expresses itself in intelligent sympathy with others in their need. The law forbade a man to steal to supply his own needs however pressing; grace impels him to work not only to supply those needs but also that he may have something to give to others, Ephesians 4:28. To turn from grace to law would result in a lowering of moral tone, and in a drying up of Christian sympathy.

6:9 And—*de*, "but," as in v. 6, suggesting a happy alternative to the selfishness which is "sowing to the flesh," and presenting in concrete form the idea underlying the metaphor of "sowing to the spirit."

let us not be weary in well doing:—see comment on *2 Thessalonians* 3:13. The warning is against discouragement, the tendency to lose hopefulness, rather than against succumbing to fatigue.

for in due season—*kairos*, as at 4:10, above; see comments on *1 Thessalonians* 2:17; 5:1; *2 Thessalonians* 2:6. The same words are translated "its own times" in 1 Timothy 2:6; Titus 1:3; "due time" is the time of God's appointment, and is neither to be hastened nor delayed by the act of any of His creatures. The reference is to the fixed relation between seedtime and harvest; it carries on the idea of the sowing.

we shall reap,—reaping is related to sowing, not only in the matter of the quality of the seed, but also in regard to the quantity sown, see 2 Corinthians 9:6. The reaping may in some cases, but certainly not invariably, and then only in a limited way, be anticipated in this life, but the promise will be completely and finally fulfilled only beyond the Judgment Seat of Christ. This reaping is otherwise presented as the reward the Lord is to bring with Him at His coming, Revelation 22:12. Diligence here produces proportionate abundance there, laxity here will mean proportionate poverty there. The same truth is declared under another figure in the words of the Lord Jesus, Matthew 6:19–21, where He contrasts the precarious treasures of earth with the immutable treasures of Heaven.

if we faint not.—*ekluō*, "to unloose, to relax"; the opposite of *anazōnnumi*, "to gird up," 1 Peter 1:13(||). *Ekluō* is used of physical faintness in Matthew 15:32, Mark 8:3; and of soul faintness in the strife with sin, Hebrews 12:3, or under the chastening of God, v. 5, or, as here, in the discharge of Christian responsibilities in obedience to the commandment of the Lord. Cp. also Deuteronomy 20:3. This warning is against the relaxation of effort. Discouragement is failure of the will. Faintness is failure of the strength, the one is the consequence of the other. Here as so often see 5:25, 26, above, and comment on *1 Thessalonians* 5:6, the apostle associates himself with those upon whom he urges the duties that pertain to the Christian faith.||

6:10 So then,—in view of the certainty of the harvest and of the fact that the nature of the seed sown, and of the ground in which it is sown, determine the character of that harvest.

as we have opportunity,—*kairos*, as in the preceding verse. The present life affords to the believer the one "due season" for sowing; that missed, the harvest is missed. As opportunity presents itself, let it be seized and used, for opportunities do not return.

let us work—*ergazomai*, see comment on *1 Thessalonians* 2:9.

that which is good—lit., "the good thing," whatever is most likely to have a happy effect in benefiting the persons concerned. "Good" here is *agathos*, as in v. 6, above. This goes beyond Romans 13:10, "Love worketh no ill." The same expression occurs again in Romans 2:10; Ephesians 4:28. This general exhortation is in effect a summing up of the particular responsibilities of the preceding context. It is good to restore the erring, v. 1; to bear the burden of others, v. 2; to share temporal supplies with those who share spiritual supplies with us, v. 6; to sow in the eternal interests of the spirit, v. 8; and to continue unwearyingly in all manner of well-doing, v. 9.

toward—*pros,* which suggests "in your intercourse with," "in your personal and active relations with"; see at 1:18, above.

all men,—the words of Peter to servants may be adopted here, "not only to the good and gentle, but also to the froward," 1 Peter 2:18. This obligation is not to be limited in any way; it is to mankind at large without distinction of race, nationality, party, creed, or character. It is elsewhere defined by the same apostle; the believer is to:
"take thought for things honorable in the sight of all men," Romans 12:17;
"be at peace with all men," v. 18;
"render to all [men] their dues," 13:7;
let his "forbearance be known unto all men," Philippians 4:5;
"increase and abound in love . . . toward all men," 1 Thessalonians 3:12;
"make supplication, prayers, intercessions, thanksgivings for all men," 1 Timothy 2:1;
"be gentle toward all men," 2 Timothy 2:24;
show "all meekness toward all men," Titus 3:2.
Similar instructions are found in other New Testament writings; the believer is to:
"follow after peace with all men, and the sanctification without which no man shall see the Lord," Hebrews 12:14;
"honor all men," 1 Peter 2:17.
God is declared to be good and to do good, Psalm 119:68, and the active life of the Lord Jesus is summed up in Peter's words that "He went about doing good," Acts 10:38. For believers who are to be imitators of God, Ephesians 5:1, and followers of Christ, Luke 9:23, their manner of life is thus marked out, and as they pursue it so do they "become sons of their Father in Heaven"; see Matthew 5:43–48.

especially—the Christian is debtor to all men to do them good by deed and word, Romans 1:14, both on the ground of the common humanity, the solidarity of the race in virtue of its origin in, and descent from, one ancestor, Adam, Acts 17:26, and because all are alike involved in sin and death in Adam's transgression, Romans 5:12–21. But in Christ the believer is brought into a new relationship, not indeed with all men, but with those who hold the same faith and share the same salvation, and who own allegiance to the same Lord; to these his obligation is accentuated. He is not, however, to relax his efforts in behalf of all; he is to increase them in behalf of those who belong to Christ.

toward them that are of the household—*oikeios,* which is used in its literal sense of one's own family in 1 Timothy 5:8. In Ephesians 2:19 the "household of God" is the same circle of the redeemed that is here called the household of the faith.||

Oikeios is derived from *oikos,* a house, which, besides its frequent literal sense, is used of Israel, i.e., of the whole nation, Matthew 10:6. In 1 Timothy 3:15; Hebrews 3:6; 10:21; 1 Peter 2:5; 4:17, it is used of believers in the Lord Jesus as *oikeios* is used here.

of the faith.—*hē pistis,* for which see comment on *1 Thessalonians* 3:2; here it may be understood of all who believe in the Lord Jesus, who trust to Him alone for salvation, and this would correspond closely with the theme of the epistle; or it may be taken as meaning all those who abide in the doctrine of Christ, 2 John 9; the result of the exhortation will be the same in either case.

6:11 See with how large—*pēlikos,* which refers to size; it is used metaphorically in Hebrews 7:4, "how great" = "distinguished."||

letters—*gramma,* which primarily means a written sign, as of the alphabet, 2 Corinthians 3:7, and here, but, as in the case of its English equivalent, this meaning has been varied and extended. Thus in John 7:15, "How knoweth this man letters?" cannot mean "How has this man become acquainted with the alphabet?" but "How has he become literate, educated? How has he obtained such knowledge of the subject he handles?" Cp. Acts 26:24, where "much learning" is lit., "many letters." In Acts 28:21, epistles, written communications, are meant; in Romans 2:27, the fact that the law of God has been committed to writing is the point; and in v. 29, and 7:6, outward conformity to the written Word, as also in 2 Corinthians 3:6. In John 5:47 the books of Moses are called his "letters," and in 2 Timothy 3:15 the whole of the canonical writings of the Old Testament are called "sacred letters."

There is no instance in the New Testament of the use of *gramma* in the plural for a single epistle, the nearest approach to that would be Luke 16:6, 7, and there "bills" may perhaps be the correct translation, since more than one transaction may have been dealt with in each case. Paul always refers to his writings as "epistles," *epistolē.* Moreover, an apparently fatal objection to the interpretation of the passage which makes him refer to the length of the epistle is that "letters" here is in the dative case *(grammasin),* not in the accusative *(grammata);* hence the translation is not "I have written a long letter," but "I have written with large letters."||

With John 7:15, cp. Acts 4;13, where "illiterate" is *agrammatos.* The Jews were puzzled by the competency of the apostles to speak, as they had been puzzled by the Lord, for it was evident that neither He nor they had qualified in the rabbinical schools.||

I have written—lit., "I wrote," a Greek idiom in which the writer of a letter put himself beside the reader and spoke of it as something done in past time; see Philemon 19, where the words are as here, "I wrote," though the apostle was referring to words then proceeding from his pen. Cp. Acts 15:27; 23:30. Hence it is quite possible that this epistle also was written by another hand, and that the apostle added these words with what follows to the end. On the other hand, he may be referring to the body of the epistle just completed as having been written by himself. It does not seem possible to determine the point finally.

with my own hand.—there were two distinct styles of writing in vogue in the apostle's days; the older, which was called "uncial," and the "cursive," or "running," which was much smaller. The oldest known copies of the Scriptures in Greek are written in the former. It may be that Paul's amanuensis used the latter, and that he himself, for distinction and emphasis, added this brief summary of the Epistle in the former. See comment on *2 Thessalonians* 3:17.

The apostle's reason for writing in large letters is not stated, nor is it suggested by the language used. It may have been because of weakness of eyesight, but the ground on which such an inference is based is precarious at the best; see at 4:15, above; moreover, *pēlikos* does not mean irregular or informed, it refers only to size. Perhaps his intention was to give emphasis to his statements, the boldness of the calligraphy matching the conviction and fervor of his mind.

To the words of the apostle thus understood a parallel is furnished by one of the papyri, in which instruction is given to put a notice on a board in large "letters," i.e., in order to draw particular attention to it.

6:12 As many as—as at 3:27, above.

desire—*thelō*, see at 4:9, above.

to make a fair show—*euprosōpeō*, lit., "to put on a good face," to make a display of religious zeal.||

in the flesh,—i.e., in external things, ordinances and rites; see at 3:3, above. It may not be without significance that the apostle at the beginning of his autograph takes up the prominent word of his last dictated paragraph. Those who, in order to escape persecution, paraded the works of the flesh were sowing to the flesh. They aimed not at the glory of God, nor at the welfare of the Galatian converts, but solely at securing their own safety. Inevitably their selfishness must bring its own retribution; they also of the flesh would reap corruption.

they compel you to be circumcised;—*anankazō*, "to put constraint upon," as in 2:3, 14, above. The continuous tense, "they are compelling you," suggests the purpose in view, but not that success would necessarily attend their efforts; see at 5:4, above. The question as yet undecided was—Would the Judaizers succeed in the Galatian churches where they had failed in the case of Titus?

only—the Judaizers cared nothing for circumcision in itself; their insistence on it was merely a means to an end.

that they may not be persecuted for the cross of Christ.—what was the motive at work in the minds of the party of the circumcision? It was certainly not concern for the spiritual welfare and the eternal safety of the believers. On the contrary, the motive the apostle discerned behind their zeal was that they themselves might escape the consequences inseparable from the preaching of the Cross, which pronounces accursed not only man the sinner, the lawbreaker, but man the religious law keeper as well. The Cross is thus an offense to Jew and Gentile alike. The addition of something as a means to, or as a condition of, salvation (such as circumcision in apostolic days, or the sacraments in later times) to the free unmerited grace of God mediated by faith in Christ alone, has proved the most effective way of avoiding that offense. But to preach a gospel without the Cross is to preach what is not a gospel at all; see at 5:11, above.

6:13 For not even they who receive circumcision—i.e., those who, whether Jews or Gentiles originally, having been themselves circumcised, advocated the circumcision of gentile converts; "the circumcision party"; see at 5:2, above.

do themselves keep the law;—*phulassō*, for which see comment on *2 Thessalonians* 3:3; it is the equivalent of "do" in 5:3, above. The apostle does not condemn the circumcision party because they did not do what was plainly impossible, observe feasts and offer sacrifices, which could be done validly only at Jerusalem, Deuteronomy 12:1-9; neither does he condemn them because they did not succeed in keeping the law fully, for that he had already shown to be impossible for any man to do, see at 3:22, above; he condemns them because they did not attempt to keep it. He impugns their sincerity; they demanded an acknowledgment of the obligation to keep the law without themselves showing any corresponding zeal in their own ways. This obvious insincerity could result only in intensified and extended hypocrisy.

but they desire to have you circumcised, that they may glory in your flesh.—i.e., in your submission to a merely external ordinance as the result of their persuasions and threats. The two reasons suggested by the apostle for this advocacy of circumcision which he so strenuously opposed are complementary. The first is negative, they thus avoided persecution at the hands of the bigoted Jews; the second is positive, they could boast of their success in proselytizing the Gentiles. Cp. Matthew 23:15. "You" stands in contrast with the preceding "they themselves"; "the motive that actuates them is not to further your growth in the Christian graces before God, but that they themselves might gain some advantage out of you in the sight of men."

6:14 But far be it from me—as at 2:17. Here "me" is emphatic; let others save themselves from persecution by disloyalty to the true gospel of Christ if they would, whatever the consequences might be to him, his own purpose to proclaim it was fixed.

to glory,—*kauchaomai*, cp. comment on *1 Thessalonians* 2:19; *2 Thessalonians* 1:4.

save in the cross of our Lord Jesus Christ,—at the close of v. 12, where he deals with those who despised it, it was sufficient for the apostle to describe the Cross in the briefest way, it is the cross of Christ. Here, speaking of his own fixed purpose, his heart kindles with passionate devotion, and his exultation finds expression in the full title, it is the Cross of the Lord Jesus Christ! To them He meant little, to Paul He was everything. To glory in a cross is a paradox; to glory in the Cross of the Lord Jesus Christ is the wisdom that comes with the fear of the Lord, Psalm 111:10; Isaiah 11:3.

through which—or, as margin, "through whom," either translation is grammatically correct, but the context is in favor of the rendering in the text. If "through whom" is preferred, then the meaning is "through whose crucifixion." The cross is here put, by metonymy, for the crucifixion of Christ.

the world—*kosmos*, see 4:3f. Here the religious world is primarily in view, for the one universal element in all world religions is salvation by human effort. But what is true of the relationship between the Christian and the world in one of its aspects is true absolutely. The absence of the article in Greek shows that the apostle is thinking of the characteristics of the world, which are at once attractive to men and abhorrent to God.

is crucified unto me, and I unto the world.—to be crucified is to be accursed, 3:13, above. Faith in Christ and recognition of his indebtedness to Christ alone for salvation, apart from any effort of his own, had made the world's religion an accursed thing to Paul, and not less had his allegiance to the crucified Savior made Paul accursed to the Jew, and to all who, like the Jew, seek salvation by works. Between the two there is no common ground, no possibility of compromise, no *modus vivendi;* the enmity is fundamental, and must continue so to the end.

6:15 For—the apostle proceeds to give the reason why he was not desirous of the applause of the world. The advocates of circumcision occupied themselves with things that, however important they may seem to men untaught by the Spirit of God, do not really and finally count at all. The one thing that does matter is not whether or no a man has been circumcised, but that he should be made the subject of the regenerating power of God, lifting him to a new plane of being by an act of new creation; cp. 2 Corinthians 4:6, "God . . . shined in our hearts."

neither is circumcision anything, nor uncircumcision,—circumcision as an act, a rite, cp. 5:6, above, where see note. Such things affect the body, not the soul; cp. the words of the Lord in Mark 7:18, 29, and those of Paul in 1 Corinthians 8:8.

but a new creature.—better, as margin, "a new creation"; the ellipsis may be supplied thus, "a new creation is what matters." The word *kainos,* which is here translated "new," means not that which is new, in time, recent, but that which is new in quality, different in character from the old with which it is contrasted. The "new tongues," *kainos,* of Mark 16:17 are the "other tongues," *heteros,* of Acts 2:4. These languages, however, were "new" and "different," not in the sense that they had never been heard before, or that they were new to the hearers, for it is plain from v. 8 that this is not the case; they were new languages to the speakers, different from those in which they were accustomed to speak.

The new things that the gospel brings for present obedience and realization are:
a new covenant, Matthew 26:28;
a new commandment, John 13:34;
a new creative act, here;
a new creation, 2 Corinthians 5:17;
a new man, i.e., a new character of manhood, spiritual and moral, after the pattern of Christ, Ephesians 4:24;
a new man, i.e., "the Church which is His (Christ's) body," Ephesians 2:15.
The new things that are to be received and enjoyed hereafter are:
a new name, the believer's, Revelation 2:17;
a new Name, the Lord's, Revelation 3:12;
a new song, Revelation 5:9;
a new heaven and a new earth, Revelation 21:1;
the new Jerusalem, Revelation 3:12; 21:2;
"And He that sitteth on the Throne said, Behold, I make all things new," Revelation 21:5, cp. 2 Corinthians 5:17,*b.*

A synonym of *kainos, neos,* means that which is recent in time though it may be just a reproduction of the old in character and quality; it is frequently translated "young," as in John 21:18. The distinctive meaning of each of these words is always observable, even where they seem to be interchangeable. Thus the new wine of Matthew 9:17; Mark 2:22, is *neos,* for the point is that it has been recently produced, but the skins are "fresh," *kainos,* they had not been used before. In Matthew 26:29, Mark 14:25, the new wine is *kainos,* for the wine of the kingdom of God will differ in character from the wine of this world. The tomb in which the Lord was laid may have been made years previously to its first use; it was new, *kainos,* in the sense that it had not been used before, John 19:41.

Neos, new in time, is also used of some of the things brought by the gospel, and which appear in the list under *kainos,* above, these are:

a new man, Colossians 3:10;

a new covenant, Hebrews 12:24;

To these is to be added "a new lump," 1 Corinthians 5:7.

The "new man" is not merely new in the sense that he is different from the old; the believer has entered upon a new experience, recently begun in him, whereas "the old man" is as old as Adam's fall. So with the new covenant, it is new in both senses; it is different from all that preceded it, as well as more recent in time. Hence both words are used.

A word formed from *kainos, kainotēs* (as "newness" is formed from "new") appears in Romans 6:4; 7:6. The believer, inasmuch as he is now in a new creation, differing in character from the old, is to behave himself in a manner consistent therewith, he is to "walk in newness of life." And for the same reason he serves God no longer in slavish fear, after the "oldness of the letter," but in the way of freedom born of love, "in newness of the spirit."||

Ktisis is primarily the creating, the creative act, as in Romans 1:20 and the present passage, but not elsewhere in the New Testament. But like the word "creation" it is also used of the product, or result, of the creative act, the "creature," as in Romans 1:25; 8:19. The same phrase appears here and in 2 Corinthians 5:17, but here, apparently, the reference is to the creative act of God, whereby a man is introduced into the blessing of salvation, in contrast with circumcision done by human hands, which the Judaizers claimed was necessary to that end. In 2 Corinthians 5:17 the reference is to what the believer is in Christ; in consequence of the creative act he has become a new creature.

This new creative act, of which a man becomes the subject when he believes in Christ, is called "new birth" in John 3:3; such as experience it are said to have been "begotten of God," 1 John 3:9, and to have been "brought . . . forth" by the will of God, James 1:18; cp. "regeneration," Titus 3:5.

Ktisis is only once used of human actions, 1 Peter 2:13, where it is translated "ordinance," with "creation" in the margin. Another form, *ktisma* = "creature," occurs in 1 Timothy 4:4, etc.; and another, *ktistēs,* occurs in 1 Peter 4:19, "Creator."(||) In Romans 1:25 "Creator" is the participle of the corresponding verb *ktizō,* to create.

6:16 And as many as shall walk—*stoicheō,* for which see at 5:25, above.

by this rule,—*kanōn,* a measuring rod of any kind, and hence, by metaphor, of anything that determines or regulates the actions of men, a standard, or principle. From it comes the English word "canon." In 2 Corinthians 10:13, 15, it is translated "province," and means the limits of the apostle's responsibility in service in the gospel as measured out and appointed to him by God; and so of the responsibilities of others in v. 16.||

The reference is to the doctrines of grace which the apostle has been expounding to, and enforcing upon, them.

Those who "walk by this rule," who make the principle of vv. 14, 15 their guiding line, seek for themselves, and preach to others, salvation through faith in Christ alone, apart from works. In Philippians 3:16, where, however, *kanōn* is omitted, the reference is to the course pursued by the believer who makes the "prize of the upward calling" the object of his ambition.

peace be unto them,—*eirēnē,* for which see comment on *1 Thessalonians* 5:3. Cp. Psalm 125:5.

and mercy,—*eleos,* is the outward manifestation of pity; it assumes need on the part of him who receives it, and resources adequate to meet the need on the part of him that shows it. God is rich in mercy, Ephesians 2:4, and accordingly He has provided salvation for all men, Titus 3:5, for Jews, Luke 1:72, and for Gentiles, Romans 15:9. But not only sinners stand in need of the mercy of God, he is merciful to those who fear Him, Luke 1:50, for they also are compassed with infirmity, and He alone can succor them. Hence they are to pray boldly for mercy for themselves in every time of need, Hebrews 4:16, and if for themselves then surely it is seemly that they should ask for mercy for one another, as Paul does here, and see 1 Timothy 1:2; 2 John 3; Jude 2. And when God brings His salvation to its final issue at the coming of Christ, His people will need and will obtain His mercy, 2 Timothy 1:16; Jude 21. Moreover, since God is merciful to men He would have them show mercy to one another, Matthew 9:13; Luke 10:37, Jude 22, and that cheerfully, Romans 12:8.

Whenever the words mercy and peace are found together, save here, they occur in this order. Mercy is the act of God; peace is the resulting experience in the heart of man; see comment on *1 Thessalonians* 1:1. Grace describes God's attitude toward the lawbreaker and the rebel; mercy is His attitude to those who are in distress.

and—*kai,* which among many uses, is frequently = "even," should be so understood here. Those who "walk by this rule" are themselves "the Israel of God."

upon the Israel of God.—the words suggest a contrast between a true and a false Israel. Circumcision could not transform a Gentile into a Jew; faith makes of any man, Jew or Gentile, an Israelite indeed, one of the true people of God, see 1 Peter 2:10, and cp. Romans 2:28, 29; Philippians 3:3. The circumcision party would have had the Galatians become Jews by submitting to a Jewish rite; let them rather by faith in Christ become of the Israel of God. But the apostle does not apologize for the Gentile converts. His challenge to the Judaizers rings out in this exultant climax—they are the very Israel of God!

The descendants of Jacob were known as Hebrews, Jews, and Israelites. These names are not always interchangeable. Speaking generally, "Hebrew" suggests their speech, see Acts 6:1, "Jew" their nationality, see 3:28, above, "Israelite" their calling to be the people of God, Matthew 2:6. The last is, therefore, the highest title of the three, connoting the dignity and the privileges wherewith God had endowed them. But the ideal to which the title pointed had been realized only by the few among their successive generations, for all that are of Israel in the course of nature are not Israelites in heart, Romans 9:6-8. The true Israelite is he who, of whatever nation born, puts his faith in God. See 3:7, 9, above, and Romans 4:12. It is not, however, to this Israel after the Spirit that the distinctive promises of national restoration and blessing, see Romans 11:26, 27, will be fulfilled, but to "Israel after the flesh," 1 Corinthians 10:18, the natural descendants of Abraham through Jacob.

There is nothing in Galatians to correspond with Romans 9—11. There is no reference of any kind to the restoration of Israel. The reason for this omission is clear. To have spoken of the restoration of Israel under the circumstances that called forth this epistle would have confused the issue which the writer had before him, and would have defeated his purpose. The epistle to the Romans is an ordered exposition of the purposes of God in the gospel; the epistle to the Galatians is a polemic directed to the maintenance of the faith once for all delivered to the saints. In Romans the apostle necessarily treats of the dispensational dealings of God; in Galatians the question of Israel's national destiny does not arise. In Romans the Israelites are the descendants of Jacob, the name retains its literal sense. Here it is used in a figure of all who trust in Christ.

6:17 From henceforth—the subject has been fully discussed, the apostle's position has been made plain, his past action vindicated, his purpose declared; now he turns to the future.

let no man trouble me;—the two words here translated "trouble" occur again in Matthew 26:10; Luke 11:7; 18:5; they mean to embarrass a person by distracting his attention or disturbing his rest, as the importunate friend did; or by giving occasion for anxiety, as some of the disciples by their criticisms perturbed the spirit of the women with the ointment. So the apostle peremptorily forbade the Judaizers to attempt to distract or disturb him further by their preaching of a false gospel and by malicious attacks upon himself. And in thus forbidding them he expresses his determination not to allow himself to be further distracted by them.

for,—introducing his reason for this emphatic assertion that he owed allegiance neither to the Judaizers nor, inferentially, to the Twelve whose mouthpiece they claimed to be, see 2:6, above. As the epistle begins, 1:1, so it ends; he is the servant, indubitably and irrevocably, of Christ alone.

I—*egō*, emphatic, "I, Paul," "I, myself"; stating not a general truth applicable to all believers, as in 2:20, above, but something peculiar to himself. The suggested contrast with the Judaizers is maintained; they feared lest they should be involved in suffering, but Paul had suffered already, how severely let his scars testify.

bear—*bastazō*, as in v. 2, above. According to the word of the Lord to Ananias, Acts 9:1-8, Paul was called "to bear the name of the Lord" among the Gentiles; to this the apostle adds that now he bears His branding marks as well. And he bears them not as a reproach is borne, but as a banner is carried by a standard bearer, with exulting pride that the honor has been conferred upon him. In this also Paul was no whit behind the Twelve; like them he rejoiced to be "counted worthy to suffer dishonor for the name," Acts 5:41. Cp. also 2 Corinthians 4:10, where, however, a different word with a similar meaning, *periphero*, "to carry about," is used.

branded—this is not separately expressed in the original.

On my body—*soma*, for which see comment on *1 Thessalonians* 5:23.

the marks—*stigma.*||

of Jesus.—this use of the personal name of the Lord alone is infrequent with the apostle, see comment on *1 Thessalonians* 1:1. Wherever it occurs, as here, his purpose is to remind his readers of the fact that in the days of His flesh He also suffered pain and shame at the hands of men.

It is probable that the apostle refers in these words to the physical sufferings he had endured since he began to proclaim Jesus as Messiah and Lord. It is probable, too, that this reference to his scars was intended to set off the insistence of the Judaizers upon a body mark which cost them nothing. Over against the circumcision they demanded as a proof of obedience to the law he set the indelible tokens, sustained in his own body, of his loyalty to the Lord Jesus. Moreover, the contrast thus suggested is heightened by the fact, which they could hardly have forgotten, that some of his wounds, and these not the least severe, had been sustained in one of their own cities, Acts 14:19.

As to the origin of the figure, it was indeed customary for a master to brand his slaves, but this language does not suggest that the apostle had been branded by his Master. Soldiers and criminals also were branded on occasion; but to neither of these is the case of Paul as here described analogous. The religious devotee branded himself with the peculiar mark of the god whose cult he affected; so was Paul branded with the marks of his devotion to the Lord Jesus. It is true such markings were forbidden by the law, Leviticus 19:28, but then Paul had not inflicted these on himself.

The marks of Jesus cannot be taken to be the marks which the Lord bears in His body in consequence of the Crucifixion; they were different in character.

6:18 The grace of our Lord Jesus Christ be with your spirit,—see comment on *1 Thessalonians* 5:28. "Spirit" is added also in Philippians 4:23; 2 Timothy 4:22, and in Philemon 25, but not in any other of this apostle's writings. See comment on *1 Thessalonians* 5:23.

brethren.—added to the benediction in this epistle only. His last word reminds them not of their differences, but of their relationship with one another because of their relationship with the Lord Jesus.

Amen.—for which see at 1:5, above.